KING OF MYSTERIES

King of Mysteries
Early Irish Religious Writings

John Carey

FOUR COURTS PRESS

Set in 10 on 12 point Ehrhardt for
FOUR COURTS PRESS • DUBLIN
Fumbally Lane, Dublin 8, Ireland
E-mail: info@four-courts-press.ie
and in North America for
FOUR COURTS PRESS
c/o ISBS, 5804 N.E. Hassalo Street, Portland, OR 97213.

A catalogue record for this title
is available from the British Library.

First edition 1998
Revised paperback edition 2000

ISBN 1–85182–572–x pbk

Note: The author and publisher wish to thank
Professor Patrick Sims-Williams, and the President and
Council of the Royal Irish Academy, for permission to
re-print material that appeared earlier in *Cambridge Medieval
Celtic Studies* 19 (1990) 13–15, and in *Ériu* 45 (1994) 17–19.

Printed in Ireland
by Colour Books Ltd, Dublin.

IN MEMORY OF MY FATHER

Quisque uelit sapiens sapientes gnoscere causas,
Sensibus in sacris sentiat artis opes.

Acknowledgements

Everything of value which has gone into this book I owe to others; but the satisfactory articulation of most of these debts would be difficult if not impossible. I do, however, wish to thank certain individuals and institutions who have helped the work forward in specific ways. Malcolm Gerratt and Yuri Stoyanov encouraged me to undertake the project in the first place; at a later stage Máire Herbert and Thomas O'Loughlin kindly looked at portions of a draft version, and offered several valuable suggestions. During the period in which the book was being written I was supported by consecutive scholarships from the Institute of Irish Studies, at the Queen's University of Belfast; and from the School of Celtic Studies, in the Dublin Institute for Advanced Studies: I am indebted to both for their generosity, and similarly to the International Sacred Literature Trust. Finally, I am grateful to Four Courts Press for the helpfulness, insight, and energy with which they have seen the volume through to publication.

Contents

ACKNOWLEDGEMENTS 6

INTRODUCTION 9

I CREATOR AND CREATION 27

Altus Prosator 29
Selections from Augustinus Hibernicus,
 On the Miracles of Holy Scripture 51
In Tenga Bithnua: 'The Ever-New Tongue' 75
Saltair na Rann, Cantos I–III 97

II THE COMING OF THE FAITH 125

Two *Loricae* 127
 Faeth Fiada: 'Patrick's Breastplate' 130
 Nuall Fir Fhio: 'Fer Fio's Cry' 136
The Pseudo-Historical Prologue to the *Senchas Már* 139

III THE SAINTS 145

Audite omnes amantes: 'Sechnall's Hymn' to Saint Patrick 147
'Broccán's Hymn' to Saint Brigit 162
Selections from *Féilire Oengusso* 180

IV THE HOLY LIFE 229

Aipgitir Chrábaid: 'The Alphabet of Devotion' 231
Stories of the Céili Dé 246

V THE LAST THINGS 259

Fís Adomnáin: 'The Vision of Adomnán' 261

TEXTUAL REMARKS 275

BIBLIOGRAPHY 281

INDEX 289

Introduction

In the *Acallam na Senórach*, a fantastic and engagingly recounted labyrinth of hero tales and place-name lore probably written close to the year 1200, Saint Patrick is joined on his travels throughout Ireland by Caílte son of Rónán, a legendary warrior who has somehow survived from the pagan past. As Caílte tells his attentive companion more and more about the old days, the saint himself comes into ever closer contact with the pre-Christian powers and influences which still linger in the landscape – a process dramatically exemplified near the close of the text, when he celebrates the marriage of a mortal king and a princess of the fairies.[1] At an earlier point in the narrative Patrick meets Cas Corach, a musician who also belongs to the race of the old gods of Ireland, and invites him to demonstrate his art:

> He took up his instrument, and tuned it, and played a strain of music upon it; and they had never heard anything so sweet unless it were the celebration of the Lord's office, and the praises of the King of heaven and earth. A stupor of sleep and slumber fell upon the clerics on account of the yearning fairy music; then he brought the entertainment to an end.
> 'Give me payment for the entertainment, holy cleric,' said Cas Corach.
> 'What payment do you request?' said Patrick.
> 'Heaven for myself,' he said, 'for that is the best payment; and grace upon my art forever, and upon all those who will practice it after me.'
> 'Heaven you will have,' said Patrick; 'and it will be one of the last three arts to be maintained in Ireland … '
> 'Good is the art which you have performed for us,' said [Patrick's scribe] Broccán.
> 'It is good indeed,' said Patrick, 'were it not for the lilt of fairy magic which there is in it: but for that, there would be nothing more like the music of the King of heaven.'
> 'If there is music in heaven,' said Broccán, 'why not on earth? It is not right to reject the entertainment thus.'
> 'I do not say that one should,' said Patrick; 'only that it should not be believed in too much.'[2]

This episode has much to tell us about the background of the pieces collected in this book, and about the polarities of native and foreign, old and new, pagan and Christian which played so crucial a role in the emergence of medieval Irish culture.

---

1 Stokes 1900, 219, 269–70. Most of the *Acallam* is translated in O'Grady 1892, 2.101–265; Stokes provides translations of passages omitted by O'Grady in loc. cit., 225–71. 2 Stokes 1900, 98–9; cf. O'Grady 1892, 2.191.

Patrick, representative of Rome, of Europe, of Christianity, gives his blessing to the arts of the pagan Irish and salutes their beauty: the minstrel from the hollow hills is promised a place in heaven. Even as he praises the music, however, the saint retains a clear sense of its subordination to the ultimate values of religion: Cas Corach's playing can never be as beautiful as the singing of the angels, and 'should not be believed in too much'.

Three important points are illustrated here. First: from a very early date the Christian Irish displayed a lively interest in the heritage which had come down to them from their pagan forebears, and a firm confidence in its perennial relevance and value. Tales about the pre-Christian past, often concerned with the Otherworld and its mysterious inhabitants, were being written already in the seventh century; and pagan heroes and demoted deities have continued to be central figures in Gaelic tradition down to the present day. The medieval Irish sought, with agile and audacious imagination, to find room for as much as possible of their old religion within the framework of the new, sometimes with exotic or indeed unorthodox results.[3]

Second: this loyalty to what was native was not yoked to any resistance of the foreign. Cas Corach does not defy Patrick, but submits to him and seeks his blessing; the old traditions continue to have a place, but it is a place within the wider framework of Christian theology and European culture. Imported learning was gathered and taught with the same enthusiasm as indigenous lore: not the Bible and the Fathers only, but apocrypha and classical writers also. The eyes of the monks were indeed turned backward, toward the riches of a hallowed past; but they were eagerly turned outward also.

My third point is closely connected to the first two. The medieval Irish were themselves aware of the hybrid character of their heritage, and reflected upon it in innumerable poems and tales. They saw themselves as a nation of converts, their identity essentially determined by the marriage of two cultures. Patrick was the agent and emblem of this marriage – perhaps indeed this was the principal reason for his status as the greatest of Irish saints. More, it may be, than anywhere else in Europe, the conversion period has always been seen in Ireland as the decisive epoch in the country's history: that time when the Irish were transformed, while still remaining ineradicably themselves. Some eight centuries later, the anecdote from the *Acallam* is yet another meditation on this theme.

Such considerations as these may be helpful in approaching the vexed and delicate question of the distinctiveness of medieval Irish Christianity. It was, indeed, enriched by inherited ideas and traditions peculiar to Ireland and carefully nurtured there. We will however do a deep disservice to the early Irish if we see them as hidebound, wilfully isolated, or resistant to the culture of the wider world: the vigour and vivid imagination of their art, literature, and spirituality were fed by a restless and visionary curiosity.

3 For two cases in point see Carey 1987 (the old gods reinterpreted as unfallen descendants of Adam), and 1989 (the Otherworld located in the southern hemisphere).

The little story which we have been considering can also be looked at from another angle. The *Acallam* appears to have been written shortly after the first Anglo-Norman penetration of Ireland, a time of far-reaching ecclesiastical as well as political change. As part of a series of developments to be described in somewhat more detail below, reformed religious orders were in the process of being introduced from the Continent; an allusion to one of the first of the new monasteries, Mellifont near the mouth of the Boyne (established 1142), is in fact the only contemporary reference in the *Acallam*. The old religious houses had been the citadels of native learning; the introduction of the Cistercians, Augustinians, and others was a result of the perception, at home and abroad, that they had grown lax and corrupt. Would the reformers prove equally hostile to the traditions of which they were the guardians?

Seen against this background, the cultural optimism of the story of Cas Corach can be seen to have a defensive edge. When he portrays Patrick, bringer of religious truth and representative of papal authority, as artistic patron of the old gods, the *Acallam's* author claims for the past a rapprochement which he may well have felt to be threatened in the present. As we shall see, these fears were justified: the reforms of the twelfth century proved to be the first in a series of historical watersheds which were radically to change the character of Irish religious life.

In what follows I shall briefly consider some of the most significant developments in the period from which the texts translated in this book are drawn.[4] I shall then look at the events which, in the eight succeeding centuries, have come between us and the culture of those times; and will conclude with some reflections on how we may best seek to approach the literature on its own terms, and to discover its relevance for ourselves.

Irish tradition abounds in tales of the conversion, centring upon the heroic figure of the national apostle Patrick. Captured as a boy by pirates in his native Britain, and sold into slavery in Ireland, he escaped only to return years later as a bearer of the Gospel. After a dramatic confrontation with the pagan king Loegaire of Tara, in which the sorcery of the court magicians was overthrown by the powers of the saint, he travelled throughout the island baptising converts, ordaining priests, and establishing churches. He fasted on the summit of the mountain Croaghpatrick in order to obtain divine blessings for the people under his protection,[5] and at last died (like Moses) at the age of one hundred and twenty. His principal foundation of Armagh was subsequently to claim metropolitan authority over the other Irish churches.[6]

---

4 Such a summary can, of course, give only a few hints concerning a rich and deeply interesting subject. There is unfortunately no really satisfactory recent guide to the ecclesiastical history of pre-Norman Ireland; Hughes 1966, although by now out of date in several respects, is still probably the best treatment available. Also dated, but still indispensable as a remarkably comprehensive guide to the sources, is Kenney 1966. 5 For one version of this episode, see the addendum to *Audite omnes*, pp. 160–1 below. 6 The earliest collection of hagiographical material on Patrick, that preserved in the Book of Armagh, is edited with translation in Bieler 1979. See also Bieler

That there is a kernel of truth in these legends is confirmed by Patrick's own writings: documents of arresting freshness and spiritual power which tell us all too little about the concrete details of his life, but do allude to the events of his captivity.[7] In general, however – and not surprisingly – the traditional picture of the conversion is now generally recognised to be a streamlined and simplified account of what must have been an exceedingly complex and piecemeal process.

Elsewhere in the literature we find traditions concerning saints who preached in Ireland before Patrick's coming; and indeed the presence in Ireland of large numbers of slaves who had been, like Patrick himself, captured in the Roman province of Britain must mean that Christians constituted a significant element in the island's population from the fourth century onward. There is no reason to doubt that Patrick's missionary efforts were of fundamental importance to the expansion of Christianity in Ireland, or that he carried its message (as he tells us) into regions in which it had never yet been heard; but he should be seen as one of the greatest in a series of which he was by no means the first.

If the process of conversion began well before Patrick, it continued for at least two centuries after him; it could scarcely have happened otherwise, in a country with no centralised political authority, dozens of petty kingdoms, and a well entrenched pagan priestly hierarchy. There is considerable disagreement regarding the stages by which the native druid priesthood gave way to the Christian church;[8] but it is at any rate reasonably clear that druids were still active in certain capacities down into the seventh and eighth centuries, a period in which they are mentioned in legal and penitential treatises.[9] That they had not yet dwindled to being mere local conjurors or 'fairy doctors' is apparent from a passage in *On the Miracles of Holy Scripture*, translated below, in which they are described as teaching what sounds like a doctrine of metempsychosis or reincarnation;[10] and a collection of canons of uncertain date, in which Christian and pagan communities in Ireland are portrayed as existing side by side, speaks of the custom of taking 'soothsayers' as witnesses to confirm legal agreements.[11] It is impossible to state with certainty when paganism became extinct in Ireland, even if we do not take at face value the claim of Gerald of Wales that there were still remote communities in the twelfth century which had never heard the name of Christ;[12] but there appears to be no good reason not to believe that the conversion had been effectively completed by the early years of the eighth century. Christians – and indeed ecclesiastics – continued however to allude to the

1971; Stokes 1887 (with a superior edition of the text in Mulchrone 1939); and Stokes 1890, 1–19, 149–67.   7 The most recent translation is that of Howlett 1994, drawing on the edition of Bieler 1952. Discussion of a broad range of questions regarding the historical and legendary Patrick, with exhaustive bibliography, is provided in Dumville et al. 1994.   8 See for instance the contrasting views of Mac Cana 1979 and of McCone 1990 (e.g. 20–1).   9 Binchy 1962, 58 §5; Bieler 1975, 160 §4; Kelly 1988, 60–1.   10 Page 58.   11 Bieler 1975, 56 §14; recent discussion of this text in Dumville et al. 1993, 175–8. Compare the testimony of Strabo (Jones 1917–32, 1244–5) and Caesar (Edwards 1917, 336–7) that the druids settled all disputes among the Gauls. 12 O'Meara 1951, 110–12.

old religion, sometimes in ways which suggest a continuing loyalty to some of its elements; a remarkable example of this is the prayer known as *Nuall Fir Fhio*, translated below.

But while it is important to remember that, in the early part of the period to which this book is devoted, the old religion still lingered on in some parts of Ireland, this knowledge should not blind us to other and equally essential aspects of that period's character. The very sources which bear witness to this residual paganism testify also to the rapid expansion and precocious intellectual fecundity of the church in Ireland: already in the seventh century religious houses had been established in the farthest and least hospitable corners of the country, and Irish ecclesiastics had produced an imposing corpus of scriptural exegesis, canon law, penitentials, saints' lives, calendrical treatises, hymns, and other works.[13]

One notable feature of this material is the scope of its learning, which draws on an impressive range of continental sources; another is its positive evaluation, unparalleled in the Europe of the time, of the vernacular language. The Irish appear to have been the first of the 'barbarian' peoples to speculate concerning the etymology and grammar of their own tongue;[14] and Irish was used for religious writing, in both prose and verse, from a very early period.[15] This literary use of the native language reflects the same cultural self-confidence which, as I suggested above, is so salient a trait in Irish tradition: that Ireland had not experienced the prestige and predominance of Latin in the same way as the territories subject to the Roman Empire is no doubt largely responsible for this.

Already in the late sixth century some divergences of practice had brought the usage of churches in Ireland, Scotland, Wales, and Brittany, and of their emissaries in other lands, into conflict with that of Rome. The most contentious of these differences proved to be in their method of calculating the date of Easter. As early as the year 600 the Irish saint Columbanus of Bobbio was writing to Pope Gregory the Great in defense of the Irish system,[16] and the Welsh retained the 'Celtic Easter' into the second half of the eighth century. The most celebrated incident in the controversy came in 664, when the king of Northumbria convened a council at Whitby to adjudicate between the Roman reckoning and the date promulgated by the Irish foundation on Iona; his verdict in favour of the former resulted in the drastic reduction of Iona's influence over the Northumbrian church.[17]

---

13 On this material see Kenney 1966, and for more recent references Lapidge and Sharpe 1985. 14 On the etymological glossaries see Mac Neill 1930–2, Russell 1988; for *Auraicept na nÉces*, the first Irish grammar, see Ahlqvist 1982. 15 The outstanding example of early Irish religious prose is the *Aipgitir Chrábaid*, included in this book. Early poems include the *Amra Coluim Chille* (composed shortly after 597?), Stokes 1899 and Clancy and Márkus 1995, 96–128; the poems of Colmán mac Lénéni (*c*.600), Thurneysen 1932; the poems in honour of Colum Cille edited by Kelly 1973, 1975; and a metrical version of the *Gospel of Thomas*, Carney 1964, 90–105. 16 Walker 1970, 2–9. 17 The classic account is that of the eighth-century English historian Bede (Colgrave and Mynors 1969, 294–309), himself a committed partisan of the Roman Easter.

The issues involved in all of this were complicated ones, and it is neither possible nor desirable to deal with them thoroughly here. It is however necessary at least to mention the Easter controversy, if only because of its symbolic importance in more recent times. Many have seen the divergent Easter reckoning as one of the main pieces of evidence for a 'Celtic church', doctrinally and jurisdictionally distinct from that of Rome: in this analysis Whitby marks a crucial step in the crushing of 'Celtic Christianity' by Rome's agents in Canterbury.[18]

In fact there is nothing – despite distinctive attitudes, peculiar customs, and occasional heterodoxy – to indicate that Irish Christians at any time believed themselves not to owe allegiance to the bishop of Rome; indeed, there is ample evidence to the contrary.[19] By the time of the meeting at Whitby, Iona represented the minority position within Ireland itself, where a synod had already been convened to debate the Easter question a generation earlier. On this occasion it was the testimony of messengers returned from Rome itself which decided the issue: having heard that Greeks, Hebrews, Scythians, and Egyptians all celebrated the feast there on a single day, the assembled clerics decided not to follow the opinion of 'an insignificant group of Britons and Irish who are almost at the end of the earth, and, if I may say so, but pimples on the face of the earth.'[20]

I have alluded to Columbanus (died 615), who established a series of important monasteries in France and Italy;[21] and to the community which Columba or Colum Cille (died 597) founded on the Hebridean island of Iona.[22] These were two of the first in a series of men who, motivated initially by a yearning for pilgrimage and voluntary exile,[23] were to play a crucial role in Britain and on the Continent as missionaries, as founders of religious houses, and as teachers. As time passed it was the last of these activities which came to predominate, reaching its high point in the ninth century in the careers of such figures as Johannes Eriugena (died *c*.877) – translator of the writings of Pseudo-Dionysius the Areopagite, and creator of one of the most brilliant and original metaphysical systems of the Middle Ages.[24]

It is however with works produced in Ireland itself that this book is concerned. Here the most important development of the eighth century was the emergence of a revival movement, usually called that of the *Céili Dé* or 'Servants of God'.[25] Reacting to what they perceived to be a falling away from the zeal and austerity of earlier times, the Céili Dé advocated a demanding regimen of fasting and prayer

18 One prominent exponent of this widespread view was Arnold Toynbee (1961, 2.324–37, 427–33). 19 On this point see Sharpe 1984. 20 Walsh and Ó Cróinín 1988, 72–5, 94–5. 21 Works edited in Walker 1970 (but cf. Lapidge 1977); Walker gives an account of Columbanus's life on pp. ix–xxxiv. 22 The best study of the network of monasteries which regarded Colum Cille as their founder is Herbert 1988. 23 The traditional background of the Irish pilgrim ethos is discussed by Charles-Edwards 1976. 24 For a useful survey of Eriugena's work, with references to the most recent scholarship, see Dutton 1992; a more detailed treatment can be found in O'Meara 1988. Although dated, Bieler 1963 provides a wonderfully readable and many-sided overview of medieval Irish activities on the Continent. 25 Detailed discussion in O Dwyer 1981.

for monks, and a more moderate but still dauntingly austere code of conduct for the layfolk who sought their spiritual counsel. Unlike the great reforming synods of the twelfth century, of which some mention will be made below, the Céili Dé did not seek to impose their programme upon society as a whole: perhaps more realistically, it was only their aim to create havens of a purer life within the framework of the status quo.

Despite the often savage self-denial of their lives (several examples of which are given below in the 'Stories of the Céili Dé'), the monks of the revival were far from indifferent to the pleasures of beauty and learning. In his *Féilire* (portions of which are also included in this book) Oengus mac Oengobann cast a calendar of saints' days into Irish verse, an undertaking requiring both extensive knowledge and considerable artistic skill. His use of the vernacular, besides reflecting that confidence in its value of which I have already spoken, was evidently motivated as well by a desire to make his work accessible to those who knew no Latin. This pastoral concern for the laity, which is also reflected in several anecdotes about the activities of the Céili Dé as 'soul-friends' or spiritual counsellors, provided a potent stimulus for the use of Irish in devotional writing; and it is probably to the reformers that the growth of this literature can largely be attributed. They also played a part in the period's spectacular achievements in the visual arts: Derrynaflan, where a magnificent hoard of sacramental vessels was discovered in 1980, was the site of a Céili Dé monastery.[26]

The movement's spread was interrupted by the arrival of the Vikings, whose raids on Ireland began at the close of the century. Their depredations must have hit the Céili Dé particularly hard, as their humble communities lacked the material resources which enabled the larger monasteries to survive repeated plundering, while their two principal houses of Tallaght and Finglas were located only a few miles from the Viking stronghold of Dublin. Although they did not entirely die out, their example and influence declined radically; and there was little to check a tendency to increasing secularisation in the Irish church in the course of the centuries which followed.

The tenth and eleventh centuries were a period of vigorous ecclesiastical reorganisation throughout western Europe. The example of developments overseas, and the direct encouragement of such influential figures as the archbishops of Canterbury, inspired a reform movement within Ireland itself in which both kings and clerics played an active part. In the great synods of Cashel (1101) and Ráith Breasail (1111) a wide range of ordinances was enacted: religious offices were not to be bought or sold, the churches were to be free of any tribute to secular authorities, the heads of monastic communities were to be celibates and in holy orders, marriage was forbidden within the degrees of kinship prohibited by canon law, and clergy (together

26 Further details in Ó Muraíle 1983.

with poets) were to be tried only before ecclesiastical courts. An organised frame-work of dioceses, divided into two great ecclesiastical provinces headed by Armagh and Cashel, was imposed on the island for the first time. Rome gave its own seal of approval to these enactments at the synod of Kells (1152), when the papal legate was empowered to create no less than four archbishoprics in Ireland.[27]

A key figure in this transitional period was Mael Maedóic Ua Morgair, better known as Saint Malachy (1094–1148). The great church of Armagh, which for hundreds of years had claimed primacy in Ireland on the strength of its traditional foundation by Saint Patrick, had since the late tenth century been ruled by members of a single family, the Clann Shínaig.[28] The last of the Clann Shínaig to enjoy unquestioned supremacy there, Cellach mac Aedo, was a zealous advocate of the reforming spirit of his time: unlike his predecessors, he embraced a life of celibacy; and he broke sharply with tradition by naming Malachy, rather than one of his own kinsmen, as his successor. It was some years before the struggle between Malachy and his Clann Shínaig rivals ended in victory for the former and for the principles he represented; once that victory was assured, Malachy retired to administer the much poorer see of Down.[29]

An important feature of the reform movement as a whole, of which the careers of Cellach and Malachy provide good examples, is its strong native element. Inspiration and exhortation came from abroad, but the initiative for change was taken by the Irish themselves, drawing upon their own traditions and spiritual resources. In Cellach's case, the cause was embraced by the head of a powerful and well-established ecclesiastical dynasty, the representative of a class which in terms of material self-interest had nothing to gain and everything to lose in the series of transformations in church organisation which he helped to bring about. Malachy, similarly, must be seen in relation to his Irish background as well as his foreign contacts. He travelled in Europe, encouraged the introduction of continental religious orders to Ireland, and died at last in the arms of Bernard of Clairvaux; but he too was a scion of the hereditary intelligentsia of Armagh, and one of his principal teachers was a local anchorite who continued in the twelfth century the ideals of asceticism which the Céili Dé had practised in the eighth.

It was thanks to Malachy that the Cistercian monastery of Mellifont was established in 1142; and the same period saw the founding of other Cistercian and Augustinian houses elsewhere in Ireland, many with royal patronage. Concomitant with this development was the decline of the older native monasteries, and of many of the traditions of which they had been the guardians: when not simply replaced by establishments belonging to one or another of the continental orders, they ceased to exist as religious communities properly so called, and the hereditary abbots became landed proprietors (sometimes in holy orders, sometimes not) whose additional duties and privileges were often the only vestiges of their earlier status.

27 A. Gwynn 1968. 28 Their origins and fortunes are treated in Ó Fiaich 1969. 29 The main source for Malachy's life, invaluable despite its obvious biases, is the biography by Saint Bernard of Clairvaux (R. Meyer 1978).

The place of the monastic schools was taken by secular learned families, who served the native chieftains and the more 'hibernicised' of the Anglo-Norman lords as historians, lawyers, physicians, and poets.[30]

Although some important exceptions exist, and it would be a mistake to argue for a clear-cut dichotomy, it remains for the most part true that the twelfth and thirteenth centuries witnessed a rupture between Irish monastic culture and the literature which it had created and transmitted in the centuries since the conversion – the fears implicit in the *Acallam* episode had been realised. This, then, is the first of the historical rifts which separate us from the works translated in this book: the disappearance of the class which wrote them, and of the literary and spiritual environment in which they first took shape.[31]

The introduction of the continental religious orders, although not far removed in time from the arrival in 1169 of the first Anglo-Norman military force in Ireland, was the result of native initiative and had no direct connection with the political aspirations of the English crown. In this it contrasts with the next events which we shall consider: the Reformation; the full subjection of the country under Elizabeth and James I; and its reconquest by Oliver Cromwell. The late sixteenth and the seventeenth centuries were times of catastrophic and pervasive change in Ireland; only a few essential developments will be noted here.

The dissolution of the monasteries, instituted by Henry VIII in 1533, was not pursued with the same zeal and thoroughness in Ireland as in England, and some religious communities managed to escape suppression or furtively to reconstitute themselves; those which survived through the sixteenth century, however, were to succumb in the seventeenth.[32] For a variety of reasons, Protestantism never took root among either the native Irish or the 'Old English' whose ancestors had settled in Ireland during the Middle Ages: many of these now withdrew their sons from universities in England, and sent them to obtain a Catholic education on the Continent. Particularly significant for the future character of Irish Catholicism was the fact that from now on candidates for the priesthood often sought training abroad: when they returned to their own country, they did so imbued with the Counter-Reformation theology of the Council of Trent.[33] Ireland's position as a Catholic country subject to a Protestant one had, ironically, placed its clergy in a particularly close relationship to the church's central hierarchy – a state of affairs which has to a great extent continued to the present day.

---

30 For a useful sketch of the history of Irish monasticism see Gwynn and Hadcock 1970, 1–12, especially 4; the emergence of a semi-laicised class of proprietors of church lands is treated in C. Mooney 1969, 10–14 and Watt 1987, 335–9. On the origins of the learned families see Mac Cana 1974; it should be noted that he posits a rather sharper division between poets and clerics in the early period than is now assumed by many of his colleagues.   31 It should be noted that there were moves in the opposite direction from the middle of the fourteenth century onward: professional poets affirmed their loyalty both to the Church and to native tradition, and members of the mendicant orders became enthusiastic students of the latter (Simms 1994, 29–33).   32 C. Mooney 1967, 22–31   33 On the Irish colleges on the Continent, and their effect on religion in seventeenth-century Ireland, see Silke 1976, 615–32.

The first years of the seventeenth century witnessed the brilliant and nearly suc-
cessful rebellion of Aodh Ua Néill, earl of Tyrone and overlord of most of Ulster.
Following his defeat by the English in 1603, what had been the most vigorously
Gaelic region remaining on the island was thrown open to confiscation and coloni-
sation – a process encouraged and greatly facilitated by the emigration of most of
Ulster's native aristocracy, the so-called 'Flight of the Earls', four years later.

These events, momentous as they were, were only a foreshadowing of what was
still to come. After a period of disorder in which the Catholics in Ireland turned
upon the Protestant population, Cromwell invaded the country in 1649. All resistance was crushed, and a far more comprehensive programme of confiscation deprived
the remaining Catholic lords of nearly all their holdings. The impoverished Gaelic
and 'Old English' nobles either fled the country or declined into poverty, and the
learned families of whom they had been the patrons faced the same alternatives.
When a Catholic king came to the English throne in the person of James II, there
were hopes of a new order; but these were dashed by his deposition, flight to Ireland,
and defeat in the battle of the Boyne (1690). The poets and scholars, whose stock
in trade had for centuries been the glorification of an elite which claimed descent
from the kings of Irish myth, were now obliged to turn for support to a peasantry
of which, when not considering it beneath their notice, they had hitherto spoken
with derision or even hatred.[34]

Two consequences of the intricate and ruinous history of this period are particularly relevant here: the loss of their former status by the native intelligentsia,
inheritors and transmitters of the literature which had been produced in the earlier
monasteries; and the tightening of the link between the embattled Catholics of
Ireland and the reinvigorated papacy of the Counter-Reformation.

Through all of these transformations, popular religion had continued substan-
tially unchanged: a rich and equivocal mixture of magic and devotion, of prayers,
charms, legends, fairs, and pilgrimages, which wove together Christian teaching
and the surviving vestiges of paganism. This vast body of traditional practice and
belief was further enriched in the eighteenth century, when scholars and poets
displaced by the collapse of the old order were obliged to seek their sustenance by
entertaining the common folk: the content of much of the earlier literature found
its way into oral culture, and even the copying of manuscripts survived as a craft
patronised by tradesmen and farmers.

With the early decades of the nineteenth century came a progressive relaxation
of the many restrictions which had been imposed on Catholics in Ireland, full
emancipation being granted at last in 1829. The same period witnessed a rapid
decline in the traditional usages, which were largely replaced by such officially
sanctioned forms of piety as novenas, religious sodalities, parochial missions, modern
developments of the Marian cult, and devotion to the Sacred Heart. Many factors

---

34 A useful summary of events in the sixteenth and seventeenth centuries is provided by Canny
1989.

were operative in this process, but the church's own improved position was surely chief among them. With the removal of governmental opposition came far greater opportunities for pastoral control; and indeed the authorities often relied upon the church as an influence promoting social stability. Priests encouraged their flocks to embrace doctrinal orthodoxy and – at least as important – a more orderly and 'respectable' way of life: the old customs, besides their semi-pagan character, were associated with violence, alcoholism, and sedition. A key figure in the 'devotional revolution' of the nineteenth century was Paul Cullen (1803–78), archbishop of Armagh and subsequently the first Irish cardinal; in 1850 he convened at Thurles the first synod to be held in Ireland since the twelfth century, at which there were enacted provisions for radical reorganisation at every level of the Irish church.[35]

Many ancient customs have of course survived in Ireland until our own times, especially in remoter areas. Nevertheless, the reforms of the last century had far-reaching effects on the Catholic population as a whole, and succeeded in stamping out many beliefs and observances which had survived the vicissitudes of more than a millennium of troubled history.

It may appear something of a digression to have dwelt at such length on the period subsequent to that which produced the texts in this collection; but I believe that it is essential to have some idea of the gulf which separates us from the times in which they were written. The disappearance of the old monasteries; the downfall of the learned families which served, so to speak, as their literary executors; the emergence of a priesthood formed within the framework of post-Tridentine orthodoxy; the attrition and widespread disappearance of the popular customs which represented the last survival of medieval Irish piety: all these things have contributed to making the Ireland of today a place radically different from the Ireland of seven centuries ago – and, more to our present purpose, have brought into being an Irish Catholicism which has only a tenuous connection with the religion of the earlier Middle Ages.

There is no point in debating whether this state of affairs is good or bad: in some ways it is one and in some the other, and in any case there is ample room for difference of opinion. What is crucial is to recognise the fact of discontinuity; unless we do so, we will only project our own ideas and preconceptions upon the texts, and can have little hope of hearing them speak in their own voices.

Such considerations constitute a challenge for anyone who seeks genuine insight into the spirit of another time or place: after all that has happened how can anyone, in Ireland or outside it, claim to speak out of the same tradition as the pre-Norman Irish?

I do not by any means want to suggest that this tradition is entirely alien; in fact of course it is simply one branch of the Christian tradition as a whole, and shares with the rest of that tradition the same Saviour, mysteries, Scriptures, and

---

35 D. Mooney 1990 provides a detailed account of the erosion of traditional popular religion in one Irish county; the decisions of the Synod of Thurles and subsequent assemblies are described by Cunningham 1970.

sacraments. On this fundamental level, all Christians have their most sacred beliefs in common with those whose writings are presented here.

This is a point of primary importance; but it does not address the question which I have in mind. For it is not Christianity as such, but the first centuries of Christianity in Ireland which are this book's concern: insofar as the faith of that period had a distinctive character it is indeed a thing apart from us, and that distinctiveness cannot be apprehended if we think only in terms of the familiar.

Ultimately, real understanding is either miraculous or impossible: either grace grants us a spark of illuminating empathy, or the Other remains closed and inscrutable. The best that we can do is to seek that understanding, to open ourselves to the possibility of that grace, with all the diligence and honesty of which we are capable.

The preparation of this book has been guided largely by these thoughts, and by the desire to come as close as possible to allowing the tradition to speak to us directly. The ideal would be to have an anthology of texts actually chosen by an Irishman of the early Middle Ages, who would also furnish supplementary comments and explanations – but such an editor, obviously, is unavailable. In the effort to go as far as I can toward supplying this lack, I have adopted the following principles:

– Texts have been selected not because of their potential appeal to a modern audience – although it is of course my hope that such an appeal will be felt – but because they were popular among the medieval Irish themselves. I have used various criteria in gauging this popularity: noting how many manuscript copies of a text survive, how many versions of it evolved over the centuries, and whether it is cited or alluded to in other works.

– I have included the medieval prefaces, commentaries, and notes which were added to the texts in the course of their transmission. This material helps us to see how they were read and understood by the culture which produced them: which of their aspects were most valued, and how in many cases the texts themselves became the subjects of further legends. We can be reminded that our way of reading is not the only way, and can attempt to enter the minds not just of the authors, but of their earlier audience.

– In the case of several of the pieces in this book, notably some of the early hymns, the words came to have at least as much importance as the meaning. To recite them verbatim was to gain supernatural rewards, in this world as well as in the next. To some of us this may seem more like magic than like piety; but whatever our judgment, it is an aspect of the texts which was of crucial importance to the tradition which preserved them. In cases where there is evidence that a composition had this incantatory value, I have therefore given the original text as well as a translation.

This collection is aimed primarily at the general reader, not the specialist; and I have omitted much discussion, and many supporting references, which would be appropriate in a more academic treatment of the material. It is my hope, though, that some of those who read the book may be motivated to pursue the subject further: to this end I have supplied references to a broad range of primary and secondary sources, both introductory and specialised, in the accompanying notes. Further details, of specifically scholarly interest, are given in the 'Textual Remarks' at the conclusion.

Like most translators, I have sought to stay as close to the original texts as possible while at the same time producing reasonably readable English versions: also like most translators, I have often found this ideal to be an elusive one. Three conventions of punctuation may conveniently be noted here. Where addition of a word or phrase has seemed necessary to bring out the sense, this addition is enclosed in square brackets [ ]; when the addition fills an actual gap in the text, representing either conjectural emendation or the use of another manuscript, angle brackets < > have been used. An ellipsis ... marks a gap which I have been unable to restore.

In light of the above considerations it will be obvious that my own personal impressions of this material, and of the culture which produced it, are of secondary importance. I certainly do not wish to impose them in any intrusive or dogmatic fashion. This having been said, and fully acknowledging the limitations of my own perspective, I would like to set down a few thoughts concerning the tradition's distinctive features and contemporary relevance.[36]

I have already mentioned the relationship between early Irish Christianity and the pagan past, and the ways in which many found it possible to achieve some synthesis between the two. It is important not to oversimplify here: much of the literature speaks of paganism with outright hostility, and rejoices in its downfall;[37] and even when a place is found in the new for some elements of the old, there is no question of compromising the former's paramount authority. What I am speaking of is a single strand within the tradition, but one characterised by creativity and vision which had a far-reaching impact. We see it at work in the visual arts, where the full repertoire of pre-Christian decorative technique was unhesitatingly applied to the new task of decorating Gospel books and reliquaries; in preaching, where at least one Irishman was condemned for having stated that Christ redeemed the pagans who had not heard his message;[38] and above all in literature, where the interweaving of pagan and Christian elements produced a rich corpus of legends. As it happens, relatively little in this book explicitly reflects this aspect of the tradition: it can however be observed in 'The Pseudo-Historical Prologue to the *Senchas Már*', with its teaching that the native legal system was inspired by the Holy Spirit; and in the bewildering amalgam of Biblical and apparently pagan allusions in *Nuall Fir Fhio*.

36 Here I enter a delicate area, where preconception, prejudice, and wishful thinking have all too often been given free rein. For a lucid look at some of the pitfalls see Sims-Williams 1986; a recent example of balanced and cautious thinking on the issue is Wright 1993, 1–48. 37 See for instance the 'First Prologue' to *Féilire Oengusso*, pp. 189–91. But even a condemnatory attitude could coexist with fascinated interest; cf. the discussion in Carey 1994. 38 Carey 1989, 10 n. 46.

Together with the self-confidence which led the Irish to preserve and develop their own traditions, mention should be made of the zeal with which they imported the writings of other cultures and made them their own. In many cases texts survive only because they were copied in Ireland – this is one reason for the great contribution which Irish scholars made, particularly in the ninth century, to preserving the literature of antiquity. Most interestingly, texts and ideas which were condemned or avoided elsewhere in Europe found a home in the fabric of Irish monastic culture. The Graeco-Roman doctrine of an inhabited southern hemisphere, viewed with suspicion or indeed antagonism in much of early Christendom, is vigorously advocated in *In Tenga Bithnua* and *Saltair na Rann*.[39] Apocryphal scriptures are better represented in Ireland than anywhere else in western Europe: an extensive body of such literature, going back in some cases to the Gnostic communities of Egypt, lies behind such texts as *In Tenga* and *Fís Adomnáin*.[40]

And so early Ireland was, as I have observed earlier, both inward-looking and outward-looking: the two perspectives fed and inspired one another; and in both we can see the same intellectual adventurousness, the same flair for creative adaptation. I believe that they had a single root as well: a faith that there is room in God's world for all in which we find value. A vivid sense of the rooted continuity of ancestral lore, of the clarity and elegance of classical cosmology, of the force of awe in heterodox Gospels and apocalypses – to feel this was to recognise that value, and the early Irish drew upon all these sources in forging their own vision of the real. Such a flexible appreciation of diversity, open to mysteries and tolerant of alternatives, is not a bad example to look to in the present time – a time in which unprecedented opportunities for intercultural understanding coexist with the murderous divisiveness of nationalist and sectarian crusades.

A keen interest in the workings of nature led the Irish to assimilate all of the ancient scientific writings to which they could gain access, and to embellish them with observations and speculations of their own. That interest is reflected in several of the pieces in this book, especially in its first section: for it was not merely an intellectual enthusiasm, but an integral part of their religious sensibility.

A name repeatedly used for God in the early sources is *Dúilem* 'Creator', and his role as Maker of the universe is stressed throughout the literature: he is King of heaven and earth, guide of the sun in its daily journey through the sky, governor of the movements of the sea. By its very existence, the whole world affirms the Divine. In the words of one of the last cantos of *Saltair na Rann*,

> All the many creatures of God –
> beloved and clever, a mighty multitude –
> after the fair shaping of each of them
> I have no true understanding of any....

39 Pages 88, 91 below; cf. Carey 1989.   40 On early Irish scientific thought see Smyth 1986, 1995. A valuable catalogue of apocryphal works is provided in McNamara 1975; many of the most important are translated in Herbert and McNamara 1989.

> My King of mysteries, of fair fame,
> wherever in his creation he dwells above the world,
> mighty and glorious – in my life
> I can do nothing but worship him.[41]

The vastness and complexity of the universe, its unfathomable secrets, fill the mind with an awe which can be the first step toward an apprehension of transcendence; or, as Columbanus puts it, 'If you wish to know the Creator, understand the creature.'[42] This same cosmic piety is conveyed in somewhat different terms in *In Tenga Bithnua*: here an exposition of God's most fantastic works is a meditation for the night before Easter; and reluctance to believe in the miraculous, in the full extravagant strangeness of existence, is tantamount to blasphemy.

A contrast to *In Tenga* is provided by the treatise *On the Miracles of Holy Scripture*, which seeks 'natural' explanations for the miracles of the Bible; but much of this contrast lies only on the surface. For the reasoning which directs the latter work is, again, predicated on a belief in God's immanence within every part of his creation: it is because of the potencies latent within their very essence that wonders can be drawn from water and air, from stone and flesh. And this pious rationalism too goes hand in hand with a reverent sense of mystery. As the author observes in the course of a discussion of the tides:

> Let whoever desires true wisdom make haste to the eternal kingdom where there is no ignorance; meanwhile, let him say in the words of the famous teacher of the gentiles, 'We know in part, and we prophesy in part' (1 Corinthians 13:9). For we barely understand even in part all of the things which we possess. The surface of the earth on which we toil, by which we are nourished, kept alive and supported, appears plainly before our eyes; yet even so we do not know what holds it up. The sun is assigned to minister to us by day, but the course which it follows in the night is hidden from our knowledge. Who has the wit to understand the changes of the moon, waxing in fifteen days and waning in the same interval? We are allowed to behold the surges of the flowing sea, but are denied knowledge of the place to which it ebbs. We know and are mindful of the place of our own birth; but the day of our death, although it is certain that it will come, is unknown to us. We are only able to contemplate in part even those bodily things which we see. Thus we know only in part, for as long as we are in this world; but if we can attain to the light of the Father of Lights, there will be nothing in the creation which we will not know.[43]

Understanding the world's mysteries can move the soul to worship, and so can failure to understand them. In finding a road to God in their experience of nature, the Irish celebrated a universe which is not sundered from its Maker – a harmony

41 Stokes 1883, lines 7997–8000, 8013–16. 42 Walker 1970, 64. 43 Migne 1844–64, 35.2159.

of being which Eriugena expresses when he writes of the immortal souls of animals, and of the final folding of all things back into the One.[44]

In certain significant ways, a concern and respect for the individual emerge from early Irish religious writing. It may seem ironic that it is in monastic rules and penitentials that this can be seen most clearly: we tend naturally to think of such texts as codifications of self-abnegation and rigorous conformity, and the stark asceticism of the Irish documents in this class does little to offset such a judgment. And yet it was the Irish who introduced the practice of private penance, opening up occasions for repeated soul-searching and introspection in the life of every Christian; and it is in Ireland that we find the figure of the *anmchara*, the 'soul-friend' or confessor.[45] Instructions for monks, found in such texts as that from which I have given excerpts in 'Stories of the Céili Dé', have none of the systematic thoroughness of the *Rule* of Saint Benedict: they consist largely of the *ad hoc* opinions of various holy men, and remarkable emphasis is laid on the degree to which people differ, and on the consequent necessity for individual judgment and responsibility. The uniqueness of each human being's experience of life is recognised as an essential aspect of the approach to God; the same sensibility of the solitary worshipper informs many of the religious lyrics which are so deservedly admired a part of medieval Irish literature.[46]

Finally, and with some trepidation, I should mention the imagination. Imagination is impossible to quantify, difficult even to characterise; yet there can be no denying that a powerful current of imaginative energy runs through all the pieces collected here. We see it most obviously in such works as *In Tenga Bithnua*, where a motley array of erudition has been transmuted into a headlong, flamboyant vision of the universe; or in the second canto of *Saltair na Rann*, where only careful probing can discover the background of the poet's elaborate portrayal of the Heavenly City. To have found some of the sources of these descriptions, or of others like them, is in no way to belittle their authors' creativity. Creativity of a different kind is present in *On the Miracles of Holy Scripture*: here the author, confronted with the full array of God's marvellous works, used all of his ingenuity in bending his rather precarious grasp of natural science to fit the demands of his theology.

I am tempted to go further. I would suggest that the almost reckless inclusiveness which I have described above, the ability to bring disparate worlds within the compass of a single faith, springs from this same imaginative sensibility. We can recognise it as well in that fondness for the extravagant, the exotic, and the superlative which – sometimes with more zest than discrimination – informs so much of the early literature. The ultimate theological justification for mankind's imaginative capacity lies in its analogy to the cosmogonic work of the Creator, of which we ourselves – God's self-portrait – are the supreme example. For Columbanus, this

---

[44] Sheldon-Williams and O'Meara 1987, 373–6, 562–3.   [45] McNeill and Gamer 1938, 23–30. For editions of the penitentials themselves, see Bieler 1975.   [46] See for instance the fine collection in Murphy 1956, 2–71.

divine shaping was not a finite incident in the world's beginning. In one of his sermons, he utters the prayer 'Let Christ paint his image in us; as he does, saying "My peace I give to you, my peace I leave to you".'[47]

Again, I offer these thoughts only as perceptions of my own. I hope that each reader will seek understanding of the Christianity of early Ireland first and most earnestly in the texts themselves. The past is gone forever, but they remain.

47 Walker 1970, 108.

I CREATOR AND CREATION

Altus Prosator

The tradition that this hymn was composed by the great saint Columba or Colum Cille (died 597) is doubtless the principal reason why it was so venerated in medieval Ireland. Colum Cille's authorship has been questioned, as it is not attributed to him in any non-Irish source; its style, however, and the archaic character of many of its scriptural citations, seem to indicate that it was at any rate written in Ireland or Britain, in his time or not long afterward.

Altus Prosator takes in the whole expanse of sacred history, from the creation to the Last Judgment. Finding a focus within this dizzying vastness, the poet concentrates so avidly on the beginning and end of the world that there is room for almost nothing else: stanzas I–XV are taken up with the origin and ordering of the universe and XVII–XXII with its final days, leaving a single stanza describing Moses on Sinai (XVI) to do duty for the rest of the Old and New Testaments. Although the Bible and the Fathers are quoted repeatedly throughout the *Altus*, the poet is primarily concerned with topics treated most fully in the apocrypha: the things hidden in the heavens and beneath the earth, the fall of the rebel angels, the events of the end time.

Even if Colum Cille did not really compose the *Altus*, it is easy to see why readers in medieval Ireland believed it to be his work. Colum Cille was famous as a poet, and innumerable verses composed centuries after his death came to be attributed to him; many of these were prophecies, and indeed the saint's prophetic powers were already being extolled by his first biographer Adomnán (died 704). The notion that he was interested in cosmology appears already in *Amra Coluim Chille*, which appears to state that he was knowledgable concerning winds, tides, and the movements of moon and sun;[1] in one early tale he converses with a mysterious youth from the Otherworld, in which they discuss 'heavenly and earthly mysteries'.[2] It was natural enough, then, that he should be credited with a hymn which (as Gregory the Great is alleged to have noted in the medieval preface below) has more to say about God's creation than about the divine nature itself.

The *Altus* has one stanza for each letter of the alphabet, and each stanza begins with the letter appropriate to it: for what is probably the earliest Irish hymn with this structure, and some general remarks on 'abecedarian' hymns, see the introductory note to *Audite omnes* below (p. 147).

By supplying most of the supplementary material which has accumulated around the *Altus*, I hope to give some impression of the ways in which it was read and appreciated throughout the early medieval period. It is interesting to contrast the scholarly approach of the person or persons who wrote the glosses – discussing the meaning or origin of individual words, explaining mythological allusions or

---

1 Stokes 1899, 254–9 §§58, 61–3; cf. Clancy and Márkus 1995, 109. 2 Meyer and Nutt 1899, 317.

theological issues, suggesting allegorical interpretations – with the almost magical attitude expressed at the end of the preface, where all sorts of rewards in this world and the next are promised to whoever recites the *Altus* regularly. Below we will find similar powers attributed to the hymn *Audite omnes*, to *Féilire Oengusso*, and to the *loricae*; as an addendum to the present text I have included an anecdote which provides further testimony concerning the hymn's devotional importance and reputed supernatural powers.

In the *Altus* itself, curiosity about the world and its fate is bound up with awestruck worship of the Creator; in the additional material, a devotional text becomes the focus both of high-flown scholarly analysis and of concrete expectations of material and personal wellbeing. All of these elements were interwoven in the fabric of the tradition as a whole, and in the religious experience of those who lived within it.

The place of this hymn's composition is Iona. The time of its composition is the reign of Aedán son of Gabrán king of Scotland, and of Aed son of Ainmire king of Ireland; Maurice or Phocas was then king of the Romans. Its author is Colum Cille, of a noble Irish lineage: he was called *Columba* ('dove'), as it is said, 'Be as shrewd as serpents and as guileless as doves' (Matthew 10:16). The reason why he composed it was that he wished to praise God.

He spent seven years meditating upon this hymn in a black cell without light, seeking forgiveness for the battle of Cúl Dreimne which he had won against Diarmait son of Cerball, and for the other battles which were won because of him.

Or, as others say, it was composed on a sudden. One day Colum Cille was in Iona, and no one with him save Baíthín, and they had no food save for a sieve of oats. Then Colum Cille said to Baíthín, 'Noble guests are coming to us today, Baíthín' – i.e., followers of Gregory[3] who came to him with gifts. And he said to Baíthín, 'Stay here to attend to the guests, so that I can go to the mill.' Then he took up his burden from a certain stone called Bláthnat which was in the enclosure; and it is still there, and the division of food in the refectory is made upon it. He thought his burden heavy, and so he composed this hymn according to the sequence of the alphabet from there all the way to the mill, i.e. '*Adiutor laborantium*', etc.[4] But when he put the first load [of grain] into the mill, he began upon the first stanza, and while the sack was being made into flour he was composing the hymn: and so it was composed on a sudden.

Colum Cille went to Iona in the five hundred and sixty-fifth year after Christ's birth, as Bede says: 'In the year of our Lord's incarnation 565, when Justin the younger took up the rule of the Roman Empire after Justinian, a priest and abbot distinguished by the life and habit of a monk, Columba by name, came from Ireland to Britain to preach the word of God in the provinces of the northern Picts.' Bruide son of Melchú was reigning over the Picts at that time, and he offered Iona to Columba; and Columba was buried there in the seventy-sixth year of his age, thirty-four years after having come to Britain to preach.

This hymn was taken eastward to Gregory, in return for the gifts which he had sent: the cross which is called 'the Great Jewel', and a hymnal for the days of the week. But those who fetched it changed three of the stanzas in order to test Gregory, i.e. [those beginning] '*Hic sublatus*' and '*Orbem*' and '*Vagatur*'. When they began reciting the hymn to Gregory, angels of God came and were standing until the [extraneous] stanza was reached; Gregory would rise in their honour until then.

3 Pope Gregory I (*c*.540–604), a figure regarded with particular reverence by the Irish. There are other legends concerning his relationship with Colum Cille, but no reliable evidence that there was in fact any direct contact between them. 4 This hymn was recently identified by Bernard Muir (1983); see also the translation and commentary in Clancy and Márkus 1995, 69–80.

When it was reached, however, the angels would sit down; Gregory too would sit, and so the hymn was finished. Then Gregory asked them to confess, for he knew that it was they who had altered it. They said that it was, and they were forgiven. And he said that there was nothing wrong with the hymn, save for how little the Trinity was praised in it *per se*, though it was praised through the creation; and that criticism reached Colum Cille, and that is the reason why he composed '*In te Christe*'.[5]

This hymn has the sequence of the alphabet, in the manner of the Hebrews.[6] The basis of this [first] stanza is drawn from the catholic faith: belief in the Oneness together with affirmation of the Threeness.[7] It was composed according to rhythm, of which there are two kinds: *artificialis* and *vulgaris*. In the *artificialis*, the feet have equal measure, equal division, and equal stress – i.e., in arsis and thesis – and the subsequent takes the place of the preceding in the resolution [of syllables]. In the *vulgaris*, however, there is correspondence of syllables and lines and couplets – and that is what is in this hymn.[8] There are six lines in each stanza except the first, and sixteen syllables in each line; and there are seven lines in the first stanza, because it is the praise of God that is therein. The uneven number is appropriate in that stanza by contrast with the others, because of the disparity between God and his creatures; the number six is that of the creatures because they were made in six days. There should be a title and an argument at the head of each stanza.[9]

The proper way to recite the hymn is to recite '*Quis potest Deo*' between every two stanzas: it is thus that its virtue will be efficacious, for that is how it was first recited.[10] This hymn has many virtues. Angels will be present for as long as it is being recited. The Devil will not find a way to the one who recites it every day, and enemies will not put him to shame on the day when he recites it. And there will be no strife in the house in which it is recited regularly. It guards against every death save death on a pillow, and there will be no hunger or nakedness in the place where it is recited often, and much else.

I

The title is 'Concerning the oneness and threeness of the three Persons of the Godhead'. The argument, however, is the [passage in] Scripture on which the

---

5 Bernard and Atkinson 1898, 1.84–6; cf. Lapidge and Sharpe 1985, 149–50 §587.   6 That is, in imitation of the abecedarian psalms; cf. the introductory discussion of *Audite omnes*, p. 147 below. 7 *Cretem Óenatad co fóisitin Tredatad*; the phrase is evidently taken from *Faeth Fiada* below, which speaks of 'belief in the Threeness, proclamation of the Oneness' (*cretim Treodataid, faísitin Oendatad*, p. 130).   8 This description is not very clear, and may reflect some vagueness on the part of the preface's author. I take the basic meaning to be that in 'vulgar' verse rhyme and regular syllable-count are all that is required; 'artificial' verse is composed according to classical standards, with account taken of the quantity of the syllables. 'The subsequent taking the place of the preceding' is perhaps a reference to elision, the dropping of a final vowel when another vowel follows at the beginning of the next word.   9 'Argument' is here used to mean the principal scriptural citation on which each stanza is based, as explained in the heading of the first stanza below. 10 A reference to the supplementary stanzas occurring after the main hymn below (pp. 48–9).

stanza is based, as it is written in Daniel (7:9) or in Isaiah (6:1): 'The Ancient of Days was sitting upon his seat.' 'The Ancient of Days' was 'the Eternal of times'. 'The Ancient of Days' signifies God, because of the multitude of the days before which God existed, or because he existed before all times. [Colum Cille] cites the Scripture of the prophets because he was a prophet himself; and he cites Daniel in particular, for he was the last and the noblest [of them], while Colum Cille was the last and the noblest of the prophets of Ireland.

> Altus Prosator, Uetustus/ Dierum, et Ingenitus,
> erat absque origine/ primordii et crepidine;
> est et erit in saecula/ saeculorum infinita,
> cui est unigenitus/ Christus et Sanctus Spiritus
> coaeternus in gloria/ deitatis perpetua.
> Non tres deos depromimus,/ sed unum Deum dicimus
> salua fide in personis/ tribus gloriosissimis.

> The exalted Creator, Ancient of Days, and Unbegotten One
> was without a first beginning, or a foundation;
> he is, and he will be for unending ages.
> [His] only-begotten Christ, and the Holy Spirit,
> are coeternal with him in the everlasting glory of Godhead.
> We do not assert that there are three gods, but speak of one God,
> retaining our faith in the three most glorious Persons.

GLOSSES 'Creator': i.e. Begetter, or the great Sower. 'Ancient': i.e. eternal, i.e. as old as time, i.e. older than our times, and preceding them. 'of Days': i.e. of times. 'without a beginning': i.e. without material, or without basis. 'only-begotten': i.e. 'first-begotten', because there is none before him; 'only-begotten', because there is none after him. 'Christ': 'Messiah' in Hebrew, 'Christ' in Greek, 'Anointed' (*unctus*) in Latin.

II

The title is, 'Concerning the creation of the nine [angelic] orders' – he has omitted three not through ignorance, but from lack of space in the stanza. The argument, however, is ' "Let there be light," and there was light' (Genesis 1:3).

> Bonos creauit angelos,/ ordines, et archangelos,
> principatum ac sedium,/ potestatum, uirtutium,
> uti non esset bonitas/ otiosa ac maiestas
> Trinitatis in omnibus/ largitatis muneribus,
> sed haberet celestia/ in quibus priuilegia
> ostenderet magnopere/ possibili fatimine.

He created the good Angels, and the Archangels, and the orders
of Principalities and Thrones, of Powers, of Virtues,
so that the goodness and majesty of the Trinity,
in all the largesse of its munificence, might not be idle,
but might have heavenly dignities in which,
with a potent utterance, it could be mightily manifest.

GLOSSES 'Angels': 'Before every day and every time, God established the angelic
creation and formless matter,' says Isidore. And this is why he omits the Cherubim
and Seraphim rather than the others: because they are farthest from men both in
knowledge and in habitation. These then are the nine orders: Angels, Archangels,
Virtues, Powers, Principalities, Dominations, Thrones, Cherubim, and Seraphim.
'idle': i.e. without action; i.e. inert or indolent, without bestowing treasures.
'heavenly': i.e. elements or agencies. 'dignities' (*priuilegia*): i.e. great distinctions, or
honours; i.e. each order above another; i.e. as if it were 'a personal law' (*priuata
lex*). 'potent': i.e. with the potent recitation; i.e. with the potent praise which the
angels give him, saying, 'Holy, holy, holy Lord.'

III

The title is 'Concerning the transmigration of the prince of the nine orders of
angels'. The argument, however, is from the Apocalypse: 'I saw a star fall to the
earth from heaven' (Revelation 9:1); and from Isaiah (14:12): 'How you have fallen,
Lucifer, who rose in the morning!'

Caeli de regni apice/ stationis angelicae
claritate praefulgoris/ uenustate speciminis
superbiendo ruerat/ Lucifer quem formauerat
apostataeque angeli/ eodem lapsu lugubri
auctoris cenodoxiae/ peruicacis inuidiae
ceteris remanentibus/ in suis principatibus.

From the summit of the kingdom of heaven, of the habitation of the
    angels,
puffed up by the brilliance of his [own] splendour, by the beauty of
    his [own] appearance,
Lucifer had fallen, whom [God] had formed.
And in that same sad downfall of the inventor of vainglory,
of unyielding envy, [fell] the apostate angels.
The others remained in their exalted stations.

GLOSSES 'apostate': i.e. they fell, i.e. the renegade angels. 'Apostate' in Greek means 'abandoner of the faith' or 'base' in Latin. 'sad' (*lugubris*): i.e. lamentable, i.e. both by themselves and by others; for the demons bewail their fall. Or *lugubrium* is the name of a tree on which even birds are unable to perch because it is so slippery; hence [its name] is given to everything slippery.[11]

IV

The title is 'Concerning the downfall of the Devil', i.e., the changing of Lucifer's name to 'the Dragon'. The argument however is from the Apocalypse: 'Behold, a red dragon having seven heads and ten horns, and its tail dragged with it a third part of the stars' (Revelation 12:3–4).

> Draco magnus deterrimus/ terribilis et antiquus,
> qui fuit serpens lubricus/ sapientior omnibus
> bestiis et animantibus/ terrae ferocioribus,
> tertiam partem siderum/ traxit secum in barathrum
> locorum infernalium/ diuersorumque carcerum,
> refugas ueri Luminis/ parasito praecipites.

> The great Dragon, worst of all, terrible and ancient –
> who was [also] the slippery serpent, wiser than all
> the beasts, and the fiercer creatures of the earth –
> dragged a third part of the stars with him into the abyss
> of the infernal places and the various prisons:
> exiles from the true Light, [hurled] headlong by the flatterer.

GLOSSES 'slippery' (*lubricus*): i.e., because one slips there; *lubrum* is a tree in the East so slippery that fleas cannot cling to it but fall off, and [its name] is given to everything slippery, and there are birds in its top from whose dung silk is made.[12] 'wiser': Wisdom can be for good or for evil: for good, as when David says 'The beginning of wisdom' (Psalm 110:10); for bad, as when Christ says, 'I will destroy the wisdom of the wise ones of this world' (1 Corinthians 1:19). 'a third': i.e. of all of the angels, or of those who sided with him. [Colum Cille] is thinking of three divisions: a third of them in the air, and a third in [the depths of] the sea and earth, and a third in the abyss, i.e. in hell. 'flatterer' (*parasitus*): i.e. by the buffoon, i.e. he is his own buffoon.

11 *Lugubris* has evidently been confused here with *lubricus* 'slippery'; cf. the gloss on the latter in the next stanza. 12 I cite the version of this gloss in Leabhar Breac, as that in the Trinity manuscript is too corrupt for me to make sense of it. Cf. the gloss on *lugubris* in the previous stanza.

V

The title is 'Concerning the creation of the elements of the world, and of man to reign over them naturally thereafter'. The argument however is, 'In the beginning God made heaven and earth,' as it says in Genesis (1:1).

Excelsus mundi machinam/ praeuidens et armoniam,
caelum et terram fecerat,/ mare et aquas condidit,
herbarum quoque germina,/ uirgultorum arbuscula,
solem, lunam, ac sidera,/ ignem ac necessaria,
aues, pisces, et pecora,/ bestias et animalia,
hominem demum regere/ protoplastum praesagmine.

The Most High, foreseeing the mechanism and harmony of the world,
had made heaven and earth, established sea and waters,
and the seeds of plants, and the bushes in thickets,
sun, moon, and stars, fire and [all] needful things,
birds, fish, and cattle, beasts and animals –
and last of all the first man, to rule them through foreknowledge.

GLOSSES 'mechanism': i.e. matter, i.e. the mass. 'heaven': i.e. the whole invisible creation. 'earth': i.e. the whole visible creation is called 'earth'. 'beasts': i.e. whatever attacks with tooth and nail is called a 'beast'. 'foreknowledge' (*praesagmen*): i.e. through prophecy, i.e. of Christ; or by supremacy over the host, i.e. supremacy over a host of men. For *praesagmen* is composed of *praesul* ('official') and *agmen* ('army')[13].... So that is what Adam had, as Cic- (?) says: 'God created all things, but Adam named them with names.'

VI

The title is 'Concerning the praising of God by the angels on the fourth day, saying "Holy, holy, holy Lord, God of Sabaoth"'. The argument is 'When I made heaven and earth, the angels praised me together,' as it is said in the Wisdom of Solomon.[14]

Factis simul sideribus,/ etheris luminaribus,
collaudauerunt angeli/ factura pro mirabili
immensae molis Dominum,/ Opificem celestium,

13 In fact *praesagmen* is a noun derived from *praesago* 'I divine, I prophesy'. 14 In fact this seems closest to Job 38:4–7; cf. perhaps Proverbs 8:22–31.

preconio laudabile,/ debito, et immobile,
concentuque egregio/ grates egerunt Domino,
amore et arbitrio,/ non naturae donario.

At the same time that the stars, the lights of the ether, were made,
the angels all praised the Lord, the Maker of heavenly things,
for his wondrous shaping of the enormous mass.
They proclaimed and exalted him without cease, as was fitting,
and gave thanks to the Lord in splendid song –
out of love and free will, not simply from inborn nature.

GLOSSES 'mass': i.e. not a physical mass. 'will': Will is the effort proper to the soul. 'nature': i.e. the praise of God was not planted in their nature, but in their will and power, as he shows already when he says 'out of love and free will'.

VII

The title is 'Concerning Adam's sin, and the second downfall of the Devil in Adam's seduction'. The argument is 'You will be an accursed serpent; you will eat earth all the days of your life,' as it says in Genesis (3:14).

Grassatis primis duobus/ seductisque parentibus,
secundo ruit Zabulus/ cum suis satellitibus;
quorum horrore uultuum,/ sonoque uolitantium,
consternarentur homines/ metu territi fragiles,
non ualentes carnalibus/ haec intueri uisibus
qui nunc ligantur fascibus/ ergastulorum nexibus.

When the first two parents were attacked and led astray,
the Devil and his followers fell a second time.
Frail men would be stupefied with fear
at the horror of their faces and the sound of their flight,
not being able with bodily vision to behold those things
which are now tied in bundles in the knotted bonds of dungeons.

GLOSSES 'were attacked': i.e. by the Devil. 'led astray': i.e. from the hour of their creation. 'parents': i.e. Adam and Eve. 'a second time': i.e. first from heaven to earth, the second time to hell. 'fell': i.e. the Devil fell from heaven through his first transgression, the second time out of the air through his second transgression. Or *ruit* ('fell') has been put here instead of *irruit* ('invaded') for the sake of the metre, as if to say 'He rose up against God'; but on the second occasion only against Adam. Otherwise it is 'fell', i.e. he fell at first through attacking God, a second time through attacking Adam. The reason for the Devil's second downfall is related [here]: the punishment imposed upon the Devil for assailing the two first parents is called 'falling' by analogy with the punishment which was imposed upon him at first for assailing God. 'and his followers': i.e. with his evil agents. 'those things': i.e. the hosts of the devils in flight. 'in bundles': in bundles and in companies: each company of them is tied up like a bundle in its own proper place. 'of dungeons': i.e. of the torture-prisons, or of the work-prisons....

VIII

The title is 'Concerning the Devil's expulsion from the community of the angels'. The argument however is from Genesis: 'Accursed serpent' (3:14); and in the Gospel it is said, 'Go back, Satan' (Matthew 4:10), and 'You shall not tempt the Lord your God' (ibid., 4:7), and 'You shall serve him alone' (ibid. 4:10).

Hic, sublatus e medio,/ deiectus est a Domino,
cuius aëris spatium/ constipatur satellitum
globo inuisibilium/ turbido perduellium:
ne malis exemplaribus/ imbutis, ac sceleribus
nullis unquam tegentibus/ septis ac parietibus,
fornicarentur homines,/ palam omnium oculis.

Plucked from the midmost [place], he was hurled down by the Lord;
the region of the air is thronged
with the tumultuous mass of his hostile followers, unseen
so that men should not, steeped in bad examples and crimes,
without the shelter of any fences or walls,
commit fornication before the eyes of all.

GLOSSES 'he': i.e. the Devil. 'plucked': i.e. from the presence of God, or from the unity of the brethren. 'hostile': i.e. 'double-fighters', i.e. among themselves, or waging [war] against God and men.... 'commit fornication': i.e. be ruined, or commit sin; 'fornication' stands for every [kind of] sin.

IX

The title is 'That clouds lift the waters into heaven'. The argument however is David's saying, 'Bringing clouds from the ends of the earth,' and again, 'Who brings forth the winds from their storehouses' (Psalm 134:7).

Inuehunt nubes pontias/ ex fontibus brumalias,
tribus profundioribus/ oceani dodrantibus,
maris caeli climatibus/ ceruleis turbinibus,
profuturas segitibus,/ uiniis, et germinibus.
Agitatae flaminibus/ thesauris emergentibus,
quique paludes marinas/ euacuant reciprocas.

Clouds carry the wintry brine from the fountains,
from the three deeper floods of the ocean,
in blue waterspouts of seawater into the heights of heaven,
to the profit of grain, of vines and seeds.
Driven by the winds which come forth from their storehouses,
they dry up the ebbing shallows of the sea.

GLOSSES 'brine': i.e. the seas. 'floods' (*dodrantes*):[15] ... i.e. the three three-quarter [periods] of retardation, i.e. the three full ... to the equinox and the sun thus. Each day, then, is retarded by three-quarters of an hour and two and a half minutes, as Bede says; but the two and a half minutes are omitted for the sake of metre, or he omits them on the authority of Philip. They are 'deeper', for it is more that they fill the estuaries and the lands, and the clouds bring waters to them more.... 'blue': i.e. from the dark blue waves, or the dark blue winds. 'grain': i.e. good men. 'vines': i.e. the just. 'seeds': i.e. base men. 'shallows': i.e. deeper fountains or store-houses, i.e. to the valleys of the winds (?) which are in storehouses. 'storehouses': i.e., it is the winds which bring....

X

The title is 'Concerning the intolerable torment of the sinners in hell'. The argument however is what Job says: 'Behold the giants groan beneath the waters' (26:5).

Kaduca ac tyrannica/ mundique momentanea
regum presenti gloria/ nutu Dei deposita.
Ecce gigantes gemere/ sub aquis magno ulcere:
comprobantur incendio/ aduri ac supplicio,
Cocitique Carybdibus/ strangulati turbentibus,
Scillis obtecti, fluctibus/ eliduntur et scropibus.

15 Much of this gloss is now illegible, and what remains is far from easy to understand. Much of its obscurity is due to an overlap of the two senses of *dodrans*, which in the Latin of Britain and Ireland at this period could mean either 'sea' or 'three-fourths (of an hour)'; the glossator naturally enough takes the reference to *dodrantes* to relate in some way to reckoning the cycle of the tides, and associates it with the doctrine that the moon lags behind the sun by a period of 47½ minutes. See further Brown 1975.

The frail, oppressive, and fleeting glory
of the kings of the present world is laid low by God's will.
See: that the giants groan in great pain beneath the waters
is made known; [and] that they are burnt by fire, are tormented.
Choked in the swelling whirlpools of Cocytus,
covered by Scyllas, they are battered by waves and cliffs.

GLOSSES 'fleeting': i.e. in a moment of time. 'giants': i.e. the mighty ones in hell.
... [They are] laid low in Mount Etna. 'beneath the waters': i.e. under waves of
torments, i.e. in intolerable torment. 'made known': i.e. in Scripture. 'Cocytus': i.e.,
the name of one of the four rivers of hell. There are four rivers in hell: Cocytus,
which means 'without joy'; Styx, which means 'sorrow'; Phlegethon, which means
'fiery'; and Acheron. Or else these are four names of a single river. 'in the swelling
whirlpools': i.e. by the swollen or harsh or boiling rocks, or by the whirlpools
which swell up. 'choked': i.e. constrained, i.e. held by the Scyllas. This is the story
which is alluded to here. Scylla daughter of Phorcys was beloved by Glaucus, a
god of the sea, which displeased Circe the daughter of the Sun. Knowing the spring
to which Scylla went every day, Circe prepared poisons. ... When Scylla came to
the spring to wash her hands, she was at once changed into a sea-monster; not
wishing to show her form to men, she cast herself into the sea. When her mother
Charybdis saw Scylla swimming in the sea, she went into the sea to catch hold of
her, but could not; and often they were assailed by the winds (?), as stories tell.
When Neptune saw that ... in the sea, he thrust his trident into the water and
made them into cliffs, setting Scylla in Sicily and Charybdis in Italy nearby; and
sailors can scarcely steer between them without danger.

XI

The title is 'Concerning the moderation of the water which comes from waters
bound in the clouds, lest they [all] flow alike'. [The argument] however is what Job
says: 'Who suspends the waters in the clouds, lest they [all] alike flow down from
above' (26:8)

Ligatas aquas nubibus/ frequenter crebrat Dominus,
ut ne erumpant protinus/ simul ruptis obicibus;
quarum uberioribus/ uenis uelut uberibus,
pedetemptim natantibus/ telli per tractus istius,
gelidis ac feruentibus/ diuersis in temporibus,
unquam influunt flumina/ nunquam deficientia.

Often the Lord sprinkles down the waters bound in the clouds
lest, the fastenings being broken, they all at once burst forth.
Streams of this [water] always, never failing, flow
in more fruitful channels, as if from breasts,
slowly through the regions of this earth,
cold and hot at different times.

GLOSSES 'all at once': i.e. when the fastenings are broken, or when the fastenings
are revealed; i.e., when the fastenings are broken by which, in some way, the water
[is held] in the clouds.... 'cold': i.e. winter and spring. 'hot': i.e. summer and
autumn.

XII

The title is 'Concerning the foundation of the earth, and the abyss'. The argument
however is what Job says: 'Who suspends the earth above nothingness' (26:7); and
elsewhere he says, 'The mass of the world is held by the power of God.' And in
the Psalm [it is said], 'Who has established the earth upon its firmness' (103:5).

Magni Dei uirtutibus/ appenditur dialibus
globus terrae et circulus/ abyssi magnae inditus,
suffultu Dei, iduma/ Omnipotentis ualida,
columnis uelut uectibus/ eundem sustentantibus,
promontoriis et rupibus,/ solidis fundaminibus,
uelut quibusdam basibus/ firmatis immobilibus.

By the divine powers of the great God
the globe of the earth is suspended, and the circle of the great abyss set,
held up by God, by the mighty hand of the Omnipotent.
Columns support it like bars,
promontories and cliffs, firm foundations,
like pillars planted and immovable.

GLOSSES 'circle': i.e. the great abyss in which was implanted the regularity of a
circle. 'hand' (iduma): i.e. 'hand'; iduma in Hebrew, cirus in Greek, manus in
Latin.[16]

16 Cirus reflects the genitive of Greek χεῑϱ. Iduma, a word for 'hand' favoured in the mannered
'hisperic' style of Latin affected by some writers in early Ireland and England, is as the gloss
claims derived from Hebrew yod 'hand'. The -m- preserves the Hebrew dual ending: yodayim
means 'two hands'. For another interpretation, see Breen 1990.

XIII

The title is 'Concerning hell, placed in the depths in the heart of the earth, and concerning its torments and its location'. The argument is 'You have rescued my soul from the lower hell' (Psalm 85:13), as it is said in the Gospel, 'The rich man is buried in hell' (Luke 16:22), and again, 'Depart, accursed ones, into the eternal fire' (Matthew 25:41), and again, 'Their worm does not die and its fire is not quenched' (Mark 9:47).

> Nulli uidetur dubium/ in imis esse infernum,
> ubi habentur tenebrae,/ uermes ac dirae bestiae,
> ubi ignis sulphureus/ ardens flammis edacibus,
> ubi rugitus hominum,/ fletus ac stridor dentium,
> ubi Gehennae gemitus/ terribilis et antiquus,
> ubi ardor flammaticus,/ sitis famisque horridus.

> None doubts that hell exists in the depths,
> where there are darkness, worms, and grim beasts,
> where sulphurous fire burns with voracious flames,
> where there are the groans of men, weeping and the gnashing of teeth,
> where there is the terrible and ancient groaning of Gehenna,
> where there are fiery heat, thirst, and terrible hunger.

GLOSSES 'hell': 'Hell' (*infernum*) is so called because it is below (*infra*); as its heart is in the midst of an animal, so hell is in the midst of the earth.

XIV

'Concerning the inhabitants of hell, who in [fear?] or shame kneel at the name of the Lord.' The argument is, as it is said in the Apocalypse, 'He has given him a name which is above every name, as it is written, "At the name of the Lord every knee bows, of the dwellers in heaven, on earth, and in hell"' (Philippians 2:9–10; cf. Revelation 5:13), and again in the same book, 'I saw a book in the right hand of the one sitting upon the throne, inscribed inside and outside, sealed with seven seals,' and as he says elsewhere in the same book, 'I saw a book in his right hand, which no one in heaven or on earth or under the earth was able to open except for the lion from the tribe of Judah' (Revelation 5:1, 3, 5).

Orbem infra, ut legimus,/ incolas esse nouimus,
quorum genu precario/ frequenter flectit Domino,
quibusque impossibile/ librum scriptum reuoluere
obsignatum signaculis/ septem de Christo monitis,
quem idem resignauerat/ postquam uictor extiterat,
explens sui praesagmina/ aduentus prophetalia.

Beneath the earth, as we read, we know that there are inhabitants
whose knee is often bent in prayer to the Lord,
and to whom it is impossible to unroll the inscribed book,
sealed with seven seals, with warnings concerning Christ,
which he himself opened after he stood forth as a victor,
fulfilling the prophecies foretelling his coming.

XV

'Concerning the Paradise of Adam, that is, the place of delights.' The argument is,
as it is said in Genesis, 'In the beginning he planted a Paradise of delights' (2:8);
and in the Apocalypse it is said, 'I will give him to eat of the fifth tree which is in
the Paradise of my God' (Revelation 2:7), and again in the Apocalypse, 'On either
side of the river was the tree of life, bearing twelve fruits month after month; and
the leaves of the tree were for the healing of the nations' (ibid. 22:2).

Plantatum a proëmio/ Paradisum a Domino
legimus in primordio/ Genesis nobilissimo,
cuius ex fonte flumina/ quattuor sunt manantia,
cuius etiam florido/ lignum uitae est medio,
cuius non cadunt folia/ gentibus salutifera,
cuius inenarrabiles/ deliciae ac fertiles.

We read in the most noble opening of Genesis
that Paradise was planted by the Lord in the beginning,
from whose spring four rivers flow,
and in whose flowering midst is the tree of life
whose leaves, bringing health to the peoples, do not fall,
and whose fertile delights cannot be told.

XVI

The title is 'Concerning Moses's ascent to the Lord on Mount Sinai'. The argument however is from the Law: 'Moses went up, and [God's] glory descended upon Mount Sinai' (Exodus 24:15–16). Or else the correct title is 'Concerning the wonders of the glory of the coming of the Lord upon the mountain'; the Scripture text however is 'There were thunders and voices and lightnings and quakings of the earth' (Revelation 16:18).

> Quis ad condictum Domini/ montem conscendit Sinaï,
> quis audiuit tonitrua/ super modum sonantia,
> quis clangorem perstrepere/ inormitatis bucinae,
> quis quoque uidit fulgora/ in gyro coruscantia,
> quis lampades et iacula,/ saxaque collidentia,
> praeter Israhelitici/ Moysen iudicem populi?

> Who has ascended Mount Sinai to speak with the Lord,
> has heard the thunder sounding exceedingly
> and the noise of the great resounding trumpet,
> has seen the lightnings flashing in a ring
> and lights and missiles and crashing stones,
> save Moses, judge of the people of Israel?

XVII

The title is 'Concerning the Day of Judgment, and its names'. The argument however is what Zephaniah says: 'The day of the Lord is near, great and very swift. That day will be a day of anger and fury and anguish, a day of disaster and misery, a day of shadows and darkness, a day of cloud and whirlwind, a day of trumpet and tumult' (1:14–16).

> Regis regum rectissimi/ prope est dies Domini,
> dies irae et uindictae,/ tenebrarum et nebulae,
> diesque mirabilium,/ tonitruorum fortium,
> dies quoque angustiae,/ meroris ac tristitiae,
> in quo cessabit mulierum/ amor ac desiderium
> hominumque contentio/ mundi huius et cupido.

> The day of the Lord is near, of the most righteous King of kings,
> a day of wrath and punishment, of darkness and clouds,

a day of marvels and mighty thunders,
a day too of anguish, of grief and sorrow,
when the love and desire of women will cease,
and men's strife and longing for this world.

XVIII

'Concerning the terrible presence of God on the Day of Judgment'. The argument
however is, as the apostle says in the second epistle to the Corinthians, 'We must
all stand before the judgment seat of Christ, so that each of us may give an account
of his own deeds for as long as he has worn a body, whether good or evil' (5:10),
and as it is said in the Gospel, 'The Son of Man will come in his glory; then he
will give to each according to his deeds' (Matthew 16:27).

Stantes erimus pauidi/ ante tribunal Domini,
reddemusque de omnibus/ rationem effectibus,
uidentes quoque posita/ ante obtutus crimina,
librosque conscientiae/ patefactos in facie.
In fletus amarissimos/ ac singultus erumpemus,
subtracta necessaria/ operandi materia.

We will stand terrified before the Lord's judgment seat
and will give an account of all our deeds,
seeing our crimes set before our faces
and the book of conscience laid open.
We will break out in most bitter tears and sobs,
having lost the material substance which is needed for action.

XIX

'Concerning the resurrection of Adam's progeny.' The argument is from the
Apocalypse: 'The Lord himself will descend from heaven, in commandment, in the
voice of the archangel, in the trumpet of God' (1 Thessalonians 4:15); and again,
'In the days of the voice of the seventh angel, when the trumpet begins to sound,
the mystery of God will be fulfilled' (Revelation 10:7).

Tuba primi archangeli/ strepente admirabili,
erumpent munitissima/ claustra ac poliandria,
mundi presentis frigora/ hominum liquescentia,
undique conglobantibus/ ad compagines ossibus,

animabus ethrialibus/ eisdem obeuntibus,
rursumque redeuntibus/ debitis mansionibus.

At the wondrous sounding of the trumpet of the first archangel,
firmly secured chambers and tombs will burst asunder,
the chill which has frozen the men of this world will thaw,
bones will come together from every side
as their heavenly souls go to meet them,
returning to their proper dwellings.

XX

'Concerning the three fiery stars which signify Christ.' The argument however is,
as it is said in the book of Job, '... He who made Orion and the inner things of
the south. Have you not established the morning and evening stars in certain
periods?' (9:9, 38:32).

Vagatur ex climactere/ Orion caeli cardine,
derelicto Virgilio/ astrorum splendidissimo,
per metas Tethis ignoti/ orientalis circuli.
Gyrans certis ambagibus/ redit priscis reditibus
oriens post biennium/ uesperugo in uesperum –
sumpta in problematibus/ tropicis intellectibus.

Abandoning the most glorious Pleiades,
Orion strays from the summit of the celestial pole
passing beyond the unknown eastern circuit of the sea.
Turning in sure revolutions, the evening star returns to its former
    courses,
rising at evening after two years have passed –
this is understood figuratively, as a type.[17]

XXI

'Concerning the Day of Judgment and the radiant wood of the Cross.' The argument however is as it is said in the Apocalypse: 'They will hide themselves in

17 The sense of this stanza seems to be that the regular return of these heavenly bodies is a
precursor of Christ's second coming.

caves and stones of the mountains, and then will say to the mountains, "Fall upon us!"' (Revelation 6:15–16); and in the Gospel: 'Immediately after the disturbance of those days the sun will be hidden and the moon will not give its light, and the stars will fall from heaven' (Matthew 24:29).

Xristo de celis Domino/ descendente celsissimo,
praefulgebit clarissimum/ signum crucis et uexillum.
Tectisque luminaribus/ duobus principalibus,
cadent in terram sidera/ ut fructus de ficulnea,
eritque mundi spatium/ ut fornacis incendium:
tunc in montium specubus/ abscondent se exercitus.

When Christ, the most exalted Lord, descends from heaven,
the most glorious sign of the Cross, and the banner, will shine forth.
And when the two chief luminaries are covered up,
the stars will fall to the earth like fruits from a fig-tree,
the whole expanse of the world will be like the blaze of a furnace:
then multitudes will hide themselves in caverns of the mountains.

XXII

The title is 'Concerning God's praise by the angels'. The argument however is from the Apocalypse: 'Around the throne I saw twenty-four thrones; and I saw twenty-four elders sitting in white garments, with golden crowns on their heads' (Revelation 4:4).

Ymnorum cantionibus/ sedulo tinnientibus
tripudiis sanctis milibus/ angelorum uernantibus,
quattuorque plenissimis/ animalibus oculis,
cum uiginti felicibus/ quattuor senioribus
coronas admittentibus/ Agni Dei sub pedibus,
laudatur tribus uicibus/ Trinitas aeternalibus.

In the fervent, resounding chanting of hymns
by thousands of angels flourishing in their holy dances,
and by the four beasts full of eyes,
and by the twenty-four blessed elders
casting their crowns beneath the feet of the Lamb of God,
the Trinity receives threefold praise eternally.

GLOSSES 'resounding': i.e., when they modulate the songs. 'flourishing': i.e. which they all used to multiply. 'beasts': i.e. the evangelists. 'twenty-four': i.e. with the twelve patriarchs and the twelve prophets, or with the twelve prophets and the twelve apostles; or else it is a figure of the four evangelists together with the twenty-four books of the Old Law.

XXIII

The title is 'Concerning the burning of the impious who do not wish to believe in Christ, and the rejoicing of the righteous'. The argument however is from the Apocalypse: 'A terrible fire will consume the enemy' (Hebrews 10:27). And elsewhere the apostle says, 'With the Father there are many dwellings,' and Christ says, 'In the house of my Father there are many dwellings' (John 14:2).

> Zelus ignis furibundus/ consumet aduersarios
> nolentes Christum credere/ Deo a Patre uenisse.
> Nos uero euolabimus/ obuiam ei protinus,
> et sic cum ipso erimus/ in diuersis ordinibus
> dignitatum pro meritis,/ praemiorum perpetuis,
> permansuri in gloria,/ a seculis in gloria.

> The wrathful zeal of fire will consume the enemy,
> who do not wish to believe that Christ came from God the Father.
> But we will straightway fly to meet him,
> and will be with him in various ranks
> of dignities and rewards according to [our] eternal merits,
> and will remain in glory forever and ever.

GLOSSES 'will consume': i.e. punishment from God the Father. 'the enemy': i.e. those who have turned away from God. 'we': i.e. the human race. 'will ... fly': i.e. on the Day of Judgment. 'to meet him': i.e. into the air. 'straightway': i.e. in the blinking of an eye. 'with him': i.e. the saints will be with Christ after the Judgment. 'in various ranks': i.e., as it is said, 'I will give to each according to his deeds' (Matthew 16:27). 'in glory': i.e. in the Kingdom.

> Quis potest Deo placere/ nouissimo in tempore,
> uariatis insignibus/ ueritatis ordinibus,
> exceptis contemptoribus/ mundi praesentis istius?
> Deum Patrem ingenitum,/ caeli ac terrae Dominum,
> ab eodemque Filium/ saecula ante genitum,
> Deumque Spiritum Sanctum/ uerum, unum, altissimum,

inuoco ut auxilium/ mihi opportunissimum,
minimo praestet omnium/ sibi deseruientium
quem angelorum milibus/ consociabit Dominus.

Who can satisfy God in the last times,
when the noble rules of truth have been changed,
save for those who scorn this present world?
I invoke God the unbegotten Father, Lord of heaven and earth,
and his Son, begotten before the ages,
and God the Holy Spirit, true, single, most exalted,
that he may grant his most helpful assistance
to me, though I am least of all the deserving,
to whom the Lord will grant comradeship with the angels in their
    thousands.

ADDENDUM: An anecdote involving the *Altus*.[18]

Three students came from Connor to study, seeking the soul-friend of Brian son
of Cennétig, that is, Mael Shuthain descendant of Cerball, of the Eóganacht Locha
Léin; for he was the best scholar of his time.[19] The three students had the same
shape, and the same appearance, and the same name, which was Domnall. They
studied under him for three years.

At the end of three years they said to their teacher, 'We wish to go to Jerusalem,
in the land of Judaea, so that our feet may walk every road on which our Saviour
travelled the earth.' The teacher said, 'You will not depart until I get payment for
my labour.' The pupils said, 'We have nothing to give; but we will be your servants
for another three years, if you wish.' 'I do not want that,' he said; 'but grant me
what I demand, or I will put you under my curse.' 'We will,' said they, 'if we are
able.' He bound them to that promise on the Lord's Gospel. 'You will go,' he said,
'the way that you desire, and you will all three die at one time on the journey. And
this is the judgment which I impose upon you: not to go to heaven after your death
until you have come to me, and told me how long I will live and whether I will obtain
mercy from the Lord.' 'We promise you that from the Lord's bosom,' they said.

Then they departed, taking with them their teacher's blessing and leaving their
own with him. They travelled every road on which they heard that the Saviour
had walked. At last they reached Jerusalem, and there they all three died at one
time, and were buried in Jerusalem with great honour.

Michael the archangel came from God to fetch them. They said, 'We will not
go until we have discharged the obligation which we accepted from our teacher, on

18 Text in O'Curry 1861, 529–31.   19 Mael Shuthain was a historical figure, who died in the year
1010; he served the great king Brian Boru both as secretary and as spiritual advisor or 'soul-friend'.

Christ's Gospel.' 'Go,' said the angel, 'and tell him that he has three and a half years left to live, and that he will then go to hell until the Day of Judgment; on the Day of Judgment sentence will be passed upon him.' 'Tell us,' they said, 'why he is to be put into hell.' 'For three reasons,' said the angel: 'for tampering (?)[20] with the Scriptures, and sleeping with many women, and despising the *Altus*.'

(Now this was why he despised the *Altus*. He had a fine son, named Mael Phátraic, who fell mortally ill. He recited the *Altus* around him seven times so that the boy should not die; but this did no good, for the boy died at once. Mael Shuthain said he would never recite the *Altus*, for God did not respect it. But God did not show disrespect for the *Altus* when he did not grant his son health; it was rather that he preferred him to be in the household of heaven, rather than in the household of earth.)

For seven years Mael Shuthain did not recite the *Altus*. Then his three pupils came to converse with Mael Shuthain in the form of three white doves, and he bade them welcome: 'Tell me how long I shall live, and whether I shall obtain a [heavenly] reward.' 'You will live for three years,' they said, 'and thereafter will go to hell until the Day of Judgment.' 'Why should I be in hell?' he said. 'For three reasons,' they said; and told him the three reasons which we have related above.

'It is not true that I shall go to hell,' he said. 'For the three sins which are upon me now ... ,' he said, 'will not be upon me henceforth; and I will renounce these sins, and God will pardon me for them, as he himself promised when he said, "The impiety of the impious, in whatever hour he change his life, will do him no harm" (Ezekiel 33:12). I will not put my own interpretation upon the Scriptures, but will follow that of the holy books. I will perform a hundred prostrations every day. I have been seven years without reciting the *Altus*: I will recite it seven times a night for as long as I live, and I will make a three days' fast every week. Go to heaven now,' he said, 'and come on the day of my death to bring me tidings.' 'We will,' they said; and the three of them departed ... , and blessed him, and he blessed them.

On the day of his death they came in the same form, and he and they blessed one another, and he asked them, 'Is my life the same in God's eyes today as when you came to converse with me before?' 'It is not,' said they; 'for your place in heaven has been shown to us, and it seemed to us very excellent. We have come to you today, as we promised, to fetch you; come with us to that place, so that you may be in God's presence, and in the unity of the Trinity and the household of heaven, until the Judgment of Judgments.'

Then he gathered many priests and clerics around him, and received the last anointing; and his pupils did not part from him until they had gone to heaven. And that good man's writings are in the church in Inisfallen still.

---

20 Literally 'making pregnant, getting with child'. O'Curry took this to mean 'interpolating', and this conjecture has been accepted by subsequent scholars; from Mael Shuthain's own words below, however, it appears to be wilful or idiosyncratic interpretation of the Bible which is meant.

Selections from Augustinus Hibernicus,
On the Miracles of Holy Scripture

Although this treatise owes its survival to its copyists' belief that it was written by the famous Saint Augustine of Hippo, it is clear from several passages in the text (none of them, as it happens, included among the selections below) that it is the work of an Irishman, writing in the year 655, probably at the monastery of Lismore in County Waterford. Composed at a time when contacts with Spain were contributing to a flowering of scholarly activity in the south of Ireland,[1] *On the Miracles* draws on a diverse array of patristic learning to formulate a bold and distinctive contribution to theology.

Augustinus sets out to provide 'natural' explanations for all of the miracles in the Bible; but in doing so he is motivated not by reductive rationalism, but by a heartfelt if idiosyncratic piety. Accepting the testimony of Genesis 2:1–3 that heaven and earth were 'perfect' after the sixth day of creation, and that God ceased from the work of creation on the seventh, he concludes that all of God's acts thereafter must have been accomplished in accordance with nature and not in contravention of its laws – if the Deity did otherwise, he would be producing 'a new creation'. The ingenuity with which Augustinus attempts to find explanations for all of the prodigies of Scripture in 'the hidden depths of nature' may strike a modern reader as fantastic, grotesque, or even comical; but his fundamental concerns deserve our attention and respect. Particularly impressive, and so far as I know unparalleled in the early Christian West, is his vision of nature as a harmonious whole whose integrity not even God will violate: I do not think that it is farfetched to see here the early foreshadowing, tentative and isolated, of an ecological sensibility.

On the Miracles of Holy Scripture is divided into three sections, dealing with the Pentateuch, with the rest of the Old Testament, and with the New Testament. I have translated several chapters from Book I, selected with a view to illustrating Augustinus's main ideas and his strategies in dealing with his material. Book III, the shortest of the sections, has been translated in its entirety; I hope that this will give the reader some impression of the range of the author's interests and approaches, which are by no means confined to his central thesis.

---

1 Hillgarth 1984.

BOOK I – ON THE PENTATEUCH OF MOSES

CHAPTER 1: On God the Creator, and the ordering of creatures

Since we wish, with the help of almighty God, to treat of those things which are miraculous, where better can we turn for a beginning than to that Creator of all things to whom Scripture often bears witness, saying 'He does great and inscrutable deeds, and miracles without number' (Job 9:10)?

He established a first foundation, as it were, for all of these miracles when he made all of his creatures out of nothing. For the eternal and omnipotent Creator of things, abiding always as Three and as One without any diminution of his power – he alone, beyond time, preceded all that he made. Then, so that he might reveal through created things all the vast goodness and power and benevolence which beforehand he had possessed within himself alone, he divided the unformed matter which he had made from nothing at the first into all the manifold species of visible and invisible things – that is, things sensible and insensible, intellectual and lacking intellect.

This, as the authority of the Book of Genesis confirms, was brought to pass in the course of the passing of six days, so that it can be maintained with complete certainty that on the sixth day everything pertaining to the disposition and arrangement of the creation was completed. For thus it is written: 'And on the sixth day God completed all his works, and blessed the seventh day, because in it he rested from all his works' (Genesis 2:2).

From this it is understood that on the sixth day God completed all things, so that on the seventh day he may be seen to have ceased, not from toiling (*a labore*), but from working (*ab opere*). But since the Lord Jesus answered the Jews who were asking about rest on the Sabbath, saying 'My Father is working until now, and I am working' (John 5:17), we both believe that he finished all things on the sixth day and rested on the seventh, and also do not doubt that he is working until now. But we must consider more carefully how the same God can be considered to have finished then, and to be working now.

On the sixth day he completed his work on the natures of created things, but even now he does not cease to govern them; and on the seventh day he rested from the work of creation (*ab opere creationis*), but he never ceases from the exercise of government (*a gubernationis regimine*).[2] For we are to

2 'Govern' is not an ideal translation here, but I hope that the context will make the sense

understand that God was a Creator then (*tunc … Creator*), but is a Governor now (*nunc Gubernator*). Therefore if among created things we see anything new arise, God should not be thought to have created a new nature, but to be governing that which he created formerly. But his power in governing his creation is so great that he may seem to be creating a new nature, when he is only bringing forth from the hidden depths of its [existing] nature that which lay concealed within.

Through such unaccustomed [acts of] government, when things reveal through the will and power of the Governor that which they do not accomplish as a part of their functioning day to day (*per efficaciam quotidianae administrationis*), there come about the miracles of which Scripture tells. But since we will speak of these miracles at greater length below, when we come to their proper place, let us [merely] stress this point for the present: that when he had finished creating the natures of things, God rested from his work on the seventh day; and that ever since, down to the present, he never ceases through all time from governing the whole creation.

Although it is said that the whole creation was arranged in the course of six days, this does not refer to the succession of days in an interval of time, but to the sequence of [God's] acts. For he who subsequently told the story divided in speech what God did not divide in the perfection of his work. For God created at once all of the things which he made, when by a single act of will he arranged the manifold diversity of all the species. In that single act of will he caused all things to come into existence at once, outside time; and since their creation he does not cease to rule over them, throughout time.

CHAPTER 2: On the differing sins of the rational natures

In that original making of all things, it was the invisible, spiritual creation which came forth at first; and then, lest that which was within should not emerge outwardly in God's works, the visible, bodily creation began to be. In that initial and universal division of all things, moreover, the Creator established two rational natures, one in the spiritual and the other in the bodily creation: the natures of angels and of men. According to the requirements of their different natures, he separated the places where they dwell, assigning heaven to the angels as a habitation, and the earth to men. When these

reasonably clear. The original meaning of the verb *guberno* is 'steer, navigate': even when extended to administration (a semantic development reflected in English 'govern'), it still denotes the directing, manipulating, or managing of a preexisting entity. Our text's influence appears to be reflected in the eleventh-century pseudohistorical treatise *Lebar Gabála*, which puts the same doctrine forward in its own account of the creation: 'Then on Saturday God rested from the completion of the new creation, but not by any means from ruling (over it)' (Macalister 1938–56, 1.16).

things had been established both natures – those of angels and of men – fell into sin.

How men transgressed against [God's] commandment is related in the Book of Genesis. To those who consider the matter, this suggests a by no means trivial question: why is Scripture silent concerning the way in which the angels sinned? For even though the prophet may be speaking of the angel's downfall in the person of the king of Babylon, when he says 'I will sit on the mountain of the testament, on the slopes of the north; I will ascend above the heights of the clouds, and build myself a throne to the north, and will be like the Most High' (Isaiah 14:13–14), these words can also be easily understood to refer literally to the king of Babylon, unless they are figuratively transferred 'from the body to the head' by allegory. So the question is not resolved by this passage; and moreover in the Gospel itself the cause of the fall, and the condemnation and punishment, are not explicitly revealed.

To be sure, someone could say that, as some think, this original sin was the tempting of man by means of the serpent, in consequence of which it was condemned to punishment, the Lord saying 'You are accursed among all the animals and beasts of the earth: you will go upon your belly, and eat earth all the days of your life' (Genesis 3:14). But far be it from us to imagine that an angel would have been able to persuade man to sin on earth, unless he himself had already sinned in heaven – in the Lord's words, 'I saw Satan falling from heaven like lightning' (Luke 10:18). For how could he envy human happiness unless he had already lost his own proper beatitude?

For we are to understand the Devil's fall not only to have preceded the fall of man but even the completion of creation which was accomplished on the sixth day, in light of the Lord's words concerning those who are to be damned on the last day: 'Depart from me, accursed ones, into the eternal fire, which my Father has prepared for the Devil and his angels' (Matthew 25:41). For when was that fire prepared, if not in the completion of the entire creation? Otherwise we would have to say that God created something else after the perfection of the sixth day; and far be that from us, lest we make a liar of Scripture – or rather of ourselves. He whose prison was prepared when the creatures were made had sinned in the beginning, before their creation; for, as Scripture says, 'He is a liar from the beginning, and has not stood in the truth' (John 8:44).

It remains for us to explain why the Lord is silent concerning the fall of the angel – since we are in no doubt that the angel, the first among God's creatures, did indeed fall. The true Physician did not wish to disclose how the angel was wounded, for he had not ordained that that wound could be healed; and he is silent concerning his condemnation and exile, since he has by no means accepted him back as a penitent. But how man sinned is described, for there is hope that he will eventually earn forgiveness; and God chose to reveal how man was banished, for in these last times he has called him back to his first state. Nor did he conceal the way in which man was condemned to punishment; for he has not refused to forgive him eventually, in the grace of his mercy.

Considering this difference between men and angels, the apostle said 'For it is not angels, but Adam's seed whom God puts on' (Hebrews 2:16). For when the gracious and merciful Creator, abiding in the supreme and unchangeable substance of God the Father, wished to empty himself in the form of a servant, he did not put on the nature of angels but that of men. But here a question arises. Seeing that God has not forgiven the sinful angels, and yet by putting on human flesh has granted forgiveness to sinful man, why is it that the highest angel was smitten with a condemnation which can never be lifted – while man, sinning and transgressing against his Maker's commandment, can through repentance obtain forgiveness? For John, and the Lord, and Peter all proclaim, 'Repent, for the kingdom of heaven has drawn near' (Matthew 3:2, 4:17; Acts 3:19).

The angel, established in the heights of his glory, could not pass on to a loftier state but could only remain in the one in which he had been created, confirmed therein by contemplating his Creator: fallen thence, he could not return, for he had plummeted from the highest condition possible to his rank. But man, set upon the earth, destined to procreate his kind and to subsist by eating, could have passed into a higher and better, a spiritual and immortal life, if while still in this condition he had continued to obey the commandment. Sin overtook him before he reached that higher state; therefore he fell from that lower rank, losing the immortality of his body – the Lord declaring, 'You are earth, and will go into the earth' (Genesis 3:19).

By his Maker's mercy, then, man is through the Lord's passion called back to that beatitude which as a sinner he never reached: had he, like the angel, fallen from that condition, he could never have been called back. Inasmuch as [man] does not attain to the immortality of the body until the death of all things has been accomplished, that beatitude to which we are summoned will be restored by the resurrection. But it will be a restoration not to the rank or state from which the first man fell, but to another loftier state, for which he hoped – as the Lord says, 'They will be like God's angels in heaven' (Matthew 22:30).[3]

3 This passage, like many others in the text, was drawn upon by the author of the pseudo-

Another thing contributes to the weight of the Devil's guilt: that immediately after sinning he fell into the trap of despair. For if he had not abandoned hope of being pardoned for his fault, he would never have persuaded man to bring about his own ruin: for someone who desires forgiveness for one sin does not by any means set out to cause another. In this way, then, he not only found a snare of perdition for himself, but was also the cause of the perdition of mankind. Yet this served to alleviate man's guilt: that he did not trangress against the commandment on his own initiative alone, but yielded to the serpent's persuasion; nor did he himself cause any other rational creature to offend against God. It is for this reason that he can more easily find the door of repentance open; if he does not enter there, he will suffer the loss of eternal life. But the one who washes his sins away with repentance will share forever in the joy of the angels.

CHAPTER 16: On Moses, and the bush on Mount Horeb

After the death of Joseph, the Egyptians began to oppress the children of Israel with the yoke of a most harsh servitude – even commanding them, lest their race grow beyond bounds, to throw their male children into the river or to kill them by various means. At this time Moses son of Amram, a man of the tribe of Levi born in the midst of this crisis, arose as the avenger of his people. Seeing an Egyptian harassing an Israelite, he killed him: when the deed became known to the king of the Egyptians, [Moses] fled from Egypt, and spent forty years in exile as a shepherd in Midian.

When the time of the promise made to the fathers had passed,[4] he was as he pastured his flock on Mount Horeb amazed to see a bush burning yet seeming not to be consumed by the fire. When he sought to investigate this apparition, and to discover why the bush burned but was not burnt up, the Lord said from the midst of the bush, 'I am the Lord God of your fathers. I will send you into Egypt, so that you may release their downtrodden descendants from the yoke of their servitude' (cf. Exodus 3:6–10).

What primarily concerns us in this terrifying vision is this: how could the fire be seen to burn, and yet not to consume that in which it burned? For if the fire took nourishment from that substance, why was that on which it fed not consumed? And if the flame which appeared did not arise from that substance, why was it necessary for it to appear in a bush at all?

Isidorian *Liber de ordine creaturarum*, a cosmological treatise written in Ireland late in the seventh century (Díaz y Díaz 1972, 136–8). Even more interesting is the reappearance of the same doctrine in 'The Pseudo-Historical Prologue to the *Senchas Már*', p. 141 below. 4 Presumably an allusion to God's prophecy to Jacob that he would bring his descendants out of Egypt (Genesis 46:4), and to the similar prophecy made by Joseph to his brothers (ibid. 50:24).

It is related that a certain shrub has the property that, the more it burns, not only is it not consumed, but in burning it is purified. Concerning this wood Saint Jerome, in the course of explaining the wooden altar which is described in the city shown by the Lord to Ezekiel in a vision, mentions that its colour is like that of linen; but although he describes its nature, he does not give its name.[5] If the fire shown to Moses was burning in a bush of this kind, what wonder if it was not consumed? For thus the nature of each, of the fire and the wood, is preserved: for the fire burns naturally from the wood, and the burning wood is naturally not consumed by the fire.

Or else, to be sure, it was not the fire which is wood's enemy which appeared in the bush, but rather that fire of which it is said that 'He makes his angels spirits, and his ministers a burning fire' (Psalm 103:4). Thus it is an incorporeal fire which is described in the bush – which, when shown to a fleshly man, must of necessity be revealed as if it were some bodily substance.[6]

CHAPTER 17: On the two signs: the hand placed in the bosom and the staff changed into a snake

When he had journeyed into Egypt it was granted to him to give a twofold sign, so that there might be three to confirm his message – the two signs, and himself. For when Moses, who up until then had been a shepherd, threw the staff which he had carried to the ground, it became a serpent; and when he thrust his hand into his bosom and drew it out again it came forth the first time afflicted with leprosy, but when he placed it in his bosom a second time it appeared whole.

Neither in the hand nor in the wood, however, did anything appear which was contrary to nature. For the nature of human flesh has both leprosy and health latent within it, as is often shown by their alternation; but so sudden a change, with a hand appearing in the same moment whole, then white with leprosy, and then again whole, appears to those who behold it as a most miraculous sign.

---

5 Augustinus Hibernicus's text of Jerome must have been defective: commenting on Ezekiel 41:22, the saint names the mysterious plant as *amianton*, stating that it is 'a kind of flax, or has the appearance of flax, (which) is found to be purer the more it burns' (Migne 1844–64, 25.421). In fact the λίθος ἀμίαντος or 'unstained stone' was a mineral, perhaps asbestos; the idea that it was a sort of flax may have been suggested by the latter's fibrous texture.   6 This second interpretation of the burning bush is also found in *The Voyage of Saint Brendan the Abbot*: as a guest in an island monastery, the saint sees the lamps in the chapel lit with a 'spiritual light' which although it burns does not cause them to diminish. When he asks, 'How is it possible for an incorporeal light to burn physically in a corporeal creature?' his host replies, 'Have you not read of the burning bush on Mount Sinai? For that bush remained unharmed by the fire' (Selmer 1959, 37).

The staff changed into a serpent, and the serpent changed back again to wood, constitute a problem for those who inquire into nature – unless it be that each, the staff and the serpent, appears to be made from earth; for being made from the same material, they could by the power of God the Governor be changed into each other by turns. But if it be conceded that all things made from earth can be changed into one another by turns – as for instance animal to tree, bread to stone, man to bird – then none of these could remain firmly within the bounds of its own nature. We would seem, indeed, to give our assent to the laughable tales told by the druids, who say that their forebears flew through the ages in the form of birds;[7] and in such cases we would speak of God not as the Governor, but as the Changer (*Mutator*) of natures. Far be it from us to do so, lest we believe that after the first establishment of the natures of all things he made anything new, or not contained by its own nature. For 'there is nothing new under the sun,' nor can anyone say, 'Behold, this is new' (Ecclesiastes 1:9–10).

Therefore many learned men say rather that the real staff, which as long as Moses held it in his hands was wood, was on various occasions changed into a serpent in appearance only, to serve as a sign – especially when it served no function save that of providing a sign. For if it had truly been a serpent, it would have remained a serpent after the sign was given. Thus it was a real staff with which Moses began to scourge Egypt with plagues, with which the sea was divided, with which the rocks were struck in Horeb and Kadesh: never changed into a serpent, it remained a staff always.

If then what appeared as a sign was only an imaginary serpent, why were those other serpents of the wizards devoured by it in Pharaoh's presence? To this objection the learned have an easy answer: the serpents which it devoured were also imaginary; and so the apparition of the divine portent was able to devour the appearance brought about by the devilish incantations of the wizards.

According to this view, then, the staff was not changed into a serpent's nature but only – in appearance, and as a sign – into its similitude. For nothing can be found in the nature of wood which could make a snake. For this reason that which was by its nature a staff only appeared as a serpent at the time when the sign was given.

---

7 This remarkable statement appears to indicate that, in the middle of the seventh century, there were still in Ireland druids (in Irish Latin the word *magus* regularly corresponds to Irish *druí*) preaching some form of the doctrine of transmigration attributed to their continental counterparts by Greek and Roman authors. The implications of this for our understanding of the pace and character of the conversion in Ireland have yet to be explored; the passage seems however to lend support to the suggestions regarding this period in the general introduction, p. 12 above.

CHAPTER 18: On the water changed into blood

Journeying into Egypt, therefore, Moses produced signs in God's presence as the Lord had commanded him, and told the king that it was God's decree that he set free the people of Israel. Since the king by no means accepted God's commandment, he scourged the land of Egypt with ten plagues as the Lord directed him. First he struck the waters and changed them into blood, so that all water throughout Egypt was turned to blood; this was death to the living things which were in them, and caused men to suffer a painful end, dying from thirst. It is appropriate that this was the first punishment to befall the Egyptians and their king: with respect to those who had commanded that the children of God's people be cast into the river, that same river's water turned to blood brought death to those who drank, and torment to those who did not.

But we must ask the question which bears upon the subject of this book: how did God, the Governor of nature, naturally change water into blood?

Water, the basis of every fluid, is by its daily operations in various creatures changed into different things, modified ceaselessly and naturally so as to provide nourishment and sustenance for every nature. For when it is infused into the wood of the vine, it is changed to the savour and colour of wine; and when it mounts to the top of an olive tree, the same water produces the fatness of olive oil; and when it is gathered by bees into their combs, it takes on the sweetness of honey; and if it is conveyed through the trunks of palm trees it produces dates, and when pressed out attains to the smoothness of cider; and when it is assigned to different animals as nourishment, it is divided into the several kinds of blood throughout the body. For it appears in the breasts with the white colour and mild sweetness of milk, for the sustenance of infants; but in all of the other parts of the body it has the red colour of blood. There are many other fluids in the body apart from blood: natural philosophers put their number at twenty-three, identifying them as urine, semen, black and red bile, saliva, tears, etc.

Water becomes all these things, through the daily workings of its nature in various creatures. What then hinders open minds from supposing that what can be achieved during a lengthy interval of time can [also] be naturally accomplished in a moment, by the command of the most powerful Governor? The changing of water to blood is not therefore contrary to nature; but what it effects in other things, and in the course of time, can also happen in water itself, and at once, if God so commands.

CHAPTER 23: On the manna falling from heaven

After they had entered the wilderness, God sustained that people – roughly six hundred thousand foot soldiers, besides the dregs of the host, that is, the miscellaneous and innumerable crowd which had come up out of Egypt – for forty years with manna, or heavenly bread. Subsequently the Psalmist commemorated that bread, saying 'He gave them bread of heaven; man ate the bread of angels' (Psalm 77:25). It came down with the dew every night, except the night of the Sabbath, and shone around the campsite with the whiteness of snow. 'For,' says Scripture, 'it was like coriander seed, and had the colour of bdellium, as white as snow' (Numbers 11:7). It could not endure the sunrise, dissolving immediately; but if it was gathered and ground in a quern it endured the heat of fire, so that it could be baked into loaves. And if anyone kept anything which was left over until the morning of the next day, it would be full of worms; nevertheless, the full measure of an omer thereof was kept for a long time afterward in the Ark of the Covenant.

Besides what is relevant to an allegorical interpretation, diligent minds must, with the Lord's help, consider how this marvellous and also needful portent can be explained.

First it may be asked whether it was bread, and how it could be called 'bread of angels'; also how, if that food is said to have had no earthly nature, it could nourish men dwelling on the earth and subject to the failings of the flesh. For in the verse quoted from the Psalmist above, it is called 'bread of heaven': this is because it comes from the clouds like rain, and clouds, as we have mentioned earlier, can be called 'heaven' in the Scriptures. The same food is called 'bread of angels' not because it nourishes the angels, who need no food, but because it was granted through the ministry of angels, just as the Law and other things were granted to the people 'by angels in the hand of a mediator' (Galatians 4:19).

How could it provide nourishment to any sort of men, if it did not have anything earthly in its substance? But how could manna, falling from the clouds, be shown to have any earthly nature – unless perhaps the nature of the lower air itself has in it something earthly? For how could air support the bodies of birds in flight, if it did not have something of the solidity of earth? For the same reason, that [aerial] substance, and clouds thickened with the nature of earth, congeal into snow and hail which has nearly the hardness of stone. What therefore hinders open minds from supposing that, just as clouds bring forth hailstones, so too they could bring forth the grains of manna – especially since when it fell to earth, like the dew with which it was generated, it would melt away like hail if the rising sun shone upon it?

And so it could be that manna, produced in those earthly parts of the air, might serve as nourishing food for earthly men. And indeed this lower region of the air is called 'earth' in holy Scripture, when in the one hundred and forty-eighth Psalm all creatures are called upon in a spirit of prophecy to praise the Lord their Creator. For having finished with all of the ornaments of the upper heaven, [the Psalm] adds the following when it comes to the lower air: 'Praise the Lord from the earth,' etc., on to 'which obey his word' (Psalm 148:7–8).[8] Thus the thicker air, full of clouds and vapours, is called 'earth' by the prophet; and this before he speaks of the regions of the lower earth, which are mentioned later.

Manna, then, was brought forth in that upper part of the 'earth' where hail and snow are produced, and was bestowed as food by angels on the men of this lower part. From this it can easily be seen that God did not go in search of anything outside of nature, but made food from the earth – not because he could not have given them bread of the usual kind every day, even in the desert; but so that man, fed from the clouds, might know that he 'does not live only by bread, but by every word which comes from God's mouth' (Deuteronomy 8:3, Matthew 4:4, Luke 4:4). For since [God] commanded nature that man should be fed with bread, so man will have wholesome food from every kind of thing if he so ordains, just as he then had rain from the clouds.

BOOK III – ON THE NEW TESTAMENT

CHAPTER 1: On the vision of Zacharias, and the birth of John the Baptist

In the forty-first year of Octavianus Augustus Caesar, when Zacharias, a priest of the Abijah class, was as befitted his office offering a holocaust in the Temple, the angel Gabriel, one of those who stand in the Lord's presence, brought him a speedy answer. Then he added, 'Your wife Elizabeth, barren until now and of a great age, will conceive and bear you a son named John, prophet and precursor of the Most High.' But the priest, not believing, accorded all too little faith to these words. 'How can this be?' he said. 'For I am old; and my wife, incapable of this thing in her youth, is now advanced in years.'

8 The full text of these verses in the Vulgate runs as follows: 'Praise the Lord from the earth, dragons and all abysses, fire, snow, hail, ice, the wind of storms, which obey his word.' Augustinus's interpretation of the word 'earth' in this passage was adopted by the author of the *Liber de ordine creaturarum* (Díaz y Díaz 1972, 128; cf. note 3 above).

The angel was not taken aback by this reply; nor did he, on account of such unbelief, withdraw the gift which had been promised. Rather, so that what the Lord had said should be fulfilled, he laid an appropriate penalty upon the priest's mouth, leaving him mute until the boy was born. Then the bonds on his tongue were loosed, when as he tried to write his son's name he said 'John is his name.'

So it was fittingly ordained that John, who afterwards was to furnish an example of repentance to all men by his diet and his dress and the place [of his dwelling], and was to be a preacher of repentance, should at the time of his conception be the occasion for a penance imposed upon his father by an angel, one which lasted until his birth. And this too was a fitting sign: that at the conception of the one who would, when he had been born, preach the kingdom of heaven, the priest, the preacher of the Old Law and of the prophets, should be condemned to silence. For the Law and the prophets extended only until John; after him, the kingdom of God was proclaimed.

After he had been conceived, and while he was still in his mother's womb before his birth, sensing that Mary the mother of the Lord had come into the house in which he was, he spoke inspired words through his mother's mouth concerning the Lord Christ who was to be born from her. For since the spirit of Moses was distributed among seventy-two councillors, what wonder if the spirit of a child still in the womb should speak through the mother?

CHAPTER 2: On the incarnation of our Lord Jesus Christ, and his birth from the Virgin Mary

Meanwhile the messenger came to Joseph's betrothed Mary, a virgin of the race of David, to tell her that through the grace of the Holy Spirit she was to bear a son without having known a man. 'This child,' he said, 'whom all the prophets have foretold, will be great in the sight of the Lord; and all of the faithful forever after will call him the Son of the Most High. For to him he has granted the throne of his father David; and he will hold sway over the kingdom of the house of Jacob forever, without any to succeed him.' Rejoicing in these words the Virgin believed, and consented thereto without any trace of incredulity or disobedience.

But when Joseph her husband saw her womb swelling his mind was troubled, for he had never known her; and so, lest this should weigh upon him, the same angel informed him concerning the boy who had been conceived and was to be born, and instructed him to accept the Virgin [as his wife]. Afterwards, when the time came, she bore a son – conceived without man's seed or carnal pleasure, and brought forth without injury to her virginity.

Although it is indeed contrary to all human experience for conception to be accomplished without a man's seed, it was not outside nature that the substance of flesh taken from a woman's womb should have come to birth. For [God] took nature naturally from nature, when with the help of the Holy Spirit he drew from the mother's flesh alone the true substance of human flesh, complete except for the vices of the passions. And lest we leave the impression, through failing to cite any examples from nature, that this was a new thing in the creation, we can point to many animals generated without the intercourse of parents. For bees have no fathers, but grow in the shelter of their mothers' bodies; and all flying things of that sort conceive their offspring in this way. Many birds, also, are able to produce eggs without males; and natural philosophers say that many kinds of fish are conceived in the same fashion. The worm is generated in meat alone, without a father; and for this reason the Lord does not disdain to be compared to it by the prophet (Psalm 22:6). Since, then, the Lord brings this about in many creatures as an established part of their natures, how can it be called contrary to nature if, through the dispensation of the Holy Spirit, a son is born from the womb of a virgin without her having had intercourse with a man?

CHAPTER 3:   On the shepherds whom the angels told of the infant's birth

When he was born in Bethlehem, the city of David, shepherds assigned to the tending of flocks were instructed by angels that the King of heaven had deigned to take on human flesh, subject to the law of birth and dwelling upon the earth among men. They then sang a song befitting this message to the listening shepherds, and ascended again into heaven. In this the angels acted appropriately, announcing the Lamb's birth first to shepherds, and the Shepherd's to [their] flocks.

The manner of the birth of the two boys John and Jesus, the precursor and the Lord, is not without a historical reason: for one was brought forth by an old woman, the other by a virgin girl. For it was fitting that John, Christ's precursor in all things, should be born of an old mother, for he was the end of the Old Law – its youngest son, as it were. But Christ took his body from a virgin girl; for he was the beginning of the New Testament, and the first of the sons who were to be born under the New Law.

Therefore in the forty-second year of Octavianus Augustus Caesar, when Herod was king of the Jews and all sovereignty had been taken away from the Jews [themselves], the Lord Jesus Christ was born in Bethlehem, a town of Judaea, to the race of David, from the Virgin Mary. This came about as was fitting: that when the succession of kings and pontiffs descending from the race of Jacob had run its course, the eternal King and Pontiff should be born.

CHAPTER 4: On the Magi led by a star from the east

When that child was born whom the prophets of the Israelites and of the pagans had foretold would be the Saviour of both peoples, Magi who had been led by a star from the land of Hevilath came to him with gifts, having made a long journey. When they had offered their gifts, and spent some time in worshipping the boy, they returned – not however taking the road by which they had come but, having been warned by a divine voice, going home by another route.

The words of the Gospel do indeed tell us of this star, which guided the Magi from Jerusalem to Bethlehem; but those who believe that the Magi had it as their guide from their own country to Jerusalem cannot support this view with the Gospel's authority. For when the Magi, still in their own land, saw a brilliant star in the heavens, they recognised – whether through their own knowledge, or the instruction of angels – that it pertained to God, and to the King whom their own prophecies and those of the church[9] declared would be born of the race of Israel. They came [therefore] to the land of Israel, and to Jerusalem where the rulership of the whole province was established, to inquire about the King and God who had been born. When they had learned what the prophets of Israel had foretold concerning the place where that child would be born, and received duplicitous instructions from the king, they journeyed onward eagerly. Leaving the city, and taking the star as their guide upon the road, they soon reached Christ.

As to whether this star is to be taken simply as a star, or as an angel, or as the Holy Spirit: if none of these views is offensive to catholic opinion, our own limited intelligence will leave it open to more qualified judges to decide between them.

For if one chooses to view it simply as a star, how did it leave the company of the other stars in order to lead [the Magi]? For we know that

---

9 Despite its anachronistic sound, this seems to be the best translation for *prophetias tam ipsorum quam ecclesiasticas*; use of the Greek word ἐκκλησία to designate the assembly of the Israelites is well attested in the Septuagint.

the nature [of the stars] was set in the beginning, and established in the firmament of heaven, as the authority of the Book of Genesis makes plain. If therefore it remained in the firmament of heaven, how could it be a guide to men walking between Jerusalem and Bethlehem? And if it flew through the air like an arrow – but moving somewhat more slowly, to match the pace of those who followed – it would in the meantime have abandoned its customary position and path in the firmament, something which the Scriptures do not describe as happening even in the case of the major luminaries when they are stationary or retrograde in the [zodiacal] signs. But perhaps it was aerial fire which performed that office, and was called a 'star' on account of its appearance, as in many other cases which we have mentioned.

If on the other hand it was an angel wearing the semblance of a star who performed this office, what would be the difficulty in that, seeing that angels transform themselves into many forms when they show themselves to men? Thus an angel with a fiery appearance spoke out of a bush to Moses on Mount Horeb; and one appeared like an armed warrior to Joshua outside the camp at Gilgal. Angels were transformed into a fiery chariot and horses when Elijah was taken aloft; and when Elisha opened the eyes of his servant, angels appeared in the same forms. They presented themselves as guests to the eyes of Abraham and Lot; and Manoah and his wife beheld an angel who spoke to them in the guise of a prophet. It would have been no wonder if on this occasion, when an angel was made the guide of the Magi, he should for the benefit of those astrologers have been transformed into the semblance of a star, and the radiance of a blazing luminary. And indeed when John describes things seen in vision in his Apocalypse he does not go against this view, saying 'The seven stars are the angels of seven churches' (Revelation 1:20). Since then angels may be called 'stars' – even if it be in ecstasy – why should not an angel have been called a star here also?[10]

Or else, if it is determined that this star was neither an angel, nor a star of the firmament, nor any kind of fire, let it be granted that it was the Holy Spirit. For afterwards, in the bodily semblance of a dove, it descended upon the Lord Jesus in the Jordan; in the same way, in the semblance of a star, it led the adoring pagans to the cradle of the Lord born in the flesh. The astrologer Balaam spoke of this figuratively, saying 'A star will arise from Jacob' (Numbers 24:17) – that is, the flaming spiritual light of Christ's grace, by which the night of pagan unbelief is illuminated. For even as the

---

10 Our text seems to be cited in a Middle Irish sermon for Epiphany: mentioning various possible explanations for the star, the homilist says 'or else, it was an angel of God that appeared in the form of a star, as is the opinion of St. Augustine' (Atkinson 1887, 473; cf. 236).

Holy Spirit later descended in fire upon the apostles, in the upper room in Zion, so in the semblance of a star it led the Magi to the Lord.

CHAPTER 5: On Christ's baptism

The boy's knowledge grew in advance of his years, until at the age of thirty he came to the Jordan. There the Lamb received baptism from that same John son of Zacharias of whom we spoke above, who was then baptising those who were to believe in the one who was to come; and the Jordan's water washed the one who was to declare himself. The Holy Spirit descended upon him in the form of a dove, and he heard the Father speaking of him from heaven: 'This is my beloved Son, in whom my soul is pleased' (Matthew 3:17, etc.). Together with these portents he saw heaven opened; then, having received baptism, he ascended from his bath in the river.

The Lord Jesus went to be baptised not because he, who was free of any personal or inherited fault, needed the sacrament and bath of baptism; but so that he might cleanse the waters which, even though God had not cursed them at Adam's fall, were tainted by the curse which rested on the earth in which they were. And lest anyone should neglect the sacrament of baptism, even he who was without sin entered the baptismal waters. And lest anyone should think ill of being baptised by an inferior, since the Lord wished to be plunged into the waters of baptism by his servant. And because he did not wish to be recognised by him until the temptation had taken place, he let the Devil see him being washed in the water among people polluted with sins, as if he himself were in need of bathing.

He saw the Holy Spirit descending upon him at baptism; and he heard the voice of his Father from the heavens, acknowledging him as his Son; and he saw heaven open before him. This was not because the Son of God did not have all of these things before his baptism, but so that the power of that sacrament might be made manifest. For he did not receive the Spirit at that time, since he and the Spirit are believed to have the same substance. Nor was it then that the Father first acknowledged him as his Son, for it is to him that he said 'I begot you from the womb before Lucifer' (Psalm 109:3) – that is, before all the angels, whom Scripture often designates [collectively] as 'Lucifer'. Nor was it then that the chamber of the heavens was opened to him, who had said 'Heaven is my throne, and the earth my footstool' (Isaiah 66:1). But the holy Trinity brought all of these things together in the baptism of the Lord, so that each of us may know what benefit there is in the mystery of holy baptism. For it is then that one who has been cleansed from the stain of his sins receives the Holy Spirit, and begins to be acknowledged as a son by God the Father through the grace of adoption; and it is then that the gates of the kingdom of heaven open for him, and he is known as a citizen of the heavenly country, and a comrade of the holy angels.

Although the Holy Spirit is said to have descended upon the Lord in bodily form, we may be certain that it did not assume [the form of] a real dove, but one of air. For it was not necessary for the Holy Spirit to take a body for itself from among the birds, since birds did not in any way transgress against the law established for their nature. But if they had transgressed in anything, still they would not merit deliverance from the punishment of their guilt through the Spirit's assumption of their flesh, as would an eternal or rational creature. But because the person of the Son was clothed in a body of human flesh, it was appropriate that the person of the Holy Spirit should descend upon him in a bodily form; and that the Father's voice, coming physically out of a cloud through the air, should be heard with the ears of the body.

Besides all this, the Father and the Holy Spirit came to the baptism in a cloud and in the shape of a dove because these things have something of water in their nature. For since the Son had chosen the substance of water for the mystery of baptism, it was necessary that the Father should speak from a watery cloud, and that the Holy Spirit should seem to take on a body which had been made from water at the beginning, and should descend from that cloud, so that thus the whole Trinity might show itself to have a single will.

CHAPTER 6: On Christ's temptation and fasting

Immediately after his baptism the Lord Jesus went up out of the water and, so that he might give the Devil the opportunity of tempting him, sought out the pathless places of the desert. There he fasted for forty days and as many nights, sustained by no human food; and there, with three replies, he triumphed over those three temptations with which Satan had seduced the first man. All iniquity was contained in the Devil's three propositions; but in the three answers with which Christ repudiated him, there was all justice.

When the Enemy was condemned and vanquished, freedom and redemption were prepared for the human race. For since Satan sought to raise himself above his Maker, therefore man, who had up until then been subject to him, rose above him through the help of the victorious Lord. And since [the Devil] sought to bind one who was free from every fault, therefore the one whom he had already conquered and now held in prison shed the chains with which he had been bound. And since [the Devil] sought to contend against one stronger than himself, therefore the one weaker than he was strengthened to resist him. And the Lord commanded [the Devil], who had up until then been exiled from heaven for his fault only as far as the earth, to flee thence into hell.

The Lord's incarnate body was able to bear forty days' hunger without danger of death; for the Lord's words, which when they came to Moses through the air revived him twice for forty days, on this occasion worked within Christ to nourish his joints and nerves. Why then is the Lord said to have been hungry after the forty days and forty nights, when it is not related that Moses and Elijah suffered hunger after fasting for that length of time? Surely our Redeemer took hunger and toil upon himself once that number of days had elapsed, both so that he might give the Tempter an opportunity to tempt, and so that it might be known that he had truly taken on the substance of human flesh. So this deed is not superhuman, nor does it require anything new, since it does not exceed the span of time for which men fasted formerly.

CHAPTER 7: On the miracles of the Gospel up to the walking upon the sea

When the Enemy had been conquered, and the forty days' fast completed, [Christ] summoned the people of Israel throughout Judaea and Galilee to the way of salvation. And from among them all, by the grace of special election, he chose for himself twelve champions. Inasmuch as he wished to make the hearts of all men trust in the health of an invisible and inner substance, that of souls, he gave even to his servants the power to heal bodies from sickness, a power which nothing could resist. Thus when he was preaching the good news of the kingdom of God throughout Galilee, and saw a miscellaneous crowd afflicted with various diseases – some made wretched because there was no light in their eyes, others whose bodies were covered with the loathsomeness of leprosy, some thwarted by the deformity of their feet – he healed them.

In [the healing of] the paralytic carried by four men, three divine acts can be discerned: his sins were forgiven; the affliction under which he suffered was healed with a word; and thoughts were answered, as by God who sees all things. And in this man it is seen how some blemishes upon the soul can be overcome through suffering.

How could a dumb man not speak, when the Word of God the Father besought him for an answer? How could he who put eloquence into the mouth of an ass not be able to strengthen a human tongue, even a mute one, so that it could utter words? And when the Light of Justice which had come into the world appeared, how could a blind man not see? And by what power could a devil remain in a man when Christ, who had banished him from heaven for his sins, came to cast him out?

There are three things to be marvelled at in the five loaves and two fishes which satisfied the five thousand: the small quantity of matter, the number of people who were filled, and the abundance of the fragments.

CHAPTER 8: On the Lord's walking upon water

The Lord, seeking disciples from the earth, was obliged to walk upon the water. This was for the sake of Peter's faith: in order that Christ should not, by doing this thing alone, give cause for doubt that he had a real body. But since Peter, the son of a man and a woman, did it with the help of Christ's command, there can be no doubt concerning the flesh of the Virgin's son.

But it may be asked whether the nature of the Lord's body, and of Peter's, was made light, so that the water could support them; or whether the substance of the water was made solid, so that it could hold up human bodies. In either case it would not be against nature for such a thing to happen at God's bidding, whether the Lord's command thickened the water or lightened human flesh.

For warriors on the Scythian coasts, as the ancients relate, practice their combats on the shores (?) of the sea, being so skilled in the art of swimming that even when plunged in the depths up to the waist they scarcely sink. If men can do this, is it to be wondered at that flesh can be made lighter at the Lord's command? All the less so, considering that at the resurrection bodies will be made so light that they will be supported not only by thick water, but even by clouds and air – as the Apostle says, 'We will be caught up to meet Christ in the air' (1 Thessalonians 4:17).

On the other hand, one might prefer to assume that it was the nature of water which was made solid, seeing that water possesses the thickness of earth – as when, shrinking with the cold, it freezes to a hardness more solid than that of earth, and can support a multitude until it is melted by warm air. And indeed, even if the flowing waves are not frozen, it is a part of water's nature to support large trees, and the bodies of men and other animals, and floating ships.

Nor is it strange that that solidity, brought about by the Lord's command, did not support Peter when he doubted, since when the Lord so wished it even the earth did not support such unbelievers as Dathan and Abiron.

CHAPTER 9: On our Lord Jesus Christ's other miracles

Two processes (*rationes*) may be discerned in the natural functioning (*administratio*) of things. Of these, the lower (*inferior ratio*) is understood to be their functioning from day to day – as when water becomes blood, or salt water becomes sweet by passing through clouds or earth. The higher of the two (*ratio superior*) comes about through that unaccustomed government (*gubernatio*) of things which may be recognised in miracles – as when in Egypt God changed water into blood in an instant, and made it sweet when it was touched with a staff.

CHAPTER 10: On the loaves and fishes, with which thousands of people
                were fed

Thus through the lower process God produces from a little grain, grown with the passage of time into a great harvest, the bread to feed innumerable men; through the higher process he multiplies a small amount of matter in an instant with his blessing. Similarly he multiplied the fishes with his first blessing, when he said 'Grow and multiply, and fill the waters of the sea' (Genesis 1:22); now their bodies are multiplied through the higher process, when he blesses them in order to satisfy the crowds.

CHAPTER 11: On the vision of the Lord upon the mountain, talking with
                Moses and Elijah

Although the Lord's face shone like the sun during this vision, it was not the flesh itself which shone: rather the divinity latent within his body granted to those who beheld it from outside a little opening through which to glimpse as much of its light as they were able. Why then did his garments have the whiteness of snow, seeing that they were neither human nor divine? Perhaps, just as divinity illuminated the outer flesh, so the flesh illuminated by that divinity shone through the garments.

   Moses and Elijah in particular were included in that vision: this was either so that they, first in the Law and first among the prophets, should meet the End of both; or so that the horned face of Moses, upon which the sons of Israel could not gaze, and Elijah, caught up in a fiery chariot, might appear dark compared with Christ. Also, because these two are said on the authority of Scripture to have fasted for forty days, it was only in their presence that the Father declared himself concerning the Lord Jesus.

   But granted that Elijah, still remaining in the body, could come to such a meeting, what is to be said of Moses? Was he once more in a body during this vision; or did he put on an illusory semblance taken from the air, like the apparition of Samuel? And if he came wearing his body, did he accomplish his resurrection then, as no one else will do until the last times? On this question the authorities, sharing a single opinion, do not differ. Since it cannot be doubted that the Lord with his three disciples, and Elijah, were present in real and not illusory bodies, it is evident that Moses too must have taken his real body back from the tomb. But since the Lord Jesus is rightly held to be 'the firstborn of the dead' (Revelation 1:5), Moses's body was restored to the tomb after this vision, so that he could put it on when the dead arise on the last day.

CHAPTER 12: On Lazarus, and the other dead restored to life

With an unshakeable determination, God has destined a fixed end and limit for every life. The lives of some appear to have been cut short by death, not so that they should die, but so that those who restore them to life might be more highly esteemed among men as being dear to God; it is for this reason that the Lord said, speaking of Lazarus to his disciples, 'This sickness will not lead to death, but [it has come about] so that the Son of Man may be glorified by means of it' (John 11:4). Shortly after this was said, Lazarus died; nevertheless he was raised on the fourth day by the Son of God, who gained glory from the deed.

For the span of his life was not accomplished; rather, the Lord often pretends to withhold that which he is unchangeably determined to bring about, as when he delayed the childbearing of the wives of Abraham and Isaac so that it might be all the more welcome when it came to pass. Moreover, the Lord so arranges things that he is asked to grant someone as a favour what he wishes to give him [in any case]; but if one of the saints should ask for what God has not ordained, that would by no means be granted – as when Moses asked to enter the Promised Land, and Paul asked that the angel of Satan withdraw from him, and they did not obtain what they requested.

Concerning all of the dead in general, then,[11] it is held that they died for the first time so that worthy men might be glorified. For it should be noted that of the eight persons whom holy Scripture, in the Old and New Testaments, declares to have been restored to life, it is said of the first, the widow's son whom Elijah raised, 'Let the boy's soul return, I pray' (1 Kings 17:21); while of the last, that Eutychus in the Acts of the Apostles who

11 Presumably Augustinus refers here to all of the dead said to have been brought back to life in the Bible.

'being raised up was found to be dead' [it is said that] Paul went down to him, lay upon him, and embraced him, saying 'Do not be dismayed, for his soul is in him' (Acts 20:9–10). Each of these cases must be considered carefully: the widow's son was dead, and the prophet asked his soul to return; the other was also dead, and Paul said that his soul was in him. In each case Scripture tells the truth, for it cannot lie. But how is it to be understood that a dead person's soul can be hidden in the limbs of his body? Unless perhaps the soul, which is immaterial, is held to be present in the body invisibly. Some, seeking to sidestep the problem, say that when Eutychus died he breathed forth his soul, and think that, when Paul said 'His soul is in him,' the soul was returning after a brief interval. But Scripture does not say whether the soul went forth or returned. The other six dead persons, whose souls are not said either to have departed or returned, may be taken as proving beyond any doubt that they were dead, and raised again by divine agency.

CHAPTER 13: On the eclipse of the sun at the Lord's passion

The sun's physical eclipse happened not when the moon was kindled,[12] as is usual, but at the full moon, the fifteenth day of the month, lest it be thought that it happened by chance. And darkness obscured the sun's light at midday to such an extent that stars were visible in the sky throughout the three hours of the eclipse.

CHAPTER 14: On the bodies of the saints, which came from their tombs
            after the Lord's resurrection

Saints came from their tombs after the Lord's resurrection; but afterwards they returned to their tombs, as we have said above of Moses, there to await the final resurrection of all – as the apostle says, 'All these have been tested in bearing witness to the faith, but have not received God's promise; for he has prepared something better for us, so that they will not be made perfect without us' (Hebrews 11:39–40).

   Are they and Moses, then, to be thought to be resurrected twice, both in this miracle and in the final resurrection of all, when they only once tasted the death incurred through Adam's sin? Far be it from anyone of catholic faith to believe that one who died once could rise twice – unless perhaps someone should say that they and Moses died twice.

12 That is, at the new moon.

But it is never written concerning those who died in this way that they were resurrected – rather that they lived, or appeared, or came from their tombs. For the word 'resurrection' applies to those who after death have returned to this life, either in the case of the Lord's own resurrection, or of the future resurrection of all. But the appearance of these persons had to do neither with human life nor with the resurrection which is to be: rather it served to move souls to accept that the Lord had risen again, and to believe in the resurrection of souls from hell. Just as the raising of the dead may be seen to involve only an appearance, not lasting death,[13] so in the case of these individuals it was a semblance of resurrection, not true resurrection, which was made manifest. For until the last day no one except the Lord will return from lasting death to unfading life; and no one will ever be thrust back again into death after the true resurrection.

CHAPTER 15: On the Lord's food after the resurrection

The learned inquire how the resurrection body could consume our fleshly food, when all the faithful know that the bodies which rise again will be spiritual, as it is said, 'It will rise as a spiritual body' (1 Corinthians 15:44). Bodies will therefore arise without any craving for food; but it may reasonably be believed that they will be able to eat it if necessary. God has by no means denied us examples of this, as in the case of the angels at Mamre. But [those who have spiritual bodies] do not, like us, deposit the food which they have chewed in their stomachs and intestines; but rather, as soon as they seem to eat what has been given them, they transform it – not in part, but entirely – into a spiritual nature.

CHAPTER 16: Peter heals a paralytic

The fittingness of the Holy Spirit's appearing above Christ as a dove, and above the apostles as fire, has been discussed; and we have spoken of the division of the languages, and of the miracles which the apostles, after they had received the Spirit, performed [in keeping with] their profession of poverty as an alternative to giving alms. When Peter said to the paralytic 'Arise and walk' (Acts 3:6), he obeyed his Master's injunction 'Have neither gold nor silver' (Matthew 10:9). For serving only God, he was freed from the Mammon of iniquity; and with a word of command to the sick man he swiftly loosed what bound him.[14]

13 Here Augustinus returns to the speculations aired in Chapter 12. 'Lasting death' (*continua mors*) is evidently to be distinguished from such brief intervals as preceded the resuscitations of Lazarus, the widow's son, and Eutychus. 14 The sequence of ideas in this little chapter is

CHAPTER 17: Peter's miracles

See how much power the apostles had in Christ! For by nothing but a word of command Peter caused Ananias – and he in full health – to perish; and he freed Tabitha, bound with the fetter of death, by the same power of command. Ananias and Sapphira died suddenly in the presence of the church, so that it might be revealed how great was the power of the apostles, and so that it might be shown how great a sin it was to take back again what had been offered to the church; and the others were chastised by this example.

difficult to follow; possibly the text itself is somewhat corrupt. In the scene in Acts 3 mentioned in the last two sentences, a paralytic at the Temple asks Peter and John for alms; instead of giving him money, Peter heals him.

In Tenga Bithnua: 'The Ever-New Tongue'

In Tenga Bithnua shares the same general interests as the other texts presented in this section: like *On the Miracles of Holy Scripture* and *Saltair na Rann*, it sees the vastness and intricacy of the universe as an adumbration of the glory of God; like *Altus Prosator*, it focusses in its portrayal of the totality of things on the world's beginning and its end. Most of the text takes the six days of creation as a basic framework; the concluding sections deal with the horrors of Judgment Day, the unimaginability of hell, and the infinity of God. These general similarities, and some more specific ones, place *In Tenga Bithnua* securely in the context of early Irish cosmological writing. It is set apart however by the extravagance of its imagery, and by the boldness of its underlying premise: far from being simply a commentary on the testimony of the Bible, it purports to be a separate heavenly revelation, unveiling all of the mysteries of the universe.

Behind this claim of direct inspiration lies a long and complicated textual history. *In Tenga Bithnua* seems to go back to a Gnostic treatise, perhaps a lost *Apocalypse of Philip*, in which the resurrected Christ explained to his disciples secrets not contained in the canonical Scriptures. The original work, probably composed in fourth- or fifth-century Egypt, was at some point translated into Latin and found its way to Ireland, most likely by way of Spain;[1] over the centuries it changed and grew, drawing upon the Bible, early travel literature, treatises on precious stones, astronomical and exegetical literature, and a variety of other sources.

Although it is possible to identify many influences on the text, there is virtually nothing in it which passively echoes any other work: its contents have been trans-formed in the crucible of the author's imagination to become part of his own unique, fantastic vision of reality. *In Tenga Bithnua* is, indeed, one of the most remarkable examples known to me of that inspired fusion of learning and creativity which distinguishes so much of early Irish literature; in another medium, we can perhaps compare the astonishing transmutations of Mediterranean Christian iconography on the figural pages of the Book of Kells. What seems to be pure invention appears in the very core of the work, in the bursts of 'angelic speech' which are presented as the verbatim utterances of the 'Ever-new Tongue' himself: these reflect no known human language, and exhibit recurrent sound patterns suggesting that they originated in free association.

The text is cast in the form of a homily, presumably to be delivered on the vigil of Easter: it is on this occasion that the revelation which forms the body of the work is said to have occurred, and emphasis is placed throughout the text on the importance both of Easter and of the hour of midnight. Cosmology and Easter are

---

1 The case for apocryphal texts having reached Ireland from Spain is argued in Dumville 1973, especially 322.

related to one another through the doctrine that all of the substances in creation went into the making of the first man: when Christ rose in a human body, the entire universe was redeemed. In this way *In Tenga Bithnua*, with its dizzying bird's eye view of all of the marvels of heaven and earth, is in its essence concerned with human salvation, and with the bonds which link God, man, and world.

'In the beginning God created heaven and earth' (Genesis 1:1), etc.[2] The High King of the world, who is mightier than every king, who is loftier than every power, who is fiercer than every dragon, who is gentler than every child, who is brighter than suns, who is holier than every elder, who is more vengeful than men, who is more loving than every mother, the only Son of God the Father, bestowed this account upon the many peoples of the world, concerning the world's form and creation.

For the form of anything which is seen in the world was not known, save to God only. For [the situation of] the race of Adam was 'a head in a bag', and 'being in a dark house'; for formerly it was not known what shape the world had, or who had made it, until this account came from heaven for the opening of everyone's mind and intellect, so that the way of life and of the saving of souls might be discovered and found.

For everything was utterly obscure to the eyes of the race of Adam. But they used to see the migration of the stars, that is, the moon and the sun and the other stars, which revolved every day without ever resting. And they saw the springs and rivers of the world flowing, which never rested at any time. And they saw the fasting of the earth, and the weakness and slumber of the light and of the fruits with the coming of winter. And they saw the resurrection of the world with its warmth and its light, with its flowers and its fruits, at the rising up of the summer once again.

Nevertheless, they did not know who made it, until there came this account of the creation of the world with its shapes and its agencies which God had established. All of that was utterly obscure until this account was related: until the Ever-new Tongue disclosed it, who spoke from the summit of heaven above the assembly of Mount Zion.

For the assembly of the east of the world had been gathered: everyone from the mountains of Abian as far as the shores of the Red Sea, and from the Dead Sea as far as the islands of Sabairn. And this was the number of the gathering: three thousand, four hundred and eighty-five bishops; and fifty-four thousand, nine hundred and sixty-six kings from among the kings of the world.

---

2 The beginning of Genesis is traditionally one of the readings for the Easter vigil mass; since at least the time of Saint Augustine, it was taken as a text for sermons preached on that vigil.

That assembly was held until the end of four months and a year, summer, winter, spring, autumn, under nine hundred canopies of white linen with golden ornaments, on the summit of Mount Zion. They used to kindle five thousand, nine hundred and fifty great torches and precious stones to illuminate the multitude, lest any storm inconvenience it at any time. Two hundred and fifty bishops, and five hundred priests, and three thousand in [the other] ecclesiastical grades, and one hundred and fifty innocent youths, and five hundred high kings with their attendants before them, used to go at midnight into Jerusalem chanting (?), and they used to return every matins with songs of the rejoicing that is hymned in heaven, that is, 'Glory to God in the highest, and peace on earth to men of good will' (Luke 2:14). Then the hosts of the assembly would rise up to meet them between two plains, with the shouts proper to each king (?), as this excursion and the multitudes returned to Mount Zion with the song of rejoicing.

Suddenly then, when it was the end of the eve of Easter, something was heard: a noise in the clouds like the sound of thunder, or it was like the crackling of a great fire; at the same time it was a stormy wind. Suddenly something was seen: a sunburst like a radiant sun in the midst of the noise. That bright sunburst was turning upon itself so that eyesight could not catch up with it; for it was seven times brighter than the sun.

Suddenly thereafter something was heard; for the eyes of the host were gazing upon the noise, for they thought that it was a sign of the Judgment. Something was heard, a bright voice which spoke in angelic language: *Hæli habia felebe fæ niteia temnibisse salis sal*; that is, 'Listen to this tale, sons of men! I have been sent from God to speak to you.'

Immediately weakness and fear fell upon the hosts. It was not terror without cause. The sound of the voice was resounding like the shout of an army, but at the same time it was brighter and clearer than the voices of men. It roared above the encampment like the howling of a great wind, which at the same time was no louder in each man's ear than the words of a friend; and it was sweeter than music.

The wise men of the Hebrews answered and said: 'Let us learn from you your name, and the reason for your name, and your essential nature.' Something was heard, the Ever-new Tongue which spoke in an angelic voice: *Nathire uimbæ o lebiæ uaun nimbisse tiron tibia ambiase sau fimblia febe able febia fuan*, that is, 'I was born,' said he, 'among the peoples of the earth, and was conceived from the union of a man and woman. This is my name: Philip the apostle. The Lord sent me to the tribes of the pagans, to preach to them. Nine times my tongue was cut from my head by the pagans, and nine times I resumed my preaching; therefore I am called "the Ever-new Tongue" by the household of heaven.'

The wise men of the Hebrews said: 'Let us learn from you in what language it is that you speak to us.' He said: 'The language in which I speak to you is that in which the angels speak, and every rank of heaven. And sea-creatures and beasts and cattle and birds and serpents and demons understand it, and all will speak it at the Judgment.

'It is this,' said he, 'which has dispatched me to you: to make plain to you the wondrous tale which the Holy Spirit related through Moses son of Amram, concerning the making of heaven and earth, together with the things which are in them. For that tale tells of the making of heaven and earth; and likewise of the creation of the world which has been accomplished by Christ's resurrection from the dead on this eve of Easter. For every material and every element and every nature which is seen in the world, they were all brought together in the body in which Christ rose again – that is, in the body of every human.

'There is in it, first of all, material from wind and air; from it proceeds the respiration of breath in people's bodies. And there is in it material from fire; that is what makes the red heat of blood in bodies. And there is in it material from the sun and the stars of heaven also; so that that is what makes the brightness and the light in people's eyes. And there is in it material from bitterness and saltiness; so that that is what makes the bitterness of tears, and the gall of the liver, and abundance of anger in people's hearts. And there is in it material from the stones and clay of the earth; so that that is what makes the mingling of flesh and bones in people. And there is in it material from the flowers and bright colours of the earth; so that that is what makes the freckling and pallor of faces, and the colour in cheeks.

'With him the whole world rose again; for the nature of all creation was in the body which Jesus had put on. For if the Lord had not contrived [that], and if he had not suffered for the sake of the race of Adam, and if he had not risen again after death, the whole world would be destroyed together with the race of Adam at the coming of the Judgment, and no creature of sea or land would be redeemed, but the heavens would burn up: save for the three heavens of the lofty *riched*[3] alone, nothing would survive unburnt. There would be no earth, nor any race of the living or the dead in the world, but only hell as far as heaven, unless the Lord had come for their redemption: all things would perish thus, without renewal.

---

3 The transcendent heaven which is the dwelling-place of God, as distinguished from the physical heavens occupied by the stars and planets; the word's original sense was 'royal throne' (from earlier *ríg-sed*), but it is only attested in the specialised sense 'heaven'. In many texts *ríched* can be used simply to mean 'sky'; in *In Tenga* however the latter is only referred to as *nem*.

'This is why I have come to you,' said Philip: 'so that I may relate this tale to you. For the making of the world's form is opaque and very obscure to you, as it has been related since ancient times.' 'It is well,' said the wise men of the Hebrews. 'Tell us some of the innumerable wonders which happened then; for it is utterly obscure to us, unless it be related to us clearly.'

Something was heard: the Ever-new Tongue which spoke in the angelic language, saying: *Læ uide fodea tabo abelia albe fab*, which means in Latin 'In the beginning God created heaven and earth' (Genesis 1:1). And he said: *Ambile bane bea fabne fa libera salese inbila tibon ale siboma fuan*. It would be tedious to recount in Hebrew everything which is related in that [utterance]: that there was no ordering of the radiant mansions; that the earth with its mountains and peoples did not exist, nor the sea with its islands, nor hell with its torments, before it was said that there should be creatures; that the circuits of the seven heavens did not exist, nor clouds for watering the earth, nor trembling (?), nor scattering of storms; that there were no lands upon which they could pour; that there was no rain or snow; that there were no lightnings, nor blowing of wind, nor thunders; that the course of the sun did not exist, nor the phases of the moon, nor the spangling of the stars; that there were no sea-monsters; that there was no sea for them to swim in; that there were no streams nor flocks nor beasts nor birds nor dragons nor serpents.

The wise men of the Hebrews asked, 'What existed at that time, when there existed none of the things which have so far been mentioned?'

The Ever-new Tongue answered, 'There was That which was more wondrous than every creature: God without beginning, without end, without sorrow, without age, without decay. There was no hour nor time nor interval when he did not exist. He is no younger, he is no older, than at first; nor was there anything which it was impossible for him to do. He thought a thought. That thought had no beginning. He thought something: that it would be nobler that his power and glory be seen – that which was inexpressible, that which existed in no other things though he existed himself.

'Suddenly then, after those thoughts, he made light. This is the light which he made: the circuit of the *ríched*, with the nine orders of angels. Seventy-two is the number of their peoples, with the 7,624 suns, with songs and radiant mansions, such as exist throughout the seven shapes of the *ríched*. In the same day he made the circuit of the shapes, that is, the material from which the world was made. For it is a round encircling shape which God first made as a shape for the world.'[4]

4 There seems to be a gap in the text here, as the Ever-new Tongue's next words appear to be answering another question even though the question itself is not preserved.

The Ever-new Tongue answered, 'Though you do not see it,' he said, 'with respect to the shapes of the world, every creature has been established in roundness. For the seven heavens were established in a round circle, and the seven surrounding seas were made in a circle, and the lands were made in a circle, and it is in a round circle that the stars go around the round wheel of the world, and it is in roundness of form that souls are seen after parting from [their] bodies, and the circuit of the lofty *ríched* is seen to be round, and the shapes of the sun and moon are seen to be round. All of that is fitting; for the Lord who has always been and who will always be, and who made all those things, is a circle without beginning, without end. That is why the world has been formed in a round shape.'

The Hebrews said: 'What was there in the many-shaped round circuit which was the material of the world?'

The Ever-new Tongue answered, 'There were,' he said, 'in the round circuit of the material of the world, cold and heat, light and darkness, heavy and light, liquid and dry, high and low, bitterness and mildness, strength and weakness, the roar of the sea and the crash of thunder, the scent of flowers and the chanting of angels and pillars of fire.

'All these things,' he said, 'were in the round many-shaped aggregation of the material of the world. And it is then that the material of hell was created; for it was not made at once, until the archangel defied the will and broke the law of the King who had made him, together with the innumerable host of the angels. And until then,' he said, 'hell had not been made, but its material was stored (?) in the round many-shaped mass from which the world was extracted, together with all of the kinds of things which exist in it. And if the angels had persevered in the nature in which they had been created, and in the angelic radiance, the material of hell would have been turned into a radiant shining kingdom.

'This, then, is what was done on the first day, in which God set about creating the world, as it is written: 'He who lives forever created all things at once' (Sirach 18:1).

Artibilon alma sea sabne ebeloia flules elbiæ limbæ lasfania lire; which means in Latin: 'And the Lord made the firmament between the waters, and he divided the waters which were above the firmament from those which were below the firmament' (Genesis 1:7). 'In the second day, then,' said he, 'God established the encircling wall of the seven heavens, together with the celestial waters. For the Lord knew when he made the world that man would transgress the commandment which was uttered to him. That is why the veil of heaven has been placed before the faces and eyes of men, so that they cannot behold the blessedness of heaven and the throne of God.'

The Hebrews said: 'Tell us the hidden natures and the mysteries of the seven heavens, and the five zones which encircle the heavens.'

The Ever-new Tongue answered, 'The seven heavens around the world concerning which you ask,' said he, '[are these]: first of all the radiant bright cloudy heaven which is nearest to you, from which shine the moon and shooting stars (?); two shining fiery heavens above that, with emissions of angels in them and scattering of winds; a cold icy heaven above those, bluer than every bright colour, seven times colder than snow, from which shines the sun; two more shining fiery heavens above those, from which shine the flaming stars which put fruitfulness into clouds and sea; a fiery splendid lofty heaven above those which is the highest of them all, upon which is placed the circuit of the *riched*. That is a sunny fiery heaven, in which the work is the singing together of songs, and choirs of angels.

'It is in the zones of the seven heavens, then, that the twelve trembling-beasts (?) conceal themselves, with the fiery heads above them in their celestial bodies, who blow the twelve winds around the world. And in the same zones sleep the dragons with breaths of fire, pillar-headed (?) dragons with plagues upon them in their flanks, who set in motion the crackling of the thunders, and blow (?) lightnings from the pupils of their eyes.

'Five zones, then, encircle heaven; and heaven is a sevenfold circuit around the earth. A cold icy zone first of all, because of which the seas are feared (?) beyond the horizon to the north. Another cold zone, which encircles great beasts beneath the seas, under the edges of the earth to the south, in the place where the nine fiery pillars have been placed to the south of heaven. A radiant zone, the noble flame of the assembly of the world, which sustains the abundant produce of the earth until it arises around the world, before it to the west (?). Two beautiful mild zones which are vital struggles (?), which give cold and heat, which cast floods of plagues from the sides of the earth in all directions.

Aibne fisen asbæ fribæ flanis leia sieth, that is, 'On the third day God made lakes and many seas and many kinds of water and many forms of salt seas; and the circuit of the earth with its plains and its mountains and its forests, and its precious stones, and its many kinds of trees.'

The wise men of the Hebrews said, 'Tell us the many kinds and mysteries of the sea.'

The Ever-new Tongue answered: 'There are,' said he, 'three bodies of sea around the world; that is, first of all a sea with seven shapes beneath the sides of the world, against which hell roars and makes an outcry around the valley. A clear blue salt sea round about the earth on every side, which sets the flood tide and ebb tide in motion, which casts up abundant produce. And then there is the third sea: a flaming sea, which we read lies in the heavens. Nine winds raise it from its sleep; its waves sing four hundred and seventy songs after it has been awakened. It gives forth a roar like thunder from the noise of its waves. Its tide has not ceased from rising since the beginning of the world, but it is never full save on Sunday. On Sunday it falls asleep, until the thunders of the winds are awakened by the departure of God's Sunday from heaven, and by the singing together of the angels above it.

'There are moreover many kinds of sea besides those, around the edges of the earth on every side. A red sea first of all, with many precious stones, with the brightness of blood, with golden colours, between the lands of Egypt and India. A roaring white sea the colour of snow, in the north among the islands of Sab. The might of its flood tide is so great that its waves cast their spray to the circuit of the clouds. A sea with poison waves, black as a beetle. No vessel which has reached it has escaped from it save for a [boat with a] single oar-bench, thanks to the lightness of its going and the strength of the wind; and [men] have found multitudes of monsters there.

'We read moreover of a sea in the ocean south of the island of Ebian. Its flood tide rises at May Day, until it begins to ebb with [the coming of] winter: half a year of flood, half a year of ebb perpetually. Its monsters and whales cry out when it begins to ebb, and fall into stupor and slumber. They awaken and rejoice with the flood, and the springs and rivers and streams of the world arise: it is through valleys that they go, until after a time they come again.

'There are moreover,' said he, 'seventy-two kinds of manifold springs in the world:

'The spring of Ebión first of all, which turns many colours in the course of each day perpetually. It has the colour of snow from sunrise to terce. It is green, with the many hues of a serpent, from terce to none. It turns the colour of blood from none to vespers. Any lips which taste of it, no smile or laughter comes upon them during life.

'The spring of Assian in the lands of Libya, which causes women to be fertile, though they were barren before.

'The spring of Seon in the lands of Dard boils up against kin-slayers and idolaters. Wrath and madness come upon any mouth which tastes of it; [he who drinks] does not speak thereafter, until he dies in sorrow and wretchedness.

'Of the spring of Zion, here in the lands of the Hebrews, it is not destined that any fool should find it. It flows without rising; it always wells up to the brim on Sunday. At night it shines like beams of the sun. More radiant colours than can be told or said appear from one hour to the next. No taste of oil or wine or honey has come into the world which could not be found therein. It never ceases from flowing, [but] its outlet is found nowhere. Whoever has tasted it has not experienced sorrow or grief of mind, and has not been given over to death.

'There is moreover a stream of water which goes across the island of torments, which rises up against every company which goes around it with falsehood; they do not escape from it.

'There are four golden streams in the valleys of the mountain of Nabuan: with the taste of wine, with the red hue of blood, with the bitterness of salt, with sands of gold.

'The stream of Alien in the islands of Tebe always resounds like thunder on the night in which the Saviour of the world was born in the lands of the Hebrews and, as you could hear tonight, on the night in which Christ arose from the dead. Three hundred and sixty-five kinds of music are in that sound. Whoever gets close to it does not speak at night for a long time thereafter. It seems that the sound comes from heaven.

'There are moreover,' said he, 'four kinds of precious stones with the intelligence and semblance of humans:

'The stone adamant in the lands of India: though it be held in winds and ice and snow, it is no colder because of that. Though there is a rain of fire and embers upon it, it is no hotter because of that. Though it is battered by axes and hammers, nothing breaks off from it because of that. Save for the blood of the Lamb with the sacrifice, there is nothing because of which it breaks. Every king who has set it on his right palm before going to battle has been victorious.

'The stone *hibien* in the lands of Hab: it burns in the blackness of night like a flaring candle. It spills every poison from the vessel in which it is placed, if it finds it therein before it. Any serpent which touches it or goes across it, dies immediately.

'The stone *istien* in the lands of Libya: it is found in the brains of dragons. The pools and great lakes in which it is put boil until they seethe forth across the lands. It shines when it comes in contact with water, and roars like thunder in the wintertime. On May Day it roars like the winds.

'The stone *fanes* in the lands of Aulol, in the stream of Dar: twelve stars and the wheel of the moon and the fiery circuit of the sun are seen in its side. It is found always in the hearts of the hot tumultuous dragons beneath the sea. Whoever has it in his hand does not tell a lie until he puts it from him. There is not enough room around it for the number that would be needed to bring it into the house of a kin-slayer or idolater. Every matins it gives forth sweet music to which nothing under heaven can be compared.'

The wise men and people of the Hebrews said: 'We ask that you tell us of the different kinds of trees which were planted by God at the creation of the world.'

The Ever-new Tongue answered, 'It is reasonable that you should ask that,' he said, 'for there are four trees in which it is thought that there are soul and intelligence like the life of angels.

'The tree Sames, first of all, at the confluence of the Ior and Dan, puts forth three fruits each year. The first fruit is bright green, that in the middle is red, the last is white. When the first fruit is ripe, the next grows from its blossoms. Anyone deranged who has tasted its fruit has regained his right wits. No leaf has fallen from it since it was made. Anyone with a blemish or a disease who lays himself in its shadow casts his sufferings from him.

'The tree of life in Paradise: whatever mouth has tasted its fruit, [the one who tasted] has not died thereafter. It is on account of that tree that Adam and Eve were banished from Paradise; for if they had tasted of that tree's fruit death would never have visited them, but they would have been alive forever. It puts forth twelve fruits every year; that is, a bright fruit every month. Its fragrance encompasses (?) Paradise, and its shade covers it, the distance of a journey of seven summer days.

'The tree Alab in the islands of Sab: its appearance is likened to the form of a man. The blossom which it brings forth quells every plague and every poison. Its fragrance and the scent of its blossoms encompass (?) a journey of six summer days, before one reaches it. The seeds of its fruit are precious stones. It quells anger and jealousy in every heart which its juice traverses.

'The tree Nathaben in the lands of the Hebrews, in the south of the mountain of Zion here; it is not far from you, in the south of the mountain where you are. Since the beginning of the world until now the sons of men have not found this tree, save only for the day when a tree was sought for crucifying Christ; and it is from its branches that there was brought the wood of the Cross through which the world has been saved. It bears seven fruits, and changes its blossoms seven times, each year. Sickness or suffering do not come to anyone who tastes its fruit; provided that he eat it before dying, nothing will separate old age and death save falling asleep (?). No honey or oil or wine have come into the world which could attain to the likeness of its flavour. The brilliance of the moon and sun, and the shining of the stars, shine from its blossoms. The tree and its blossoms sing seventy-two kinds of song together, when the winds meet them, ever since the beginning of the world. Three hundred and sixty-five birds, with the brightness of snow, with golden wings, with gleaming eyes, sing many songs in many languages from its branches; it is known that it is rational speech which they sing together, but that the ears of men cannot recognise it.'

The wise men of the Hebrews said, 'Lord, save that we dare not [say it], there is much in what we are being told which it is difficult to believe.'

Something was heard, the Ever-new Tongue: *Abia feble abia alitrian afen alpula nistien erolmea leam*, that is, 'Patient,' said he, 'is the gracious heart of the King of heaven, in that he does not hurl the world into the nethermost torments on account of what is done in every hour, considering all the blasphemy and reviling and enmity which every tongue casts into his face.

'Why do you not see,' said he, 'that it is harder to believe in the horned beast that the sea cast up on the shore of Cephas, on the night when Christ was born in the lands of the Hebrews? Streams of wine burst from its mouth before death. The hosts of the island who gazed upon it thought that it was a mountain or a lofty island which [the sea] had cast upon the shore. A stream burst forth for them from the cliff, as if from a vessel; and mead [came] from its mouth as it expired. Three hundred and fifty horns, shining like ice, [grew] from its head at the front. The length of its form upon the shore of Cephas extended fifty-six times farther than the eye could see. As for the horns, there is room in each of them for drink for a hundred and fifty men; they remain in your cities up to the present day,' he said. 'It is no harder to believe this tale than to believe and acknowledge the other.

'[There is] a bird of vast size in the lands of India whose name is *hiruath*. So great is its form that it is a journey of three winter days by sea or land [when] it beats its wings as it is hunting whales. Mountains of sand and the sun, it is they which heat the egg which is deposited after being laid. A ship with sails and oars is made of half of that egg after hatching. It bears one hundred and seventy thousand, together with their weapons and their provisions, across the sea; and a great many of the host which is here in this assembly came across the Red Sea in half of that egg. Do not be incredulous concerning God's abundant miracles, like a child in a lightless house.'

Suddenly then there arose a warrior of the tribe of Judah from the encampment in the east: Judas Maccabaeus son of Gomer son of Saleh son of Judas Iscariot who betrayed his Lord, one damned from of old. He arose and said: 'A lie,' said he, 'is the tree with birds with golden wings, and with the songs, of which this man has told. I do not believe that it exists. What would conceal the tree, in the middle of the plain, from the eyes of all?'

He turned withershins before the host of the assembly on the south, to the south of Mount Zion. Immediately he saw something: a fiery cloud. That cloud dissolved (?) before his eyes, so that he saw the tree with its radiant fruits. Its flowers were shining like the sun. Then he heard the mingled singing of the shining golden birds in many languages, and of the leaves of bright colours stirred by the voices of the winds.

Then all at once his sinful eyes could not endure gazing upon the holy colours. His eyes burst in his head. Then the blast of a fiery wind assailed him, driving into his chest and face so that they became as black as a beetle; and it cast him down half dead in the midst of the encampment. And he said: *Eui falia faste, eui falia faste, eui falia faste, maria fablea nelise nam*; that is, 'I am a faithless scoundrel.' And he said: 'Harsh are the torments which await me and are in store for me. Hauntingly beautiful is the bright plain which I have seen, which no one had ever seen before. Great blasphemy have we spoken: woe to the one who has committed it!' He had scarcely spoken when he fell dead to the ground.

Thereupon the hosts of the entire encampment arose, and they did penance, and this is what they were saying: 'O my holy Lord, for the sake of your own mercy and the feebleness of the substance from which we were made, let not the reproach of [your] anger fall upon our lack of faith! We have done things deserving of punishment (?); but dark to our eyes was the wondrous thing we did not know.'

Something was heard, the Ever-new Tongue: *Na itho adnacul lenisteia tibon talafi aia asfa bibo limbia flaune*, that is, 'If you were to put all your kindred to the sword – sons and daughters, mothers and fathers – and then set them to roast so that you might eat their flesh, it would be seven times easier to forgive that than to forgive blasphemy against God, and disbelief in his creatures and his miracles. There is not in heaven or earth any turning to repentance which can atone for blasphemy against God, and disbelief in his creatures and in the Trinity and in the wonders which God has wrought – only eternal existence without an end in the nethermost torments.'

The wise men of the Hebrews inquired, saying: 'Tell us what you began [to say].'

Something was heard, the Ever-new Tongue: *Alea fas uide uala nistien alme ama faus elobi reba*, that is, 'On the fourth day God made seventy-two kinds of wandering heavenly stars, together with the fiery circuit of the sun which warms the world, swift as the wind, with the intelligence and radiance of the angels. It illuminates twelve plains beneath the edges of the world in its shining every night. That is the circuit because of which the fiery sea and the flocks of birds cry out, the circuit because of which the hosts of angels assemble and rejoice after the brightness of night.'

The wise men of the Hebrews said: 'Tell us of the twelve plains beneath the edges of the earth, on which the sun sheds light every night; for knowledge of this matter is obscure to us.'

To that the Ever-new Tongue replied: 'It is thus that the sun goes every evening. First it shines on the stream beyond the sea, with tidings of the waters in the east. Then it shines at night upon the lofty sea of fire, and upon the seas of sulphurous flame which surround the red peoples. Then it shines upon the hosts of youths in the playing-fields, who utter a cry to heaven for fear of the beast which kills many thousands of hosts beneath the waves to the south. Then it shines upon the mountain with streams of fire, which traverse (?) the plains of clay with hosts of followers in them. Then it shines upon the enclosure of the great beast against which the twenty-four warriors arise, against which they invoke (?) the valley of torments. Then it shines upon the terrible populous enclosure which has closed around the hell-dwellers to the north. It shines in the black valleys with melancholy streams across their faces. Then it shines upon the enclosure of the beast who brings the many seas around the flanks of the earth on every side, who sucks the many seas back again so that he leaves the beaches dry on every side. Then it shines on the mountain of fire which was formed from the fire of Judgment, to triumph over every created thing. Then it shines upon the many thousands who sleep the tearful sleep since the beginning of the world in the valley of flowers. Then it shines upon the dark tearful plain, with the dragons who have been placed under the mist. Then it shines upon the flocks of birds who sing many songs together in the valleys of the flowers. Then it shines upon the bright plains with the wine-flowers which illuminate the valley. Then it shines upon Adam's Paradise until it rises from the east in the morning; it would have many tales to relate upon its journey, if it had a tongue to disclose them.'

'Tell us,' said the people of the Hebrews, 'of the many kinds of stars which you declared to us earlier. What nature is in them; and is the nature of all the stars similar?'

The Ever-new Tongue answered: 'It is not similar. First of all, [there are] the ten stars of Gabuen: trembling seizes them and manes of fire cover their faces, foretelling pestilence and mortality upon the earth. Other stars circle the world between the hours of terce and none; then they lapse into weakness until the same hour comes [again]. Other stars bring excessive heat or cold or ... upon the earth. Other stars run to incite the dragons which breathe upon the world. Other stars run until the end of fifty years, when a time of slumber comes to them. When sleep takes them, they set to the north of the sea of fire, in the valley of the tears, for seven years; they sleep until they are awakened by the shout of the blessed angels and by the voices of the dragons who call upon (?) the valley. Other stars run for six days and six nights, until Sunday comes. With the beginning of Sunday they embark upon many songs, and fall asleep until God's Sunday hastens from heaven; then they embark upon the same course.'

Alimbea fones arife aste, boia fiten salmibia libe lib ebile nablea fabe, that is, 'On the fifth day God made seventy-two kinds of flocks of birds, and seventy-two kinds of sea-beasts, each with its own form and behaviour and nature.

'First of all, the birds of the island of Naboth: there does not shine forth upon the surface of the earth any bright colour or radiance which does not shine from their wings. They shed tears at cold and snow, and rejoice at warmth and the bright colours of summer. They awaken always in the middle of the night, and sing songs together which are as sweet as the music of stringed instruments.

'The bird-flocks of Sabes: their wings shine at night like burning candles. Any pestilence touched by their wings, or by their shadow in flight, is healed. They fall into a state of dormancy in the time of winter and of cold, and awaken with the coming of May. They sing a noble gentle song in their slumbers, like the roar of the wind.

'The bird-flocks in the islands of Ebothen, between the east of Africa and heaven: there has not come upon the earth any bright colour which does not shine from their wings, nor since the beginning of the world has a feather or plume fallen from their wings; nor has their number or count increased. The fragrance and the scent of the flowers, and the taste of the seven rivers of wine which traverse (?) the bright plains, that is what sustains them since the beginning of the world. They do not rest from singing songs together, nor would they be weary, until midnight should come with the chanting of the angels from the cloud.

'Then the three bird-flocks divide themselves; there are 1572 birds in each flock. The first flock lift up their voices at midnight and sing praise to God in song, telling of the secret innumerable hidden wonders which not even the angels of heaven know. Then the middle flock arises with its threefold song, marvelling at the wonders which God has wrought from the beginning of the world until the Judgment. The last flock takes it up (?) at the end of the night: chanting a septiform song they tell of the tumults

which will come upon the world with the terror of the Judgment; and
thereafter they tell of the seventyfold division of the torments, and those who
will deserve them, and they tell of the seventy-two seats of the bright
dwellings in the heavens, and of everyone who will deserve them. *Et diresir
alba sibe alea alibme lis* – that is, if the race of Adam heard the song of
those bird-flocks, there would not be joy or pleasure after they ceased listening to them, but grief (?) and longing and sorrow until they died of
lamentation.'

Efi lia lasien ferosa filera leus dissia nimbile nue bua faune intoria tebnæ,
that is, 'Let us make man in our image and likeness, and let him be over
the fishes of the sea and the birds of the air and the beasts of the whole
earth' (Genesis 1:26). So versatile (?) is the power of the Lord that there
are twenty-four shapes upon the race of Adam after the Fall.

'The warriors of the island of Ebia first of all: we read that the body of
each of them is fifty-six feet long. They do not awaken from their sleep
unless a tempest of the sea, or the shout of battle or an army, or the noise
of music causes it. When they arise from their sleep, their eyes shine like
the radiance of stars. They grow great in the seas in which they are, so that
[the seas] cast their monsters and whales up onto the land as food for them.

'White fiery tribes in the islands of Odaib: flames of fire come from their
mouths when they grow angry. At night their eyes shine like burning
candles. Their hair and bodies gleam like snow: they are very white. Fish
from the many seas, neither boiled nor cooked, is what sustains them.

'The tribes of Ithier north of Mount Caucasus: they have their mouths
in their breasts, and four eyes in their backs. Burning and great heat are in
their bodies, such that no other race can endure it.

'There are other bright tribes in the lands of the Assyrians: gazing upon
their faces is nobler than every people (?). Such is the sweetness of their
speech that the noise of their armies is sweeter than music.

'The tribes of southern India, with the smallness of their form: the
tallest of them only reach [the height of] a cubit of five hands.

'The host of women which there is in the mountains of Armenia: their
bodies are greater than those of any men. They never bear [any children]
save daughters. Their wrath and their valour when going into battle are
fiercer than those of any men. They arise from their sleep in the middle of
the night. They release sparks of fire from their mouths. Their beards
reach as far as their navels. Gold which is finer than that of any smelting is
always found in their right hands when they are born.

'The tribes of Fones in the lands of Libya: their eyes burn like sparks of
fire when they grow angry. There is not enough room around one of them

for the number of men which it would take to overcome him. Such is the magnitude and sweetness of their voice that it is louder than voices and trumpets. When they die they pour forth a stream of wine from their mouths. They sing a haunting song in their sleep, to which no likeness has been found.

'Many shapes besides those were set upon the race of Adam after the Fall. For the first man that God made in the beginning, he made him in his own image and likeness; and the offspring begotten by him would have been the same, had he not transgressed.'

The wise men of the Hebrews said: 'Tell us in order the number of kindreds which God set upon his creatures.'

'They will be reckoned up for you,' said he: 'seventy-two kinds of creatures beneath the seas; seventy-two kinds of bird-flocks in the air; seventy-two kinds of predatory (?) beasts; seventy-two kinds of snakes which crawl upon the earth; seventy-two kinds of fruits of the trees; seventy-two kinds of appearances of stars which have been set throughout heaven; seventy-two kinds of companies of angels in heaven; seventy-two kinds of torments as punishments in the hells; seventy-two kinds of music and bright dwellings in heaven; seventy-two kinds of languages upon the tongues of men; seventy-two kinds of men of the race of Adam. If one reckons according to the number of peoples, however, this is their number: one hundred and fifty-seven peoples throughout the world; but throughout the world there are many peoples beneath the seas.'

The wise men of the Hebrews said, 'Tell us of the prison which God ordained for the punishment of sinners.'

The Ever-new Tongue answered: 'It is difficult to tell of it,' said he. 'Even if I had set about telling of it since the beginning of the world, I would not have related the nature of all the distress which you ask about before the Day of Judgment. To begin with, such is the greatness and depth of the valley that even though the bird which is swiftest and strongest in flight should set out, it would scarcely reach its bottom at the end of a thousand years.'

Elestia tibon ituria tamne ito firbia fuan. 'I do not know,' he said, 'which of the two is more numerous: all the sand beneath the seas, or all the kinds of beasts that there are to maul souls in hell.

'So great is [their] despair among the torments that they cannot speak the name of God, such is [their] grief and despair at the magnitude and number of the torments. So great is the fire and the burning and the heat, that if all the bodies of water in the world – clouds and streams and rivers and the seas encircling the earth – were to be poured into the valley of torments they would not quench it; for it is the wrath of God that seethes in the hells. So great is the intense cold there, that if a gust of cold resembling it were conveyed into this world through the hollow of a pipe, there would perish all the birds in the air, and all the beasts beneath the seas, and every living animal which it could find upon the land. Such is the brilliance of the fire that if any of it were conveyed through a pipe, all the waters in the world which it would encounter would ebb before it, and it would burn up all the animals which it encountered, splitting the earth around them. So great is the darkness that if any of it were conveyed into the world – even as much as the pupil in a man's eye – all the birds that it encountered in the air, and men and beasts upon the earth, would not see radiance or light [again] until the day they died. So great is the stench in the lakes of the torments that if a single drop of it were placed in the midst of the world, all the animals which it reached in the world, in sea and land and air, would perish.

'So great are the hunger and thirst there, that if any of it were conveyed into the world for a single hour, all the beasts and men and birds that it encountered would perish in a single hour of hunger and thirst. So great is the fear which the souls have of the torments there that if a pang (?) of such fear came into the world, whatever animals it encountered in sea and air and land would all become mad and senseless with fear, so that they died of it. So great are the melancholy and sorrow and grief there that if some of it were conveyed into the world through a pipe there would not be joy or pleasure in the world nor in the faces of friends, nor would welcome nor wine affect them, but every heart which it visited would perish of melancholy and lamentation.

'Wherever I begin the task (?), I could not relate it all even if I were not to rest before the Day of Judgment: [it is] a place in which ears heard no voice save woe and fear and melancholy; a place in which there was no pause for respite, nor look of joy upon a face; a place in which there was no honour nor dignity nor consolation of friends nor gentle voice, but abundance of lightning and foul winds and fiery black snow, together with extreme cold. Gnashing of teeth, smothering of faces, oppression of breaths, much coughing, hands beaten in grief, shedding of tears, woe with groans, hearts full of terror, horrible shapes, the infliction of merciless, savage, shameful torments. Burning everywhere. Horror everywhere. Wailing and outcry everywhere.'

The wise men of the Hebrews said: 'Tell us of the Day of Judgment, and how the world will be destroyed, and at what time it will be destroyed.'

The Ever-new Tongue answered: 'It is not pleasant,' said he, 'even to be reminded of the Judgment concerning which you ask. Trembling and fear come upon even the angels of heaven when it is remembered and brought to mind; for it is cause for much trembling and fear. The three hundred and sixty-five eruptions (?) from the mountains of fire, bursting upon the lands before the face of the great King whose power will destroy the world. The tottering and breaking of the seven heavens as they bend down upon the lands. The rising and the tumult of the four fiery winds from the four cardinal points of heaven, with roaring and the coming of thunder and lightning from every side. The thundering of the 3,375 stars as they fall from heaven. The moon turning the colour of blood. The sun quenching its light. The hosts of heaven will be so numerous on that day that no mortal will be able to see them all, or to reckon their number, but only God. The woods and mountains dissolving (?) in a fiery blast from every side. The crying out of the beasts, and of all the animals of the land. The raining down (?) of fire in every land. The flocks of birds in the air crying out because of the streams of fire. The bellowing of the whales and the fish in the seas because of the ebbing away of the salt seas before the heat of the fire. The descent of the nine orders of heaven, and the crying and singing of the souls as they come to take their bodies from the earth. The wailing and outcry of the sinners as they plead for mercy from the Lord whom they have afflicted; and it will be a 'cry into the void' for them, and 'repentance too late'. The outcry of those in hell, as the souls are vomited up to the assembly, so that judgment may be passed upon each one according to its deserts. The smiting together of the seven heavens as they dissolve in the winds of fire. The shaking of the earth as it is knocked backwards and upside down. The wailing and outcry of the demons and the souls of the sinners, as hell closes over them forever.'

The wise men of the Hebrews said: 'At what time of the day or night was the world made, and [at what time] will it be destroyed, and [at what time] did the Lord arise from the dead?'

The Ever-new Tongue answered: 'At midnight,' said he, 'the Lord arose and the world was made; and at midnight the circuit was made which was the material of the world; and at midnight the Adversary (that is, the Devil) was exiled from heaven; and at midnight the body of man was made in Paradise. At midnight Cain performed the first kin-slaying that was perpetrated in the world. At midnight sulphurous fire was poured down upon the five cities, upon which the sea of fire is inflicted until the Judgment. At midnight the Flood began to pour over the world. At midnight the Passover of the lamb was celebrated at Rameses in Egypt. At midnight the People of God crossed the Red Sea, and Pharaoh was drowned with his army. At midnight Babylon was conquered. At midnight the Saviour of the world was born in Bethlehem in Judaea; and he was crucified at midnight, for the sake of the sins of Adam and his descendants; for the thick darkness of night covered the world from terce to none. At midnight a company of angels came across the islands of Sab, so that they scattered pestilence across the world. At midnight the Lord came to harrow hell, and he freed the souls from the imprisonment and misery in which they were, and he bound the enemy and the destroyer of creation, the thief and robber and ancient traitor – that is, the Devil – in the lowest depths of the hells. At midnight the material of the world was formed. At midnight it will be destroyed.

'As for the Lord who arose from the dead on this eve of Easter, his power and his might and his dignity and his deeds and his workings in his creation, from the beginning of the world until the end of the Judgment, cannot be told. For even if all the monsters beneath the seas and all the birds in the air and all the cattle and beasts and people upon the earth and all the angels in the heavens and all the demons in hell had begun at the beginning of the world, they would not before the Judgment have related even a seventh part of the deeds of God.

'So terrible is his wrath, first of all, that if his mind were to be vexed to the point of bestirring itself against the household which he has created, earthly things could not endure that anger. For if he were to show his face in anger, the heavens would cast themselves down upon the earth and the seas would ebb away around the world. The earth would wither, so that nothing would remain therein. The kingdom of heaven and the angels would fall into a stupor, and would appear nowhere. Hell would increase exceedingly, so that its torments would be seven times worse than they are; for it is the wrath of God that seethes in the hells.

'What thing could be more wondrous than the Child to be asleep in the arms of the Virgin, and yet a trembling upon creation and the angels? He has closed his fist around the seven heavens and the earth and hell and the many surrounding seas. The Child asleep in the arms of the Virgin, and yet a trembling upon the angels, and the heavens, and the lands with their inhabitants, and the whales in the seas, and upon the dwellers in hell – for fear of his power, and in hopes of deliverance from vexing [him] (?).

'Such is the beauty and radiance of his face that if all the souls in hell were to gaze upon the radiance of his face, they would not notice the suffering and punishment and torture of hell.

'Such is the sanctity of his form, that whoever gazed upon his face would be unable to commit a sin thereafter.

'Such is the radiance and splendour and brilliance of his face that when the nine heavenly orders shine forth, and every angel in them is seven times brighter than the sun; and when the souls of the saints shine forth with the same semblance; and when the sun is seven times brighter than it is now – the radiance of the face of the great King who made every created thing will [still] outshine them all, so that the brightness of the Lord will surpass the angels and the stars of heaven and the souls of the saints just as the sun's brightness and radiance surpass the other stars.

'Such is the versatility of his power that even if all the angels in heaven and devils in hell and humans upon the earth and beasts beneath the seas were to address God, each one of them speaking in a separate language, it would be easy for God to answer every creature among them simultaneously, [each] in its individual language and in accordance with its own nature.

'Such is the beauty of the Lord's appearance that if it were revealed and uncovered (?) in the hells, the hells would turn into radiant dwellings and into the radiance of the *ríched*, like the heavenly Kingdom.

'Such is the brilliance and brightness of his face, that were it told to every impure soul to whom God has given destruction – [that is,] going into the infernal habitation – in payment for its lust, that would be harder for the souls to bear than any torment: departure from God's presence and perpetual banishment from beholding his face [would be harder to bear] than all the crosses and many torments of hell.

'As the Lord is ineffable, so his kingdom and its blessedness are as ineffable as he is: the sweetness of the songs, the joy of the faces, the beauty of the forms, the brightness and fieriness of the host, the purity of the innocent thoughts of the souls. A place in which no voice of anger or jealousy is heard, nor sorrow nor hardship.

'Happy, then, is the one who will be summoned to that kingdom when the Lord says to them: "Come, blessed ones of my Father, possess the kingdom which has been prepared for you since the beginning of the world" (Matthew 25:34). Where there is no need for the light of the sun, or of the moon or stars, but the Lord will be [its] light since he is the source of light. Where there will be health. Where there is tranquillity of the seas. Where there is a great peace. Where there is unconquerable love. Where there is eternal life. Where old age will not appear. Where gladness is found. Where meanings will be declared. Where there is Paradise, plentiful and sweet. Where there is the splendour of the angels. Where there is the radiance of justice. Where there is the royal palm. Where there are golden streams. Where there is the melodious praise of the angels, and the assembly of all the saints. Where the heavenly Jerusalem is. Where there is no grief or sadness after rejoicing, but perpetual happiness. Where the good has not been lacking, and is not lacking, and will never be lacking.

'What could be more wondrous to someone than that kingdom? A place where poverty and nakedness and hunger and thirst will not be seen. A place where no desire nor need for clothing or food will arise (?), but rather being at the great exalted feast forever in the presence of the Father and the Son and the Holy Spirit. A place where there are the three best lights of which one reads: the light of the King who bestows the kingdom, the light of the saints on whom it is bestowed, the light of the kingdom which is bestowed there.

'May we all reach that kingdom, may we deserve it, may we dwell in it! World without end, Amen.'

Saltair na Rann, Cantos I–III

Saltair na Rann ('The Psalter of the Quatrains') is the title of a series of poems covering the full sweep of Christian sacred history, from the world's creation down to the calamities which will overtake it in the last days. The main body of the work consists of one hundred and fifty cantos – hence the title, which alludes to the hundred and fifty psalms of the Bible. These are followed by two devotional poems, and the 'ten songs of the Resurrection', which last deal with the end of the world. Most of the *Saltair* follows the Bible's testimony fairly closely, but in some of its sections the poet has drawn freely on a wider repertoire of sources – classical, patristic, and apocryphal.

In style the *Saltair* is formulaic and often repetitive, relying heavily on stock phrases (often quite difficult to translate) to supply rhymes and to fill out the metre. Often, however, the author manages to turn this standardised diction into a vehicle for truly moving passages of poetry: an example is the final part of Canto I below. Probably the most interesting aspect of the *Saltair* as a whole is the way in which, in the process of putting the Bible story into medieval Irish verse, it transforms it and imbues it with an Irish flavour. The *Saltair* gives us an unparalleled opportunity to look at the panorama of the Scriptures through the eyes of the tradition to which this book is devoted; and to experience some of the vivid, colourful, imaginative sensibility which that tradition brought to the church's teachings.[1]

I here translate the first three cantos, which deal with the physical universe, the divine realm or *ríched*, and the angelic hierarchies. Although the outlines of the creation account in Genesis can be recognised at various points in Canto I, they have been overshadowed by a wealth of cosmological detail which bears eloquent witness to the avid interest in the natural world which so often went hand in hand with early Irish piety. With Cantos II and III the Bible is left almost entirely behind as the author's imagination takes flight toward the splendours of heaven; some imagery from the Book of Revelation, however, appears toward the end of II. The poet drew on many and very varied sources in piecing together his picture of the cosmos: among them are Pliny the Elder, Augustine, Gregory the Great, *1 Enoch*, Ezekiel, and a treatise on the Holy Land by Adomnán of Iona.[2]

[1] For another, earlier collection of poems which are also very illuminating in this respect see Carney 1964. [2] For detailed discussion of the background of these cantos, see Carey 1985, 1986, 1987a.

I

Mo Rí-se, Rí nime náir,
cen uabur, cen immarbáig,
dorósat domun dualach,
mo Rí bithbeó bithbuadach.

My King, the King of noble heaven,
without pride, without boasting,
made the world with its true nature –
my King ever living, ever triumphant;

King over the creation, on which the sun looks down,
King over the depths of the ocean,
King south, north, west, and east,
against whom no struggle can be maintained;

King of mysteries, who has been, who is,
before the creation, before the ages,
King living forever still, fair his semblance,
King without beginning, without end.

The King made glorious heaven –
he is not proud, he is not changeful –
and the earth, with its abundant beauties,
equally strong, equally firm, equally mighty.

The King made the noble light
and the grim darkness:
the one is full day,
the other complete night.

The King shaped the firm dwelling of God
from the first substance of the elements;
... [3] to a fecund appearance,
the wondrous formless mass.

3 Manuscripts illegible at this point.

From it the King shaped every creature;
he established them, without the fair mystery of enchantment:
both smooth and rough, with beauty,
both dead and living.

The illustrious mighty King carved
from the noble first substance
the heavy fertile earth – the tale is certain –
established upon its foundation in length and breadth.

The King, unstinting in his designs, created
in the hollow of the firmament
the beautiful world, which multitudes affirm,
like a fine round apple.

Thereafter the King skilfully shaped
further masses around the earth:
a subtle circling above the world, a radiant achievement,
the cold watery air.

The King sprinkles bright cold water
upon the mass of the land, with its mighty kindreds,
in torrents, with quantities of streams,
according to measure and proportion.

The King arranged the eight winds,
raising them up without blemish to their beauty:
there are four chief winds
and four fierce secondary winds.

Learned authors speak
of four more secondary winds:
the exact number
of the winds is twelve.

The King formed the colours of the winds,
arranging them in their beauty side by side (?),
they were skilfully arranged in a circuit (?)
with the mingling of every colour.

White, pure purple,
blue, mighty green,
yellow, red, precise in skill –
no discord comes between them in their fair assemblies.

Black, grey, piebald,
dark, hard jet,
dun: the dark colours
are not bright or easy to embrace.

Above every plain the King arranged
the eight fierce secondary winds;
he formed without defect, a refuge from hardships,
the boundaries of the four chief winds.

The bright pure purple from the east,
the bright wonderful white from the south,
the stormy harsh (?) black from the north,
the noisy dun from the west.

The red and yellow together
between white and purple;
the green, and the sea's valiant blue,
between dun and shining white.

The grey and jet, terrible their ardour (?),
between dun and jet-black;
the dark and the piebald, in the east,
between black and purple.

Their form was fitly arranged,
their ordering was accomplished
according to wisdom, according to *glésa*[4] without concealment,
in divisions and stations.

The twelve winds, with their several forces,
east and west, north and south:
the King harmonised them,
binding them under seven *glésa*.

---

4 *Glés* (plural *glésa*) usually means 'arrangement, contrivance, device', but its sense here is obscure. Cf. p. 161 below, where the word is again used of a mysterious aerial phenomenon.

The King harnessed them according to divisions
around the earth, with many *glésa*:
a bright *glés* between every pair of winds,
and one *glés* over them all.

The King assigned them their conduct, according to *glésa*,
according to custom, without transgression:
at one time gentle, so it is said,
at another time stormy.

The King revealed the measurement of the height
from the earth to the firmament:
by it they measure, a pure quantity,
the thickness of the earth.

He established the course of seven stars
from the firmament to the earth:
Saturn, Jupiter, Mercury, Mars,
Sol, Venus, stately Luna.

The King reckoned – noble the tale –
from the earth to the moon:
the pure quantity which they measure
is one hundred and twenty-six miles.

That is the cold air,
with many wandering breezes.
Its swift name, certainly,
is 'the bright airy[5] heaven'.

The King reckoned, with pure clear splendour,
the space from moon to sun:
two hundred and fifty-two miles –
his power is great.

That is the lofty ether,
without wind, without moving air,
whose name – a tale without stammering –
is 'the wondrous ethereal heaven'.

---

5 Reading *aierda* with 24.P.27; Rawlinson B 502 has *airerda* 'delightful'.

Thrice the same amount, clearly,
is between the firmament and the sun:[6]
truly, my mighty King of the stars
granted it to the reckoners.

That is virginal Olympus
without movement or stir,
according to the noble account of the ancient sages;
its name is 'the third holy heaven'.

One thousand, five hundred, and twelve miles,
a bright measurement:
the fair course of the stars which they traverse
from the firmament to the earth.

The measure of the space, a fixed path,
from the earth to the firmament –
that is the measure, in layered strata (?),
from the firmament to the *ríched*.[7]

It is three thousand
and twenty-four miles
from here to the *ríched*, a great distance,
without counting the firmament.

The measure of that whole distance,
from the earth to the seat of the King,
is the same as that from the firm earth
down to the depths of hell.

The King of every populous swift ruddy company,
it is he who stitched the firmament;
as he deemed right, above every plain,
he shaped it from the formless mass.

The King of every splendid substance,
our mighty tree (?), illustrious and great forever:
the glorious one, with fair ... (?)
divided it into five zones.

---

6 That is, three times the sun's height from the earth.   7 For this word's sense see p. 79, note 3 above.

My King traced the fifth zone,
which burns the skin, in the far south;
to satisfy the needs of multitudes (?)
there are two frigid zones surrounding two which are temperate.

Frigid in the south and frigid in the north;
then the two which are temperate, a great triumph;
the torrid zone, it is certain,
between the two which are temperate.

The King who surpasses every splendid over-king
established dominions wholly subject to his will:
he made them, without bright wantonness,
as the first shape of the firmament.

As its shell is around an egg,
save that it moves with many turnings,
is the veil of the firmament around the world
revolving perpetually and forever.

He measured it all around,
following a bright band of eternal light (?).
It is harder to estimate the distance around it:
it is not measured through it or across.

A circuit was divided, according to plan,
as authors have described:
twelve intervals subject to seemly law,
twelve 'parts' corresponding to them.

The space of a solar month to each 'part',
according to those noble gentle authors;
running in its journey, a splendid tale,
it goes around every year.

In the firmament, with splendour,
are seventy-two windows;
by day there shine together
six windows for each 'part'.

There is, through the mysteries of the bright King
who created man wholly subject to his will,
a covering upon each window,
fastened without haste or delay.

A firm strong mantle, a splendid feat,
like a fair capacious hide,
a rounded garment – he stretched it
around the earth and the three heavens (?).

Surrounding the three heavens on this side of it,
with three perfect heavens surrounding it,
it was itself the seventh heaven
established between the heavens.

It is not the fair abode of the angelic host
but a perfect, enduring sphere
which moves like a mill wheel
perpetually turning forever.

The firmament, with abundant fame,
and the seven noble stars,
have a single motion – a splendid tale –
since the hour when they were created.

The King divided the red colour above the surface
of the firmament, it is not. ... (?):
a carving in equal (?) smooth sections
into twelve correct divisions.

The King over every place, over every height,
named each single constellation:
without doubt, according to due rights,
he named the twelve constellations.

The shape of each constellation, a bright course,
encircling the firmament:
as famous elders affirm[8]
they are named from their shapes.

8 'Elders' (*sin*) preserved only in 24.P.27.

Aquarius, Pisces, Aries, Taurus of the herds,
noble Gemini and Cancer,
Leo, Virgo, Libra, Scorpio ... (?),
Sagittarius, Capricorn.

The King of mysteries disposed them
in their vast clusters:
the row of heights, above every plain,
which the sun and moon traverse.

It is thirty days, an ample movement,
together with ten and a half hours
which are in the ... (?) journey above every height
which the sun traverses in each constellation.

The noble sun, according to rule,
in the circuit of each year,
enters each constellation
on the fifteenth before the calends, a fair place.

The sun's time in Aquarius, an interval without disgrace,
was situated in January;
and in Pisces ... (?), brightly,
it is reckoned in February.

The sun appears, gaining dignity thereby,
in Aries in March;
and shines, as it wishes,
in Taurus in April.

The sun is in Gemini in May:
it is certain, it has not changed.
It is not gently that the sun in Cancer
heats every household in June.

In July the sun is in Leo;
it is then that it pours down its full radiance.
The sun goes for a while on its journey
into Virgo in August.

The sun shines for every company
in Libra in September;
the sun bathes itself, it does not conceal itself,
in Scorpio in October.

The sun takes shelter in Sagittarius
in November, above every sea;
in December, enduring the tale,
the sun is in Capricorn.

These are the twelve constellations
which the bright white Lord created.
They revolve across the world above every sea;
the sun makes its full circuit through them.

Five things each day, without deception,
should be known by each intellectual:
by everyone, without the appearance of reproach,
who is in holy orders.

The day of the solar month, the phase of the moon,
the tide, without folly,
the day of the week, the feasts of the pure saints,
related with exact clarity.

The King who arranged the fleeting multitude
of circuits and movements of the stars:
even as he assembled them in divisions
he named them with their names.

Although the side of the many-starred firmament
which faces us is dear to us,
the other side, delight without prohibition,
would be no uglier if we could see it.

The King accomplished a feat (?) which does not fade
in the circling of the firmament:
its face appears equally close
to the earth on every side.

The King formed the true firmament
with its stars, without weakness;
from one hour to the next it turns
around the earth, without bright falsehood.

The King made a great expanse of waters
above the perfect firmament;
the other expanse of waters is the sea
which encloses the earth.

The bright King whom every prophet has foretold,
the Lord who established every fair dignity,
created the sun with its pure form
which sheds light upon heaven and earth.

The King made the glorious moon
and the wide sea:
the King made them according to rule
so that they act rightly and in harmony.

A sixth part of the whole earth
is the amount which is in the moon;
and the sun, with purity,
is sixteen times the earth's size.

The King made many beasts
beneath the vast unreckonable sea:
none save my King can reveal
their names or their numbers.

The King made multitudes of hosts
of birds in flight,
of wild beasts in the mountains,
of herds on the smooth plains.

The number of their splendid names
and of their great various forms:
none in the flesh can reckon that,
but only the King from holy heaven.

The King made cold air,
and bright red fire,
and the illustrious mighty earth,
and pure flowing water.

Thereafter the King sowed the earth
with herbs, with forests:
the world is full of their fragrance
and the abundance of their many fruits.

The King who rules over cold and heat,
my true King who watches over me:
it is he who has established every division,
the King beyond reckoning, beyond telling.

With grace the bright King of mysteries
has revealed to us every wonder,
that through them we may understand him – a bright protection –
and through the multitude of his miracles.

The King who has made each creature in turn,
visible and invisible:
save for the King who made those things
there is no king upon the earth.

There is not, among strong men,
among angels or archangels,
anyone who could bring forward ... (?)
anything which is marvellous set beside my King.

II

Rí *dorigne ríched réil*
cona chríchaib dia choimréir:
treb thogach duanach daingen,
do shluag amra árchaingel.

Through his will, the King made
the bright *ríched* with its boundaries:
a peerless mighty dwelling, filled with songs,
for the wondrous host of the archangels.

The *ríched* with its companies,
noble, peaceful, not narrow,
a sturdy stronghold with a hundred graces:
a tenth part of it is the size of the world.

There are three walls there, without decay,
which encircle the *ríched*:
a wall of green glass – a fair deed –
a wall of gold, a wall of purple.

The green wall is outermost, without distress;
the wall of gold is next to the stronghold;
in the middle, with fair bright fame,
is the vast wall of purple glass.

There is there, with the surging of tumults (?),
a perfect symmetrical stronghold.
Within it, in bright peace,
is a long path of four chief doorways.

The size of each single one
of the four chief doorways,
side by side, a number according to reckoning,
is a mile for each doorway.

There is a cross of gold in each doorway
upon which a bright eternal company gazes.
The King made them, without effort (?):
they are broad and very high.

A bird of red gold upon each cross,
a great voice overhead which does not falter;
in each cross, as a part of the arrangement (?),
is a huge precious jewel.

Each day an archangel – a fair journey –
[comes] with his troop from the *ríched*'s King:
with choral singing, with splendid music,
he goes around each cross.

For each doorway there is a courtyard,
whose dimensions it is pleasant to record:
I compare each of them
to the earth with its seas.

The circuit of each courtyard,
with its silver sands,
with its territories in lovely bloom,
with its radiant plants:

Though the size of the vast courtyard
seem great to you – a brilliant array –
a wall of silver, without slackening in the work,
was made around each courtyard.

Porches are set outside the walls,
around the fortress on every side,
with wholesome, peaceful, innumerable
dwellings for the many thousands.

There are eight porches set side by side,
until they meet going around the stronghold.
I have no comparison or venerable likeness
for the size of each porch.

Each porch is full of herbs,
with sands of bronze;
a wall of fair bronze was established
solidly around each porch.

The twelve walls – a bright division –
of the porches and courtyards,
together with the three outer walls,
are around the chief stronghold.

There are forty doorways into the abode
of the *ríched*, with its royal thrones:
three for each smooth courtyard,
and three for each porch;

In addition there are four doorways outside
the outer porches,
set against the firm enclosure, with many strengths,
against the first watchtower.[9]

A door of silver, fair to see,
is in each doorway of that courtyard;
bronze doors, with grace,
are in the doorways of the porches.

The ramparts of all the porches
outward from the fortress
are likened to the illustrious distance
from the earth to the moon.

The walls of the courtyards, as is fitting,
were made of *findruine*:[10]
their vast height, in splendour,
is that from the earth to the pure sun.

The three walls which go around the chief stronghold,
[this is] the size of their shaping (?):
their height is revealed, without decay,
as that from the earth to the firmament.

In the placement of the outer walls
around the fortress, around the stronghold,
each wall clearly surpasses the next
by a third – a brilliant feat.

The King established
the abodes around the chief stronghold:
certain is the testimony concerning
the courtyards and porches [extending] outward from the fortress.

---

9 The word in the text is *athchomarc*, which otherwise means 'enquiry, request, question'; for the considerations on which the present translation is based see Carey 1986, 97–100; 1988, 128–9.
10 The composition of the precious alloy *findruine* is not clear from the sources; that it consisted largely of silver seems indicated by the first element *find* 'white'.

The hosts of the race of Adam, with mighty deeds,
rightly divided into companies:
glory comes to them according to their deserts
in each separate abode.

Each host of them dwells
in its own porch, its own courtyard,
with fair abundance of radiance,
of peace, of prosperity.

Saints and holy virgins, with grace,
showered with bliss after the grievous struggle:[11]
they will be parted from the host outside
and borne into the great stronghold.

The shining stronghold of God:
though its chief doorways are great,
none enters in from the habitations of the earth
save three persons.

The person who keeps God's law;
the person who is truly a virgin;
the noble penitent
who admits and does not conceal his deeds.

Lovingly they will be summoned
into the plain of the saints in the chief stronghold,
glorious in light – glad the tidings –
each through his chief doorway:

The beautiful pure doorways
shining with precious stones,
with great fame which multitudes relate,
with their doors of red gold.

11 A conjectural translation, emending *braenchath* 'dew-battle' (?) to *brónchath* 'battle of sorrow'. Alternatively, *braen* 'dew' may here (as elsewhere) refer to blood, in this case the blood of martyrdom.

Three watchtowers for each doorway,
measuring a fair pure *togairt*[12] in breadth;
for every illustrious corner (?), an exact reckoning,
a watchtower upon each wall.

The stairs up to the pure doorways,
a fair bright path of red gold:
they are radiant, a bright assembly,
with each step higher than the last.

From step to step, an exact reckoning,
there is an easy ascent into the chief fortress.
The fair host of peace which has attained the path
numbers many thousands, a hundred hundreds.

Around the walls in a great swath,
in the midst of the chief stronghold,
are splendid glass platforms,
sturdy bridges of red gold.

There are delightful regions there,
perpetually fresh in every eternal season,
bearing every kind of delicious fruit,
with honeyed fragrances.

There is sanctuary there without sorrow,
there is light which never fades;
songs which are pure, fair, skilful,
enduring, tender, delightfully sweet.

There is there that which satisfies every company
in the vast royal *ríched*:
the sound of the [angelic] orders, of the bright songs,
the scent of the fragrant flowers.

There are many noble wholesome abodes there,
many firm dignified choirs,
many companies – a skilful tune –
many songs to each choir.

12 Perhaps for *togairm* 'summons, invocation'; but this too gives no clear sense in this context. For discussion see the references in note 9 above.

There are broad lakes there –
delightful are their waves, their holy expanses –
around which sing bright choirs,
glad, noble, delectable.

There are narrow streams there
of every kind of delightful liquour;
to content the eternal multitude with honours (?)
there are there many bright fountains.

There are abundant jewels there;
there are golden platforms
which he has erected for the sake of the hosts;
there are there many royal streams.

There are there many mighty trees,
many choice lands,
many precious, perfect, incomparable treasures,
many hundred abundant plains.

There are many delightful songs, without flaw,
in the great plain of starry heaven,
many pleasant tunes, many strains of music,
which no reckoning or description can convey.

There are there, in order (?), in mighty ranks,
a hundred and forty-four rewards
in the presence of the King,
according to reckoning.

From the beginning of the world until Judgment
the race of Adam, though they were speaking of it, would not be able
to describe – a splendid account –
even one of those rewards.

Besides those, there are
as many rewards in heaven
as there are drops of rain – a swift sound –
or flakes of snow that fall.

The splendid marvellous dwelling of my King
is in the midst of the chief stronghold:
many hundreds of thousands
are around his footstool.

The throne of the King of the *ríched*
was made all of red gold:
the King of mysteries raised it
above the golden ramparts.

The abode of the radiant Angels[13]
is nearest to the chief doorways;
the Archangels, with their companies,
are next to the holy Angels.

The Virtues, a power above every plain,
are next to the Archangels;
the Powers, with divine compassion (?),
are nearest to the Virtues.

The Principalities, whose music is sweet,
are next to the Powers;
the Dominations, a fierce company,
are beneath the shelter of the footstool.

Marvellous is the company which surpasses them all
upon the footstool of the royal seat:
holy the King who has established
the Thrones with their great throngs.

He has placed the hosts of the Cherubim
around the royal abode;
above everyone save the bright King
stands the noble host of the Seraphim.

Holy is the state of the nine heavenly orders,
surrounding the King of all substances:
without failure of their mighty virtue,
without mutual pride or jealousy.

13 Here and below I capitalise the names 'Angel', 'Archangel', etc., when the celestial orders are
being enumerated; elsewhere I have left the terms in lower case.

In numerous companies subject to the King of laws,
this is their exact number:
seventy-two hosts, with excellence,
are in each of the orders.

The number in each host, a glad tale without decay,
cannot be known to any
unless the King knows it
who made them from nothing –

The King exalted above them all,
King of the firm-established *ríched*,
excellent, truthful, steadfast King,
King royally noble in his royal abode;

King of great youth, King of remote age,
King who formed heaven around the pure sun,
King of all the saints, with grace,
dear King, fair King, beautiful King.

The King made the pure house of heaven
for the angels who did not transgress;
the land of the saints, of the sons of life,[14]
a bright plain both long and broad.

He established a peaceful noble abode,
a halting-place from journeys on royal roads (?),
a fair, pure, perfect, bright region
for the noble penitents.

It is my King, like the chief above the host,
sanctus Dominus Sabaoth,
for whom there resounds above the height, lovingly chanted,
the song of the twenty-four white saints.

The King established the skilful choir
of the twenty-four white saints:
beautifully they sing a chant to the host:
'*Sanctus Deus Sabaoth.*'

14 This phrase is common throughout the period covered by this book, in both Irish (*maic bethad*) and Latin (*filii uitae*): it designates the virtuous, the blessed, those who lead godly lives. Its opposite, equally widespread, is 'sons of death' (*maic báis, filii mortis*).

King of noble, excellent, radiant dwellings,
of peaceful settled abodes, of rare diadems,
whose is the flock of lambs – a radiant tale –
which surround the pure unblemished Lamb.

The bright King set that Lamb
to wander upon the mountain;
a pure multitude of one hundred and forty-four thousand
youths follows after it.

A perfect choir
of unstained virgins, with lovely voices,
sings a bright song together
following the shining Lamb.

Equally dear, equally swift, radiant,
following the Lamb across the mountain:
on their faces were written, with grace,
their own name and the Father's.

The King made the voice
to sound from the heavens:
great and terrible, a radiant feat,
like the roar of many waters;

Or like the voice of a harp, whose sound they love –
they sing nobly, without flaw,
like a flood-tide in their multitudes, above every division –
or like the mighty sound of thunder.

The King of the flowering tree of life,
a path for the ranks of the noble orders:
its canopy, and its dropping dew,
extended on all sides across the plain of the *ríched*.

Upon it perches the splendid bird-flock,
a radiant gift of abundant songs;
no decay comes, with spreading grace,
to its fruit or foliage.

Fair is the bird-flock:
every beautiful bird has a hundred wings.
They sing without fault, with radiant glory,
a hundred songs for every wing.

The King made many glorious habitations,
and accomplished many beautiful, fitting, ample deeds.
With my cherished King, above every plain,
there is every great dignity, without lack.

His are the seven heavens in unblemished power –
a bright tale without prohibition, without fault –
surrounding the earth, with floods of fire,
each heaven with its name:

Air, ether above every host,
Olympus, the firmament,
the heaven of water, the heaven of the pure angels,
the heaven in which is the bright noble Lord.

Many wondrous companies are his,
and many dwellings without error:
his are the nine orders [of angels], a noble multitude,
and the abode of each order.

The tenth order is his, without any evasion:
the race of Adam.
The shining white Lord protects
those who endure (?) a time of sadness.

There is peace there, and great joy,
without lament or reproach;
for the ranks of the host, noble companies,
there is enduring, perpetual life.

The good which our dear God has in store
for his saints in his holy dwelling –
there is not, after tracing its secrets (?),
anyone who can relate a hundredth part of it.

Lord, chief of every brilliant rank,
who gazes down upon the multitude of the eternal world –
may the King who made the *ríched*
save me after I depart from the embattled flesh.

III

Rí *dorósat na noí ngrád*
nime fri cumtach coemnár,
fo glanblad a chrotha glain,
fria adrad, fria airmitin.

The King created the nine orders
of heaven, as a noble shrine (?),
according to the pure glory of his own pure form,
to worship and honour him.

The three orders – a pure division –
which are nearest to the earth
are the Angels, drawn up in ranks,
the Archangels, the Virtues.

The three middle orders
are the Powers of radiant fame,
the Principalities – a boast which is not contested –
and the Dominations.

The three highest orders,
in the presence of the High King,
are the Thrones next to the royal seat,
the Cherubim and Seraphim.

The tenth order, as it is related to you,
is the race of Adam, without any evasion.
Above the world, without the troubles of the flesh,
my holy King created them.

The King established the orders,
apportioning to each its own fair gift,
with the many bright plains of their fair deeds
to seek them out, to honour them.

There are seven orders, a noble achievement,
particularly [devoted] to the High King:
perpetually, without any appearance of distress,
they sing to him without ceasing.

There are two orders, established in companies,
to minister to the race of Adam,
[attending] to every clear customary hardship –
the Angels and Archangels.

The bright pure Angels, the deed is certain,
bear messages at God's behest;
the Archangels, without fault,
are the chief messengers.

The Virtues are powers ever ready
to perform bright pure miracles;
the Powers, with shapely beauty,
are skilled in governing.

The Principalities, with pleasant semblance,
[attend] to the swift accomplishment of commands;
the Dominations, whose forms are holy,
are a noble host of rulers.

The Thrones, more fiercely vehement,
are before the royal seat of the High King;
the Cherubim and Seraphim
perpetually sing innumerable bright songs.

Perfect and unfading is the choir
which sings in the noble starry *ríched*.
A bright chorus which was nurtured upon the plain of stars:
the twenty-four white elders.

The perfect hosts answer them
when the many orders bear witness (?);
this is the chant of the multitude:
'*Sanctus Deus Sabaoth.*'

The King has revealed to me, a splendid tale,
something of the magnitude of the many orders,
of their rich populous abodes,
of their companies, of their many virtues;

Of the arrangement (?), above the turmoil of the world,
of the many serried courses of the stars,
beautiful like beams of the sun,
holy and radiant;

Of their ... (?) excellence in humility,
of their kindness and perpetual harmony,
of their fair yearning without sin,
of their charity and compassion;

Of their wholesomeness, no small thing to tell,
of their glory, of their brilliance,
of their bright, charming, pure appearance,
of their holy wondrous semblance;

Of their peace, in ranks, in courses,
of their deeds, of their pure songs,
of their fair wondrous works,
of their habitations and many dwellings.

[This is] the number of the Angels in heaven
according to our bright white Lord,
made manifest, and confirmed through grace (?),
according to the Spirit's revelation.

The number is not, my King,
that of the whole of their radiant host,
but only that of the troop which arises
·to accompany each Archangel.

One, two, three by turn:
two added to them makes five.
Two fives – it is clear when it is proclaimed –
make up the number ten.

Exactly two tens, a swift measurement,
go into an exact twenty;
and three tens, progressing firmly,
go into thirty.

After thirty, the living ones
disclose and reveal around you, my King,
four tens, in proper strength:
that is the number forty.

Five tens, related in sequence,
go into fifty;
six tens, without doubt or miscounting,
are the number sixty.

Seven tens go fitly into seventy,
eight tens are mighty eighty,
nine tens go into ninety after that,
and ten tens into a pure hundred.

There are ten hundreds in a thousand, a great feat,
and ten thousands in a legion;[15]
ten legions always, every day,
go into a *cunea*.

Ten *cuneae* clearly, whatever their arrangement (?),
go into a myriad;
ten myriads, a dignity which grants fame to thousands,
belong properly to a *caterva*.

Ten *catervae*, it has been heard,
go into an *exercitus*;
ten *exercitus*, firmly,[16]
go properly into a *turba*.

Ten *turbae*, the certain [measure] of the pure multitudes,
go into an *agmen*;
ten *agmina* of Angels, bright ranks,
accompany each Archangel.

---

15 Medieval Irish had no words for numbers higher than a thousand; the poet accordingly adopts an idiosyncratic reckoning based on Latin military terminology. **16** Reading *tenn* 'firm' with 24.P. 27.

There are seven Archangels in heaven
with the Over-King of the star-bright *riched*:
with each Archangel, individually,
are seventy *agmina* of Angels.

That is the ninth order
which was made in noble holy heaven:
that of the bright pure Angels, without blemish,
who accompany the Archangels.

The other eight orders
which God created with clear precision –
save for my shining glorious King in heaven
none can reckon their number.

Let us count, calling them out before the King of laws,
the names of the twenty-four white men,
the generous throng of the troops of angels,
of the lofty ones, of the archangels.

Gabriel, Michael, good their authority,
Raphael, fair Panachel,
Babichel, Raguel, it has been heard,
Mirachel, Rumiel the royal champion.

Fafigial, perfect Sumsagial,
Sarmichiel, Sarachel of noble rank,
Uriel, good and noble Hermichel,
Sarachel, Barachel of mighty fame.

Lihigiel, Darachel without sin,
Segiel and noble sturdy Sariel,
Lonachel and Arachel,
Stichiel, bright pure Gallichiel.

Let us pray to them, a sure unfading protection,
for the sake of the King who formed the *riched*:
that I may live without sorrows, a fair semblance,
forever in their company.

Whoever takes part with the nine orders
between nocturns and matins
will possess heaven, a secure sanctuary,
in perpetual unity with the archangels.

They are two thirds of the host, it has been heard,
which was in heaven before the transgression:
an entire third, under grievous blight,
went to hell.

Fair Lord, I pray to you
concerning my excesses and deficiencies:
grant me forgiveness here
for my misdeeds, my ignorance.

Though it was a sin to relate
the vast number of the many ranks,
what I have said, a lengthy recitation,
has been in praise of my great King.

Even if I had a hundred strong tongues
with which to speak faultlessly,
I could never relate
one hundredth of the wonders of my High King –

The eternal Over-King of the varied world,
who has numbered every skilful multitude,
our Pillar, our Patron, our Abbot,
the lofty King who has created.

II THE COMING OF THE FAITH

Two *Loricae*

The two prayers translated below are specimens of the so-called *lorica* or 'breast-plate' (Irish *lúirech*): the term, and the underlying inspiration, evidently derive from the references to spiritual armour in the writings of Saint Paul (Ephesians 6:11–17, 1 Thessalonians 5:8). *Loricae* are protective prayers whose efficacy, like that of many incantations, depends on exhaustive enumeration: God and all the powers of heaven are invoked to protect every part of the suppliant against a multitude of spiritual and physical dangers.[1] The *Faeth Fiada* and *Nuall Fir Fhio* are not the earliest of the *loricae*, nor are they very typical examples of the form: on the contrary, they develop its conventions in fresh and sometimes surprising ways, revealing imaginative and spiritual possibilities for the genre which rise well above the semi-magical pragmatism of many of its other surviving representatives.

Besides the power of God, and the merits of angels and the righteous, the author of the *Faeth Fiada* girds himself with the virtues of a series of natural phenomena, arranged in a sequence heaven-fire-air-water-earth that reflects the classical cosmology which the Irish had enthusiastically adopted as a part of Christian culture.[2] In seeking to absorb these into his own person, he goes considerably beyond such possible Biblical models as Psalm 148 and Daniel 3:52–80, where all of creation is exhorted to unite in praising the Creator, and approaches the actual identification of the self with various aspects of the outer world found in compositions attributed to legendary poets of Ireland and Wales.[3]

In subsequent sections of the prayer the suppliant appeals in analogous ways to God and to Christ: God's mind, eye, ear, and hand are to minister to him; Christ is to be present on all sides of him, and also with him and within him. Although he never goes so far as to speak of a radical fusion with the Godhead, he stops only just short of doing so: all of his faculties are suspended in prayerful submission to an ubiquitous Deity.

---

1 The best survey of the subject is probably still Gougaud 1911–12 (in French); for a recent discussion in English see Herren 1987, 23–31. 2 Compare the sequence of chapters in the early Irish cosmological treatise *Liber de ordine creaturarum*: 'Faith in the Trinity', 'The spiritual creation', 'The waters which are above the firmament', 'The firmament of heaven', 'The sun and moon', three chapters on the atmosphere, 'The nature of the waters and the course of the ocean', 'Paradise', and 'The situation of the earthly sphere', followed by chapters on hell and punishment (Díaz y Díaz 1972). A comparable ordering can be observed in *Altus Prosator*. 3 A well-known example is the poem attributed to the legendary poet Amairgen, beginning 'I am a wind in the sea' (Macalister 1938–56, 5.110–13). Although ambitious claims have been made for this composition as a relic of Irish paganism, metrical and linguistic evidence indicates that it can scarcely be earlier than the end of the ninth century; this is not, of course, necessarily a denial of the antiquity of its traditional background.

Almost all of the dangers from which the speaker prays to be protected are spiritual ones: demons, vices, and the doctrines of false prophets, pagans, heretics, and idolaters. Taken in this context, his request to be guarded against 'spells of women and smiths and druids' may reflect anxiety regarding the errors of superstition rather than belief in the pernicious efficacy of magic.

Some scholars continued to defend the traditional ascription of the *Faeth Fiada* to Saint Patrick down to quite recent times, but it is now generally held that it was composed in the eighth century. The antiquary George Petrie claimed that oral versions were still current in the 1830s,[4] but it is not certain that the 'breastplate of Patrick' of which he heard mention then was the same prayer as that under consideration here. Evidence of its use in the intervening period is provided by the Middle Irish preface. In assigning supernatural benefits to the prayer's recitation the preface is by no means unusual; we may compare the more elaborate list of benefits to be obtained by reciting the *Altus Prosator*. Considerably less common is the stipulation that the suppliant's mind must be firmly fixed upon God if these benefits are to be obtained: spiritual engagement, and not mere recitation, is essential to the *lorica*'s efficacy. The story about Patrick disguising himself and his followers as deer, which has at least one close analogue in Irish heroic legend,[5] is found in earlier sources without any explicit reference to our text; I have included one example below immediately following the prayer itself.

Almost nothing has been written about *Nuall Fir Fhio* since the first full edition appeared, for the simple reason that no one has known quite what to make of it. Despite references to 'the King of all things' and the Holy Spirit, and a possible allusion to a saint Laisrén, pride of place is given to beings who seem to be pagan deities: the daughters of the sea, a silver warrior, and someone named Senach who is described as having been reared by fairy women. This led Kuno Meyer to suggest that 'an ecclesiastic ... recast an ancient and probably popular pagan prayer by adding Christian tags to it,' while Calvert Watkins, untroubled by the text's Christian elements, describes it simply as 'a druid prayer for long life, run through with Indo-European poetic phraseology.'[6] But can the Christian references really be simply brushed aside? This has not yet been convincingly demonstrated. If the mysterious beings invoked really are old gods and goddesses, moreover, they have left no traces elsewhere in the literature, a fact which makes the references to them here even harder to interpret.

These puzzles need to be considered in conjunction with another curious circumstance: *Nuall Fir Fhio* seems to have been composed by a learned cleric. Its title seems to mean 'Fer Fio's cry', and the Irish annals record the death of 'Fer Fio the wise, son of the blacksmith, abbot of Comraire in Meath' in the year 762.[7]

---

4 Petrie 1839, 69.   5 In *Táin Bó Cuailnge*, fairy musicians are pursued by the army of Ireland 'until they went before them into the pillar-stones at Lía Mór in the north, transformed into deer, for (in reality) they were druids possessed of great occult knowledge' (O'Rahilly 1976, 151).
6 Meyer 1914, 227; Watkins 1976, 271.

Whatever may have been the reason for *Nuall Fir Fhio*'s composition, and the beliefs of its author – and we may well never know these – it provides unique and fascinating evidence of the complicated interrelationship between native tradition and Christian spirituality at the highest levels of the early Irish ecclesiastical hierarchy.[8]

The *Faeth Fiada* is one of the most popular and highly regarded productions of the medieval Irish church; the religious orientation of the *Nuall Fir Fhio* is problematical at best, and even specialists have generally avoided discussing it. Yet the two prayers may have originated in the same milieu. Not only do both seem to have been composed in the eighth century, but both conclude with words from the final verse of Psalm 3. The psalm as a whole, in which the speaker prays to God for protection against a multitude of enemies, accords well with the concerns of *loricae* in general and with the tenor of these two specimens in particular; but I am not aware of any other instances of its employment in this way. Curiously, it is *Nuall Fir Fhio* which follows the Biblical text most closely.

7 Mac Airt and Mac Niocaill 1983, 214–5, 762.6. 8 No comprehensive general study of early Irish spells, and of the mingling of pagan and Christian elements to be found in them, has yet been undertaken. For editions of individual texts see Stokes 1873–5; Stokes and Strachan 1901–3, 2.248–50, 293 (and for the latter cf. Oskamp 1977–9, 387–8); Meyer 1916; Meroney 1945; and Best 1952.

FAETH FIADA: 'PATRICK'S BREASTPLATE'

Patrick made this hymn; it was composed in the time of Loegaire son of Niall. It was composed in order to protect him and his monks from deadly enemies, who were lying in wait for the clerics. And it is a breastplate of faith, to protect body and soul against demons and men and vices. If anyone recites it every day, with his mind fixed wholly upon God, demons will not stand against him, it will protect him against every poison and jealousy, it will guard him against sudden death, it will be a breastplate for his soul after death. Patrick recited it when Loegaire had set an ambush for him, lest he come to Tara to spread the Faith, so that it seemed to those who lay in wait that they were wild deer, with a fawn following them (that was Benén).[9] And its name is *Faíd Fiada* ('the Deer's Cry').[10]

Atomriug indiu
niurt tréun:
togairm Trindóit,
cretim Treodatad,
faísitin Oendatad,
i nDúlemon dáil.

Today I gird myself
with a mighty power:
invocation of the Trinity,
belief in the Threeness,
affirmation of the Oneness,
in the Creator's presence.

Atomriug indiu
niurt gene Críst cona bathius,
niurt a chrochtho cona adnacul,
niurt a essérgi cona fhresgabáil,
niurt a thoíniudo fri brithemnas mbrátho.

9 *Benén* is the Irish form of Latin *Benignus*. The saint of this name was traditionally held to have been Patrick's first successor as bishop of Armagh, having become his disciple while still a young boy. 10 This seems to be a reinterpretation of *féth fía*, a term of uncertain derivation used in Middle Irish and later sources to designate some kind of spell of invisibility. In light of this prayer's links with *Nuall Fir Fhio*, mentioned above, it is interesting that the latter is ascribed to a man named Fer *Fío*.

Today I gird myself
with the power of Christ's birth together with his baptism,
with the power of his crucifixion together with his burial,
with the power of his resurrection together with his ascension,
with the power of his descent to pronounce the judgment
    of Doomsday.

Atomriug indiu
niurt gráid hiruphin,
i n-aurlataid aingel,
i frestul inna n-archaingel,
i freiscisin esséirgi
ar chiunn fochraicce,
i n-ernaigthib uasalathrach,
i tairchetlaib fáithe,
i preceptaib apstal,
i n-iresaib foísmedach,
i n-enccai noebingen,
i ngnímaib fer fírén.

Today I gird myself
with the power of the order of the cherubim,
with the obedience of angels,
with the ministry of the archangels,
with the expectation of resurrection
for the sake of a reward,
with the prayers of patriarchs,
with the predictions of prophets,
with the precepts of apostles,
with the faith of confessors,
with the innocence of holy virgins,
with the deeds of righteous men.

Atomriug indiu
niurt nime,
soilsi gréne,
étrochtai éscai,
áni thened,
déni lóchet,
luaithi gaíthe,

fudomnai mara,
tairismigi thalman,
cobsaidi ailech.

Today I gird myself
with the strength of heaven,
light of the sun,
brightness of the moon,
brilliance of fire,
speed of lightning,
swiftness of wind,
depth of sea,
firmness of earth,
stability of rock.

Atomriug indiu
niurt Dé dom luamairecht.
Cumachtae nDé dom chumgabáil,
ciall Dé dom imthús,
rosc nDé dom remcisiu,
cluas Dé dom étsecht,
briathar Dé dom erlabrai,
lám Dé dom imdegail,
intech Dé dom remthechtas,
sciath Dé dom imdítin,
sochraite Dé dom anacul,[11]
ar intledaib demnae,
ar aslagib dualche,
ar forimthechtaib aicnid,
ar cech duine mídúthrastar dam,
i céin ocus i n-ocus,
i n-uathud ocus i sochaidi.

Today I gird myself
with the strength of God to direct me.

---

11 I take all of the phrases in this sequence, apart from the first, to begin with independent nominatives: oblique forms for *ciall, cluas, briathar, lám* occur in none of the manuscripts; and nasalisation follows the old neuters *cumachtae* and *rosc*. Against this must be set the instances of unhistorical nasalisation in the London and Oxford manuscripts; even so, I think that the balance of the evidence inclines toward the interpretation adopted here.

The might of God to exalt me,
the mind of God to lead me,
the eye of God to watch over me,
the ear of God to hear me,
the word of God to speak to me,
the hand of God to defend me,
the path of God to go before me,
the shield of God to guard me,
the help of God to protect me,
against the snares of demons,
against the temptations of vices,
against the tendencies (?) of nature,[12]
against everyone who will wish me ill,
far and near,
among few and among many.

Tocuiriur etrum indiu inna uili nert-so
fri cech nert n-amnas n-étrocar fristaí dom churp ocus dom anmain,
fri tinchetla saíbfháithe,
fri dubrechtu gentliuchtae,
fri saíbrechtu heretecdae,
fri imchellacht n-ídlachtae,
fri brichtu ban ocus gobann ocus druad,
fri cech fiss arachuille corp ocus anmain duini.

Today I interpose all these powers between myself
and every harsh pitiless power which may come against my body
      and my soul,
against the predictions of false prophets,
against the black laws of paganism,
against the crooked laws of heretics,
against the encirclement of idolatry,
against the spells of women and smiths and druids,[13]
against every knowledge which harms a man's body and soul.

---

12 I here emend the manuscript variants *airnechtaib, foirmdechaib* to *forimthechtaib*. Greene and O'Connor suggested *airrechtaib* 'assaults'.   13 The phrase *brichtu ban* 'spells of women' is particularly interesting here: it recurs in an early tale about a young man lured away by a woman from the Otherworld (Oskamp 1974, 223, 226); and an exactly cognate expression is found in a pagan Celtic inscription from southern France (Meid 1992, 40–6).

Críst dom imdegail indiu
ar neim, ar loscud, ar bádud, ar guin,
condom-thair ilar fochraicce.
Críst limm, Críst reum, Críst im degaid,
Críst indium, Críst ísum, Críst uasum,
Críst desum, Críst tuathum,
Críst i llius, Críst i sius, Críst i n-erus,
Críst i cridiu cech duini immumrorda,
Críst i ngin cech oín rodom-labrathar,
Críst i cech rusc nodom-dercathar,
Críst i cech cluais rodom-chloathar.

May Christ protect me today
against poison, against burning, against drowning, against wounding,
that many rewards may come to me.
May Christ be with me, Christ before me, Christ behind me,
Christ within me, Christ beneath me, Christ above me,
Christ to my right, Christ to my left,
Christ where I lie down, Christ where I sit, Christ where I stand,
Christ in the heart of everyone who thinks of me,
Christ in the mouth of everyone who speaks to me,
Christ in every eye which looks on me,
Christ in every ear which hears me.

Atomriug indiu
niurt tréun:
togairm Trindóit,
cretim Treodatad,
faísitin Oendatad,
i nDúlemon dáil.

Today I gird myself
with a mighty power:
invocation of the Trinity,
belief in the Threeness,
proclamation of the Oneness,
in the Creator's presence.

Domini est salus,
Domini est salus,
Christi est salus;
salus tua, Domine, sit semper nobiscum.

Salvation is of the Lord,
salvation is of the Lord,
salvation is of Christ;
may your salvation, Lord, be always with us.[14]

[The story of how Patrick and his followers appeared as deer to the men waiting to attack them is recounted more fully in an early Middle Irish life of Patrick (Mulchrone 1939, 30–1), itself an elaboration of a much briefer account in the seventh-century life by Muirchú (Bieler 1979, 90–1). The former version runs as follows:]

> ... Loegaire said to Patrick, 'Come after me to Tara, cleric, so that I may accept belief from you in the presence of the men of Ireland.' But he had placed an ambush in wait for Patrick at every pass from Ferta Fer Féicc to Tara, to kill him. God, however, did not grant him his will. Patrick came together with seven young clerics, with Benén accompanying them as a serving-lad. Patrick blessed them before they set out: concealment came upon them, so that no one noticed them. The pagans in the ambush only saw eight stags go past them across the upland, with a fawn following them which had a spot on its shoulder: that was Patrick and the seven, followed by Benén with his writing-tablets on his back. Loegaire came to Tara that evening, downcast and humiliated, together with the few who had waited with him.

---

14 These words are, as noted above, adapted from the last verse of Psalm 3: *Domini est salus, et super populum tuum benedictio tua*; compare the conclusion of *Nuall Fir Fhio* below. In the present case they seem to have been modified in imitation of one of the principal responses in the mass: *Kyrie eleison, Kyrie eleison, Christe eleison* 'Lord have mercy, Lord have mercy, Christ have mercy'.

NUALL FIR FHIO: 'FER FIO'S CRY'

May Fer Fio's cry protect me upon the road, as I make my circuit of the Plain of
Life.

> Admuiniur secht n-ingena trethan,
> dolbte snáthi macc n-aesmár.
> Trí bás uaim rouccaiter,
> trí aes dam dorataiter,
> secht tonna tocid dom dorodálter.
> Ním choillet messe fom chuairt,
> i llúrig Lasrén cen léniud.
> Ní nascar mo chlú ar chel.
> Domthí aes,
> ním-thí bás
> corba sen.

> I invoke the seven daughters of the sea
> who form the threads of the long-lived youths.
> May three deaths be taken from me,
> may three life-times be granted me,
> may seven waves of luck be poured out for me.
> May spectres[15] not harm me upon my rounds
> in the breastplate of Laisrén,[16] without injury.
> My fame is not bound to perish.
> May long life come to me,
> may death not come to me
> until I am old.

> Admuiniur m'argetnïa,
> nád ba, nád beba.
> Aimser dom dorindnastar
> findruni feba.

15 The rare word *messe* 'spectres, phantoms' must not have been understood by an early scribe, as the word is glossed 'i.e., the female sins' (sins of women? sins with women?) in both manuscripts of the text. 16 *Lasrén* here has generally been taken as an adjective meaning something like 'radiant'; the only other potential instance, however, occurs in a context at least as obscure as this one. It does not seem unreasonable to interpret it as designating a person: several saints were named Laisrén, and there is a story about a monk of that name who made a visionary journey to hell in the course of which he was protected against the attacks of demons (Meyer 1899).

Ro órthar mo richt,
ro soerthar mo recht,
ro mórthar mo nert.
Níb ellam mo lecht,
ním-thí bás for fecht,
ro fírthar mo thecht.
Ním-ragba nathir díchuinn,
ná doirb dúrglas,
ná doel díchuinn.
Ním-millethar teól,
ná cuire ban,
ná cuire buiden.
Domthí aurchur n-aimsire
ó Ríg na n-uile.

I invoke my silver warrior,
who has not died, who will not die.
May time be granted me
with the virtue of *findruine*.[17]
May my shape be made golden,
may my rank be ennobled,
may my strength be magnified.
May my burial not be swift,
may death not come to me upon the road,
may my journey be confirmed.
May the senseless snake not seize me,
nor the harsh grey worm,
nor the senseless beetle.
May no thief destroy me,
nor a company of women,
nor a company of warriors.
May an extension of time be granted me
by the King of all things.

Admuiniur Senach sechtaimserach,
conaltar mná síde
for bruinnib Buais.
Ní báitter mo shechtchaindel.

17 Cf. p. 111, note 10 above.

Am dún díthogail,
am ail anscuichthe,
am lia lógmar,
am sén sechtmainech.
Ropo chétach, cétbliadnach,
cach cét diib ar uair.
Cotagaur cucum a lessa;
rob é rath in Spirto Noíb form-sa.

I invoke Senach of the seven ages,
whom fairy women fostered
on the breasts of inspiration.[18]
May my seven candles not be quenched.
I am an impregnable fortress,
I am an immovable rock,
I am a precious stone,
I am a weekly blessing.
May I live a hundred times a hundred years,
each hundred of them in turn.
I summon their benefits to me;
may the grace of the Holy Spirit be upon me.[19]

Domini est salus, ter.
Christi est salus, ter.
Super populum tuum, Domine,
benedictio tua.

Salvation is of the Lord (three times).
Salvation is of Christ (three times).
May your blessing, Lord,
be upon your people.

18 Or 'on the banks of the Bush' – one of the rivers traditionally held to convey supernatural knowledge from the Otherworld.   19 That the Holy Spirit is invoked at the end of the third section may be due in part to the fact that it is the third person of the Trinity. There is also almost certainly an implicit association between the sevens mentioned throughout the section and the seven gifts of the Holy Spirit derived by the Fathers of the Church from the Vulgate text of Isaiah 11:2: other Irish texts speak of the 'seven-formed Spirit' (*Spirut sechtndelbach*).

The Pseudo-Historical Prologue to
the *Senchas Már*

At some point in the eighth century more than two dozen separate law tracts were brought together to form the massive collection known as the *Senchas Már* or 'Great Tradition', a body of material comprising roughly half of the early Irish legal treatises now known to us. At a later date the short tale translated here was placed at the head of the entire compilation, to tell the story of how the *Senchas Már* – and, indeed, the laws of Christian Ireland in general – had come to be codified. In my own view our tale originated as an independent composition, probably in the ninth century, and its connection with the *Senchas Már* is a secondary one.

Underlying the specific legal issues on which the story's action turns is a cultural dilemma of fundamental importance: the confrontation between pagan Irish law, here represented by Loegaire king of Tara, and the new dispensation represented by Saint Patrick. The story predictably resolves their rivalry in Patrick's favour; but it is significant that it does so in a way which allows for the retention of as many as possible of the old ways, and indeed provides divine ratification of their value. When the tension latent between the two systems erupts into crisis, Patrick refers judgment to a member of the native poetic order – and Dubthach, far from being a mouthpiece of paganism, speaks words inspired by the Holy Spirit. In his speech, and in the story as a whole, an effort is made to reconcile the 'law of nature' followed by the virtuous pagans of the past with the new law of the Gospel: the legal code of Christian Ireland emerges from the harmonisation of the two, 'the knitting together of church and kingdom'.

When the Faith in its fullness had been established among the men of Ireland, and Christ's Gospel had been preached to them all, and Loegaire with his druids had been bested by the miracles and great wonders which Patrick had wrought in the presence of the men of Ireland, so that thereafter he believed, and submitted to all of Patrick's will – then the best of the men of Ireland were commanded by Loegaire to assemble for a conference regarding the proper ordering of their usages and laws. A message was sent by them to Patrick, that he should come to the assembly.

On the day before Patrick came to them, the men of Ireland conferred among themselves. 'What,' Loegaire asked them, 'is most difficult for you in what the cleric has preached to you?' 'Not hard to answer: the law of forgiveness,' they said; 'for as soon as every man expects to be forgiven for whatever evil thing he does, there will be no restraint upon plundering, and every man will smite his fellow, for he will have no fear of being blamed for it.' 'What then will you do regarding this?' asked Loegaire. 'What is your own advice concerning it?' said they. 'This is what I have devised,' said he, 'if you agree: let his own temperament be tested, that is, let someone from his household be slain in his presence. If he pardons him, we will submit to that law; if he does not pardon [him], however, we will not submit to that law.'

Thus the plan of Loegaire and the men of Ireland was decided upon: that a certain man would slay the charioteer who was in front of Patrick when he came to the assembly. This was fulfilled through Loegaire's pronouncement (?). After the man of Patrick's household had been slain in his presence as he was alighting from his chariot, Patrick gazed toward heaven, for that is where his help was. Thereupon a trembling and a great earthquake seized the island of Ireland and its men, and knocked the host gathered at the assembly sprawling. And they feared with a great fear and were made like dead men.

Then Loegaire and the best of the men of Ireland prostrated themselves in full submission to God and Patrick. 'Patience, patience, cleric!' said the men of Ireland. 'You have preached forgiveness: grant forgiveness to us!' 'Well, then,' said Patrick. All the men of Ireland sat down. Then the men of Ireland said to Patrick, as we have said, 'Give an opinion concerning [this matter].' Then Patrick said, 'I place it,' said he, 'under the jurisdiction of the royal poet of the island of Ireland, namely Dubthach moccu Lugair, a vessel full of the Holy Spirit.'

'Well, then,' said Dubthach. 'Alas that you have said this to me, cleric,' said Dubthach. 'It is difficult for me to be in this debate between God and man. For if I say that compensation should not be exacted for this deed, perhaps that may affront your honour, and you may not think it good. But if I say that it should be paid for and avenged, that may not seem good to God. For this is what is in the Gospels: full forgiveness of every evil deed by every neighbour to his fellow.'

'Well, then,' said Patrick; 'whatever God may give [you] to say, speak thus. It is not you who speaks, but the Spirit of your Father who speaks in you' (Matthew 10:20). Then Patrick blessed his mouth, and the grace of the Holy Spirit came upon his speech so that he said:

> An evil deed which is not punished is a relapse into paganism.
> For it is to preserve faith in the Lord that the power of correcting every iniquity, of chastising, was left with a foreign name.
> An unpunished sin is an evasion of baptism: it diminishes righteousness, it assists the guilty.
> For a demon does not merit forgiveness when he sins.
> Likewise a man from whom God is expelled: he is forfeited to death, death which burns, in transgressing the High King's commandment.
> For a limit was set on the merit of everyone's repentance after Christ's crucifixion: that he should not lapse into another misdeed.

Why is it that a man is pardoned when he has committed a sin, provided that he does penance; but a demon is not pardoned when he has committed transgression, even though he betakes himself to penance? This is the reason. It is a feeble mortal body which is around the man, and there is with God an abode higher than the abode in which he is. But it is a subtle pure body which is around the angel, and there is not with God an abode higher than the abode in which he is; and therefore he does not grant pardon to him when he has committed transgression, even though he betakes himself to penance.[1]

> I pray to God that he make straight my path.
> Older than the fathers, the fathers of Noah, is the power which God did not deem wicked, so that the bloodshed of men does not swell to excess.

---

1 With this passage, and the immediately preceding section of the judgment, compare the discussion of the fall of Lucifer in *On the Miracles* (p. 55 above); also Carey 1990, 15–16. The portion of the judgment which follows may be a separate composition; thus Binchy 1975–6, 18.

May the Lord's truth, the testimony of the New Law, aid me in the
  case of Nuadu.
[The case] has been submitted to me; I assert the good; I know divine
  knowledge, if it be with sanctity of conscience.
Everyone dies in his guilt.
The example (?) of vengeance upholds two laws.[2]
I prove by my cheeks, which will not bring a blush to pure dignity,
  that I have judged a sound judgment.[3]
I follow Patrick after my baptism.
Let the hand which has deserved it be punished fully: every living
  thing gives the judgment which it chooses (?).
There was in the first law of the men of Ireland that which God has
  not pardoned in his New Law.
The Trinity, which did not protect Adam, does not permit mercy
  through the might of heaven. For it was in perpetual renewal that
  God in his mercy created him, so that he has earned death again
  according to merit.
Let everyone die who kills a man in the image of the King who arrayed
  them in multitudes.
Death pursues bloodshed, if someone dies of it.
Neither the trifle of a needle nor the nobility of elders protects the
  living man who dispenses death.
When killing by foul play is pronounced, let deaths be died.
Whoever releases the guilty is guilty. I sentence the guilty to death.
A lawful judgment has guided me, according to my knowledge: the
  misdeed which kills him is evil.
I pronounce a sentence of death: let everyone die in his guilt.
Nuadu was judged for the sake of heaven; and he was not judged for
  the sake of death.

Thus the two laws were fulfilled: the culprit was killed for his crime, and his
soul was pardoned. This was established by the men of Ireland: everyone [to
die] for his crime, so that sin might not increase again in this island.

And then the men of Ireland said, 'It is needful for us to establish and
arrange all our laws, as well as this matter.' 'It is better to do it,' said
Patrick. Then all the people of skill in Ireland were convened, so that each

2 That is, vengeance is still appropriate in the new, Christian dispensation.   3 An allusion to the
ethos of personal honour which was already of fundamental importance to the pagan Celtic
peoples. The cheek, as the place where a blush can appear, figures in Irish sources as a correlative
of honour; similarly, 'face' can be used to designate dignity or status.

exhibited his skill to Patrick, in the presence of all the princes in Ireland. Then it was entrusted to Dubthach to display judgment, and all the poetry of Ireland, and every law which had held sway among the men of Ireland, in the law of nature and the law of the prophets, in the judgments of the island of Ireland and among the poets who had prophesied that the white language of the *Beati* would come, i.e. the law of Scripture.[4] For the Holy Spirit spoke and prophesied through the mouths of the righteous men who were first in the island of Ireland, as he prophesied through the mouths of the chief prophets and patriarchs in the law of the Old Testament; for the law of nature reached many things which the law of Scripture did not reach. As for the judgments of true nature which the Holy Spirit uttered through the mouths of the righteous judges and poets of the men of Ireland, from the time when this island was settled until the coming of the Faith, Dubthach revealed them all to Patrick. Whatever did not go against God's word in the law of Scripture and in the New Testament, or against the consciences of the faithful, was fixed in the system of judgment by Patrick and the churches and the princes of Ireland severally. The whole law of nature was acceptable, save [in what concerns] the Faith, and its proper dues, and the knitting together of church and kingdom.[5] So that that is the *Senchas Már*.

Nine men were chosen to arrange [the laws]: Patrick and Benignus and Cairnech, three bishops; Loegaire son of Niall king of Ireland and Dáire king of Ulster and Corc son of Lugaid king of Munster, three kings; [and] Dubthach moccu Lugair, and Fergus the poet, and Ros son of Trechem the expert in legal language. *Nó-fís* ('nine-knowledge'), then, is the name of the book they arranged, i.e., the knowledge of nine men; and we have seen an example of it above. This then is the law of Patrick. No human judge of the Gaels can undo anything which he may find in the *Senchas Már*.

Until Patrick came, [authority in] speaking was only granted to three men: the historian with a good memory for explanation and narration; the man of art for praise and satire; the judge for giving judgments with *roscada*[6] and maxims. After Patrick's coming, however, all of these [kinds of authoritative]

---

4 'The *Beati*' is the abecedarian Psalm 119, which begins with the words *Beati immaculati in uia*. Particular sanctity was attributed to it in early Ireland; cf. the first anecdote in 'Stories of the Céili Dé' below, and the introductory discussion of the hymn *Audite omnes*. For an anecdote illustrating its supernatural efficacy see Stokes 1890, x.   5 This passage, from the words 'every law which had held sway' above, is based on the eighth-century law tract *Córus Béscnai*, one of the treatises which make up the *Senchas Már*. *Córus Béscnai* contains a brief account of Patrick's meeting with Dubthach, which presumably provided the initial inspiration for our tale.   6 A *rosc* or *roscad* is a type of stylised composition which is neither normal prose nor syllabically regular verse; it was commonly used as a vehicle for legal or ethical teaching, in prophecies and spells, and in set speeches in the sagas.

speech are subject to the possessor of the white language, i.e., of the Scriptures.

From the time when Amairgen Glúngel gave the first judgment in Ireland, judgment was in the hands of the poets alone until the 'Colloquy of the Two Sages' in Emain Macha, i.e., [the colloquy] of Ferchertne and Néde son of Adna concerning the sage's mantle which had belonged to Adna son of Othar.[7] Dark was the speech which the poets spoke in that case, and the judgment which they gave was not clear to the princes. 'Their judgment and their understanding belong to these men alone,' said the princes.... 'Moreover, we do not understand what they say.' 'It is plain,' said Conchobar: 'henceforth everyone will have a share [in judging]; except for what pertains properly to them therein, it will not fall to their lot. Each will take his own portions of it.'

So poets were deprived of the power to judge, save for what pertained properly to them; and each of the men of Ireland took his own portion of judgment. Such are the Judgments of Eochu son of Luchta, and the Judgments of Fachtna son of Sencha, and the False Judgments of Caratnia Teiscthe, and the Judgments of Morann, and the Judgments of Eógan son of Durthacht, and the Judgments of Doet Nemthine, and the Judgments of Bríg Ambue, and the Judgments of Dian Cécht concerning physicians (although those were given first). At that time the nobles of Ireland adjudged the measure of law-suit and speech to each man according to his rank, as they are reckoned in the *Bretha Nemed*, etc.

7 This is the earliest known allusion to the riddling dialogue *Immacallam in Dá Thuarad* (Stokes 1905).

III THE SAINTS

Audite Omnes Amantes:
'Sechnall's Hymn' to Saint Patrick

Whenever this hymn was really composed, it was believed throughout the Middle Ages to be the work of Saint Secundinus or Sechnall, one of Patrick's disciples and first successors as bishop of Armagh. It was evidently a popular and important text from an early date: several other Irish hymns reflect its influence, as does the late seventh-century life of Patrick by Muirchú moccu Macthéni.

It is easy to see how *Audite omnes* came to be attributed to one of Patrick's contemporaries, as the saint is spoken of in the present tense throughout. A subtler and more interesting link between the hymn and its subject can be observed in the use which both make of the Bible. Patrick's surviving writings are remarkable for the extent to which they are permeated with Biblical diction: it is almost as if he has no language of his own to use, only that of the Scriptures. But in submitting so completely to the words of revelation he paradoxically makes them his own, manipulating and deploying the sacred texts with an astonishing mastery.[1] The author of the hymn not only draws upon the Bible in the same way, but takes Patrick as his model in doing so, for various of his scriptural citations echo those made by the saint himself.[2]

Each of the hymn's twenty-three verses begins with a consecutive letter of the alphabet, a feature also found in the hymn *Altus Prosator* above. In composing 'abecedarian' hymns of this type, the Irish followed the example of such psalms as 118, *Beati immaculati in uia*, which has just this structure in the Hebrew original.[3] The tradition that all of the spiritual merit to be obtained by reciting the hymn could be gained by reciting its last three verses only, mentioned in the medieval preface, was already current a century or so earlier in the life of Patrick known as *Bethu Phátraic*; I have given the relevant passage as an addendum below. One eleventh-century manuscript gives only the last three verses, followed by the first: for many readers, presumably, what the hymn could do was more important than what it said.

The preface provides an account of the hymn's form and of how it was believed that it had come to be written; to this other stories about Patrick and Sechnall have been added, some of them more concerned with their power than with their holiness as such. The most interesting of these anecdotes is probably that in which Sechnall is described as tricking Patrick by reciting a hymn in praise of him without revealing the identity of the dedicatee, then bargaining with him concerning the number of souls which he is to receive in payment for it; in the excerpt from *Bethu Phátraic*, it is Patrick who bargains in this way with God himself.

---

1 The most recent translation of Patrick's works, together with a provocative discussion of their literary sophistication, may be found in Howlett 1994. 2 Biblical quotations and allusions in the hymn are so ubiquitous that I have not noted them below, although I have done so in the case of the later glosses. For complete references see Orchard 1993. 3 Great sanctity was attributed to this psalm by the Irish; cf. the reference to 'the white language of the *Beati*' as a designation for the Christian revelation as a whole in 'The Pseudo-Historical Prologue to the *Senchas Már*', p. 143 above.

Audite omnes. The place of this hymn's composition is Domnach Sechnaill; and it is Sechnall who composed it in honour of Patrick.

<Patrick's origin was among the Britons of Dumbarton: his father was named Calpurnius, and his grandfather was a deacon named Potitus; his mother was Conchess, and his two sisters were Lupait and Tigris.> Patrick had four names: his parents called him Succat; he was called Cothraige when he was in service to four men; Saint Germanus gave him the name Magonius; and he was named Patrick by Pope Celestine.

<As for the reason for Patrick's coming to Ireland, this is how it happened: the seven sons of Sechtmaide king of the Britons went on a voyage, and ravaged Brittany. It happened that at that time a number of Britons from Dumbarton were in Brittany: Patrick's father Calpurnius son of Potitus was killed there, and Patrick and his two sisters were taken captive. Then the sons of Sechtmaide crossed the sea to Ireland. Lupait was sold there, in Conaille Muirthemne; and Patrick was sold in Dál nAraide, to Míliucc moccu Buain and his three brothers. They sold his two sisters in Conaille Muirthemne, and they had no knowledge of one another.>

<It is four men who bought Patrick, Míliucc among them: hence he got the name Cothraige, because he was serving four households (*cethar-threib*). But when Míliucc saw that he was a trustworthy slave, he bought him from the other three, so that he served him alone for seven years according to the custom of the Hebrews (Exodus 21:2, Deuteronomy 15:12); and he suffered many hardships in the wilderness of Sliab Mis in Dál nAraide, keeping watch over Míliucc's swine.>

<Now it came about that Míliucc had a vision in the night: it seemed to him that he saw Cothraige approaching him in the house where he was, and there was a flame of fire above his head, and coming from his nostrils and ears; it seemed to him that the flame threatened to burn him, but he drove it away from himself so that it did him no harm. But the fire burned his son and daughter, who were in the same bed with him, so that it reduced them to ashes; and the wind scattered those ashes throughout Ireland.>

<Then Cothraige was summoned to Míliucc so that he could tell him of his vision, and Cothraige interpreted it: 'The flame which you saw in me is faith in the Trinity, which burns within me. And I will preach it to you hereafter, and you will not believe; but your son and daughter will believe, and the fire of grace will burn them.'>

<When the holy Patrick was born, he was taken to a blind faceless[4] youth to be baptised, a priest named Gorianus. He had no water with which to perform the baptism, and so he made the sign of the Cross with the infant's hand upon the ground,

4 Literally 'plank-faced' (*clárenech*); his face was apparently perfectly flat.

and water came forth. And Gorianus washed his face, and his eyes were opened, and he read the office of baptism although he had never learned the alphabet.>

The time of the hymn's composition, then, was the reign of Loegaire son of Niall king of Ireland.

The reason for its composition was to praise Patrick, <for Sechnall had said to Patrick, 'When shall I compose a eulogy for you?' Patrick said, 'I do not wish to be praised in my lifetime.' Sechnall said, 'I did not ask whether I should do it, but when I should do it.' Patrick said, 'If you do it, the time has come,' for he knew that the time of his death was near.>

<It is Sechnall son of Restitutus who composed this hymn to Patrick, for he was Patrick's fosterson, and the son of Patrick's sister.> He belonged to the Lombards of Italy, as Eochaid grandson of Flannucán said:

> Sechnall moccu Baird, he of virtue,
> a paragon of the men of the world,
> belonged to the pure fierce race, white their colour,
> the Lombards of Italy.

The Lombards (*Longobardi*) are so called because they have a long beard (*longa barba*). <'Secundinus'[5] is taken to mean 'cutting away the faults' (*secans delicta*) of others, or himself 'fleeing from faults' (*secedens ... a delictis*).>

<When Sechnall was composing this hymn, a fair was being held near Domnach Sechnaill; he went there to prohibit it, but was not successful. After that Sechnall returned home, and raised his hands to God, so that the earth swallowed up thirteen chariots together with their riders and all the rest scattered in flight.>

Or else this is the reason for its composition: the offense which Sechnall gave to Patrick [when he said], 'Patrick is a good man save for one thing: how little he preaches charity.' When Patrick heard that, he came to Sechnall in great anger. <Sechnall had finished celebrating the mass, apart from approaching the body of Christ, when he heard that Patrick had arrived full of rage against him; he left the eucharist on the altar, and prostrated himself before Patrick. Then Patrick drove his chariot over him, but God raised the earth up around him on this side and on that, so that it did him no harm.>

<'Why are you vexed with me?' said Sechnall. 'What is that one thing,' said Patrick, 'which you have said that I have not practised? For if I have not practised charity, I am guilty of violating God's commandment. My God of Doomsday[6] knows that> it is for charity's own sake that I have not preached it: for sons of life will come to this island after me, and they will have need of that service from

---

5 The original form of his name, of which 'Sechnall' is the Irish version.   6 An old tradition, which may be genuine, holds that *Mo Dia brátha* ('My God of Doomsday' or 'By the God of Doomsday') was Patrick's favourite oath. In some texts it is preserved in the form *Modebroth*, perhaps a fragment of the ancient British speech which was Patrick's native language. For the expression 'sons of life' see p. 116, note 14 above.

men.'7 <'I did not know,' said Sechnall, 'that it was not out of negligence that you acted thus.' Then the angel said to Patrick, 'You will have all of that.'8>

Patrick and Sechnall made peace then. <As they were walking around the church-yard, they heard a choir of angels singing around the eucharist in the church. They were singing the hymn which begins 'Come, you saints, to the body of Christ,'9 and that is why that hymn has been sung ever since in Ireland at the time of approaching the body of Christ.>

<Thereafter Patrick sent Sechnall to Rome, to fetch back some of the relics of Paul and Peter, and of other martyrs: that is the penance which he gave him. Those are the relics which are in Armagh, in the shrine of Paul and Peter.>

When Sechnall had finished composing the eulogy, he went to show it to Patrick. When he came where Patrick was, he said to him, 'I have composed a eulogy on a certain son of life, to which I would like you to listen.' Patrick said, 'Welcome be praise of a man of God's household.' Sechnall began the hymn with 'He keeps Christ's blessed commandments,' so that Patrick should not know for whom the hymn had been composed until he had finished reciting it.10 When Sechnall said, 'For he will be called greatest in the kingdom of heaven,' Patrick shook to and fro and said, 'How can a man be "greatest" in the kingdom of heaven?' Sechnall answered, '[The superlative] is used for the positive here; <or else it is because he has surpassed many of his own kind.' 'A good answer,' said Patrick.>

<When Sechnall had finished reciting the hymn, a man and woman arrived with food for Patrick: curds and butter. The man's name was Bera, and the woman's Bríg. Patrick said, 'There will be no scarcity of food in the house in which this hymn is recited before eating.'>

<And a new house in which it is recited before [eating] will have Patrick watching over it, together with the saints of Ireland, as was revealed to Colmán Elo and to others with him; and it was revealed to Coemgen along with his followers. When [Coemgen] came on Sunday from the church into the refectory, and sang this hymn, Patrick appeared to him with many elders. He sang it three times, and then some fool said, 'Why do we sing this hymn thus?' 'That is not good,' said Coemgen: 'it is because Patrick appeared with his disciples for as long as we were singing the hymn.'>

When Sechnall had finished reciting the hymn, he said, 'Give me payment for it.' <'I shall,' said Patrick: 'as many days as there are in a year, so many souls of

7 Other versions of this episode make Patrick's sense clearer: if he had preached the virtue of charity, all of the wealth in Ireland would have been given to him, and nothing would have been left for those who came later.   8 This sentence seems out of place here; it may have slipped in from an account of Patrick's fast atop the Cruachán, described in detail in the addendum attached below.   9 The text of this hymn has survived in the seventh-century *Antiphonary of Bangor*, where it is said to have been sung 'when priests take communion' (Kenney 1966, 262).   10 That is, Sechnall began with the second stanza. Had he started with the first, in which Patrick is named, his ruse would of course have been unsuccessful. Another legend relating to the problems involved in praising a saint in his own lifetime occurs in the preface to *Amra Coluim Chille* (Stokes 1899, 132–5).

sinners will go to heaven in exchange for composing the hymn.' 'I will not accept that,' said Sechnall; 'for it seems little to me, and the eulogy is a good one.'> 'You will have,' said Patrick, 'as many sinners going to heaven as there are hairs in the cloak of your habit, in exchange for composing the hymn.' 'I will not accept that,' said Sechnall; <'for what devout person could not bring that amount with him to heaven, even without any praise to such a man as yourself?' 'You will be able to bring to heaven,' said Patrick, 'seven every Thursday and twelve every Saturday from among the sinners of Ireland.' 'That is little,' said Sechnall.> 'You will obtain,' said Patrick, 'that everyone who recites it when lying down and when getting up will go to heaven.' 'I will not accept that,' said Sechnall, 'for the hymn is long, and not everyone can remember it.' 'All of its grace,' said Patrick, 'will be in the last three stanzas.' 'Thanks be to God,' said Sechnall.

    <The angel promised the same thing to Patrick on the Cruach: that everyone who recites it when lying down and getting up will go to heaven; as it is said,

> The hymn which you have chosen while still alive
> will be a breastplate (*lúirech*) of protection for all.[11]>

This is the first hymn to be composed in Ireland. It has the sequence of the alphabet, in the Hebrew fashion, but not in all respects (?).[12] It contains twenty-three stanzas, with four lines in each stanza, and fifteen syllables in each line: if anyone finds more in it, or less, it is an error. There are two or three places in it where *in* occurs without sense or metrical justification, etc.

    <[It is written] in imitation of Moses, saying 'Hear what I shall say, you heavens' (Deuteronomy 32:1); and of David, saying 'Hear these things, all you peoples' (Psalm 49:1).>

Audite omnes amantes Deum sancta merita
uiri in Christo, beati Patricii episcopi,
quomodo bonum ob actum simulatur angelis,
perfectamque propter uitam aequatur apostolis.

Hearken, all you lovers of God, to the holy merits
of a man blessed in Christ, the bishop Patrick:
how through his good deeds he is like the angels,
and on account of his perfect life is made equal to the apostles.

---

11 A quotation from an Old Irish hymn about Patrick's life (Stokes and Strachan 1903, 2.319, line 51). On the concept of the *lúirech* or *lorica* see the introductory remarks to 'Two *Loricae*', pp. 127–9 above.   12 This last phrase (*sed non per omnia*) is peculiar to the manuscript on which I base this translation. I take it to be an allusion to the fact that the words beginning the stanzas for K, Y, and Z are here spelled *castum*, *imnos*, and *sona*; in the other manuscripts they are written *kastam*, *ymnos*, and *zona* in accordance with the overall abecedarian scheme.

GLOSS 'Patrick' (*Patricius*): i.e., 'he who sits beside the king' (*ad latus regis*), or 'father of citizens' (*pater ciuium*); 'patrician' is the name of a class among the Romans, which rules the patriciate (?).

> Beata Christi custodit mandata in omnibus,
> cuius opera refulgent clara inter [h]omines,
> sanctumque cuius sequ[u]ntur exemplum mirificum,
> unde et in caelis Patrem magnificant Dominum.

> He keeps Christ's blessed commandments in all things,
> his bright deeds shine forth among men;
> and they follow his holy miraculous example,
> so that they [too] magnify God the Father in heaven.

GLOSSES 'example': As it is said, 'Let your light so shine before men that they may see your good deeds, so that they may glorify your Father who is in heaven' (Matthew 5:16). 'magnify': i.e., men 'making great' (*magnum facientes*) in the name of the Lord.

> Constans in Dei timore, et fide immobilis,
> super quem edificatur, ut Petrus, ecclesia;
> cuiusque apostolatum a Deo sortitus est,
> in cuius porte aduersus inferni non preualent.

> Constant in the fear of God, and immovable in faith,
> upon whom, as upon Peter, the church is built:
> whose apostleship has come from God,
> and against whom the gates of hell do not prevail.

GLOSSES 'faith': i.e., in the Trinity; as Paul said, 'Brothers, be firm,' etc. (1 Corinthians 15:58). 'Peter': As it is said, 'You are Peter, and upon this rock (*petram*) I will build my church' (Matthew 16:18). 'Peter' is interpreted as meaning 'he who recognises': let whoever desires to enter the kingdom of heaven, then, recognise God through faith as Peter did.

> Dominus illum elegit ut doceret barbaras
> nationes, ut piscaret per doctrine retia:
> ut de <saeculo> credentes traheret ad gratiam,
> Dominumque sequerentur sedem ad etheriam.

> The Lord chose him so that he might teach the barbarian
> nations, so that he might fish with the nets of doctrine;

so that he might draw believers out of the world to grace,
and they might follow the Lord to a heavenly seat.

GLOSSES 'barbarian': i.e., it is interpreted as meaning 'foreign', because they are
foreign to the Roman tongue. 'to grace': i.e., to faith, or heaven (?).

Electa Christi tallenta uendit euangelica,
quae Euernas inter gentes cum usuris exigit;
nauigi huius laboris tum opere pretium
cum Christo regni celestis possessurus gaudium.

He sells the precious talents of the Gospel of Christ
and demands them back, with interest, from the pagans of Ireland.
As his payment for the toil of this laborious voyage
he will share with Christ the joy of the kingdom of heaven.

GLOSSES 'talents': i.e., commandments. 'voyage': i.e., this voyage of the church.
The sea is this world, the ship is the church, the pilot is the teacher who brings it
to the haven of life, the haven of life is life eternal. 'with Christ': As the Lord says
in the Gospel, 'Where there is a body, there eagles will gather' (Matthew 24:28);
as if he were to say plainly, 'Where Christ will have been according to the flesh,
there the just will be; and thus they will be with him forever in heaven.'

Fidelis Dei minister, insignisque nuntius,
apostolicum exemplum formamque prebet bonis,
qui tam uerbis quam et factis plebi predicat Dei,
ut quem dictis non conuertit, actu prouocet bono.

A faithful minister of God, and a splendid messenger,
he gave to the good the example and form of an apostle,
preaching to the people of God with both words and deeds
so that he might with a good act inspire the one whom his words did
    not move.

Gloriam habet cum Christo, honorem in saeculo,
qui ab <omnibus> ut Dei uen[er]atur angelus,
quem Deus misit [ut] Paulum ad gentes apostolum,
ut hominibus ducatum preberet regno Dei.

He has glory with Christ and honour in the world,
being revered by all as an angel of God

whom God has sent, like Paul, as an apostle to the pagans,
that he might show men the way to God's kingdom.

GLOSSES 'whom': i.e., as God sent Paul to the gentiles, so [he sent] Patrick to the Irish.

Humilis Dei ob metum spiritu et corpore,
super quem bonum ob actum requiesc<i>t Dominus,
cuiusque iusta in carne Christi portat stigmata,
in cuius sola sustendans gloriatur in cruce.

Humble in spirit and body out of fear of God,
upon whom the Lord rests because of his good works,
bearing in his righteous flesh the stigmata of Christ
and carrying his Cross, in which alone he glories.

GLOSSES 'cross': i.e., the cross of suffering.

Impiger credentes pascit dapibus celestibus,
ne qui uidentur cum Christo in uia defici<a>nt,
quibus erogat ut panes uerba euangelica,
in cuius multiplicantur ut manna in manibus.

Tirelessly he feeds the faithful with heavenly feasts,
lest those who are seen with Christ should fail upon the way:
he gives them the words of the Gospel like loaves,
multiplied in his hands like manna.

GLOSSES 'feasts': i.e., sermons. 'are seen': i.e., in the retinue of Christ. 'on the way': i.e., in faith. 'manna': i.e., it is called *manna* in Hebrew, 'what is this?' in Latin (cf. Exodus 16:15).

<Kastam> qui custodit carnem ob amorem Domini,
quam carnem templum parauit Sanctoque Spiritui,
a quo constanter cum mundis possidetur actibus,
quam ut hostiam placentem uiuam offert Domino.

He keeps his flesh chaste for love of the Lord,
flesh which he has prepared as a temple for the Holy Spirit
(by whom it is constantly moved to pure deeds),
and which he offers to the Lord as a pleasing living sacrifice.

GLOSSES 'by whom': i.e., by the Spirit. 'constantly': i.e., because he does not depart from the Spirit. 'which': i.e., the flesh. 'offers': i.e., in chastity, and truth, and the absence of the death of sin. 'pleasing': i.e., to God, not to men. 'living': i.e., in virtues.

Lumenque mundi accensum ingens euangelicum,
in candelabro leuatum, toti fulgens saeculo;
ciuitas regis munita supra montem possita,
copia in qua est multa quam Dominus possidet.

He is the light of the world, the great burning light of the Gospel,
raised aloft on a candlestick, illuminating the whole age;
the fortified city of a king, set atop a mountain,
in which there is great abundance of the Lord's possessions.

GLOSSES 'light': i.e., he has lifted up the light of wisdom in the world; as it is said in the Gospel: 'No one lights a lamp unless he places it upon a candlestick, so that it may give light to all who are in the house' (Matthew 5:15), unless it be the Son of God, who is Jesus Christ. 'of a king': i.e., of Patrick. 'a mountain': i.e., Christ is a fruitful mountain. 'in which': i.e., in the city. 'abundance': i.e., of virtues.

Maximus nanque in regno celorum uocabitur
qui, quod uerbis docet sacris, factis adimplet bonis;
bono procedit exemplo formamque fidelium,
mundo<qu>e in corde habet ad Deum fiduciam.

For he will be called greatest in the kingdom of heaven,
who fulfils in good deeds what he teaches in holy words;
who by his good example exceeds the standard of the faithful,
and guards faith in God in his pure heart.

GLOSSES 'greatest': i.e., as if best, or as if greatest; or the greatest of his race. 'fulfils': i.e., he fulfilled in act whatever he taught in speech.

Nomen Domini audenter annuntiat gentibus,
<qu>ibus lauacri salutis eternam dat gratiam,
pro qu<o>rum orat dilictis ad Deum cotidie,
pro quibus, ut Deo dignas, ymolatque hostias.

Boldly he announces the Lord's name to the pagans,
giving them the eternal grace of the bath of salvation,

praying daily to God on account of their sins,
offering sacrifices for their sake, as befitting to God.

GLOSSES 'bath': i.e., of baptism: *baptisma* in Greek, *tinctio* ('dipping') in Latin.
By that dipping all filth is washed away, both what is original and what is caused
by deeds. 'their': i.e., the pagans'. 'sacrifices': i.e., as Christ is called both sacrifice
and priest: sacrifice according to the flesh, priest according to the spirit; for he was
offered up in the flesh.

Omnem pro diuina lege mundi spernit gloriam,
quae cuncta ad cuius mensam estimat ciscilia;
nec ingruenti mouetur mundi huius fulmine –
sed in aduersis laetatur, cum pro Christo patitur.

He rejects all the world's glory for the sake of the divine law,
considering it all mere scraps at its table;
nor is he disturbed by the hurtling lightning of this world,
but rejoices in hardships since he suffers for Christ's sake.

GLOSSES 'it all': i.e., rewards. 'its [table]': i.e., [the table] of the law. 'scraps'
(*ciscilia*): Ambrose says that *supercilium* ('eyebrow') means 'superabundance'; [for] *cilon*
is a Greek word which means 'abundance'. 'hurtling': i.e., by the noisy or very
heavy lightning. 'in hardships': i.e., in tribulations. 'suffers': i.e., this is the one
who suffers for Christ's sake: the one who 'denies himself, and carries his cross
daily' (Luke 9:23).

Pastor bonus ac fidelis gregis euangelici,
quem Deus Dei elegit custodire populum,
suamque pascere plebem diuinis dogmatibus,
pro qua ad Christi exemplum suam tradidit animam.

A good and faithful shepherd of the Gospel's flock,
whom God has chosen to guard the people of God
and to nourish his folk with divine teachings –
for whom, following Christ's example, he has offered up his life.

GLOSSES 'shepherd': i.e., a good shepherd is one like Christ, who said, 'I am the
good shepherd, offering my life for my sheep' (John 10:15). 'to nourish': i.e., he
satisfied [them]. 'teachings': teaching, i.e. precept. 'for whom': i.e., for [his] folk,
as the apostle says, 'I would willingly be condemned for the sake of my brothers'
(Romans 9:3).

Quem pro meritis Saluator prouexit pontificem,
ut in celesti moneret clericos militia,
celestem quibus annonam erogat cum uestibus,
quod in diuinis impletur sacrisque affatibus.

The Saviour has, for his merits, exalted him as pontiff,
that he may instruct the clerics in celestial warfare,
giving them heavenly food and clothing
filled full of divine and holy speeches.

Regis nuntius, inuitans credentes ad nuptias,
qui ornatur uestimento nuptiale indutus,
qui celeste [h]aurit uinum in uassis celestibus,
propinnansque Dei plebem spirituali poculo.

The King's messenger, inviting believers to the wedding,
himself adorned with a wedding garment,
he draws the heavenly wine in heavenly vessels,
and serves God's people with drink from a spiritual goblet.

GLOSSES   'the wedding': i.e., of the kingdom of heaven; as it is said, 'Be like
men awaiting your lord's return to his wedding, so that when he comes and knocks
they may speedily open for him' (Luke 12:36). 'draws': Bede says '*Bria* is a vessel
for wine; hence one who is drunk (*ebrius*) is one who drinks from a *bria*, but on the
other hand he who is called sober (*sobrius*) is as if he were *sibrius*, i.e. without a *bria*
(*sine bria*), i.e. without wine.' 'wine': i.e., the wine of the doctrine of the Gospel. 'in
... vessels': i.e., in the saints.

Sacrum inuenit thesaurum sacro in uolumine,
Saluatorisque in carne d<ei>tatem preuidit,
quem thesaurum emit sanctis perfectisque meritis;
Hisraël uocatur, huius anima uidens Deum.

He has found a holy treasury in the holy book,
he has prophetically seen the Saviour's Godhead in the flesh.
He has bought that treasure with his holy and perfect merits:
he is called 'Israel', for his soul sees God.

GLOSSES   'treasury': i.e., Christ; or the reward or mystery of the Gospel. 'book':
i.e., in holy Scripture, or in the Gospel. 'Godhead': i.e., he believed Christ to be

the Son of God, according to his divinity. 'treasure': i.e, the heavenly kingdom. 'Israel': 'Israel' either has two syllables, and means 'a man fighting with God',
or has three syllables, and means 'a man who sees God'.

> Testis Domini, fidelis in lege catholica,
> cuius uerba sunt diuinis condita oraculis
> ne humane putrent carnes, esseque a uermibus,
> sed celeste saliuntur sapore ad uictimam.

> He is the Lord's faithful witness in the catholic law,
> whose words are seasoned with the oracles of God,
> that the bodies of men may not rot, eaten by worms,
> but may be salted with heavenly savour for the Sacrifice.

GLOSSES   'heavenly': i.e., the teaching of God. 'savour': i.e., of body and soul.

> Verus cultor et insignis agri euangelici,
> cuius semina uidentur Christi euangelia,
> que diuin<o> serit ore in aures prudentium,
> quorumque corda ac mentes Sancto arat Spiritu.

> True and illustrious husbandman of the field of the Gospel,
> whose seeds are seen to be the Gospels of Christ
> which, with his godly mouth, he sows in the ears of the wise,
> ploughing their hearts and minds with the Holy Spirit.

GLOSSES   'field': i.e., the field is the bodies of the faithful. 'seeds': i.e., the seeds
are the teaching of the Gospel.

> Xristus illum sibi legit in terris uicarium,
> qui de gemino captiuos liberat seruitio,
> plerosque de seruitute quos redemit hominum,
> innumeros de zabuli obsoluit dominio.

> Christ has chosen him as his representative on earth,
> who frees captives from a twofold servitude:
> very many men has he redeemed from slavery,
> countless are they whom he has loosed from the Devil's dominion.

GLOSSES 'Christ': i.e., *Christos* is said in Greek, *Messiah* in Hebrew, *Unctus* ('Anointed') in Latin. 'representative' (*uicarius*): i.e., 'heir';[13] for Jerome says in his letter concerning the ranks of the Romans that the *uicarius* is the man who remains in the city after the *comes* ('count') has gone, until he comes together with the king. The king is God, the *comes* is Christ, the *uicarius* is Patrick.

> <Y>mnos cum Apocalipsi, psalmosque cantat Dei,
> quosque ad edificandum Dei tractat populum,
> quam legem in Trinitate sacri credit nominis,
> tribu[s]que personis unam docetque substantiam.

> He sings hymns and the Apocalypse, and the psalms of God,
> which he expounds to build up God's people.
> Belief in the Trinity of sacred name is a law to him,
> and he teaches one Substance with three Persons.

> <Z>ona Domini precinctus, diebus ac noctibus
> sine intermissione Deum orat Dominum,
> cuius ingentis laboris percepturus premium:
> cum apostolis regnabit sanctus super Israël.

> Girt with the belt of the Lord, by day and night
> he prays to the Lord God without ceasing.
> He will receive the reward of his vast labour
> when he will reign as a saint with the apostles over Israel.

GLOSSES 'with the belt': i.e., with chastity. 'without ceasing': Augustine says: 'If each day [one] worships at fixed times, then he prays without ceasing.' 'will reign': i.e., Patrick will reign over the Irish on the Day of Judgment; as it is said to the apostles, 'And you will sit on twelve thrones, judging the twelve tribes of Israel' (Matthew 19:28).

> Oratio:
> In memoria eterna erit iustus;
> ab auditione mala non timebit.

> Patricíi laudes semper <dicamus>,
> ut nos cum illo defendat Deus.

---

13 The Irish word here is *comarbae* 'successor'. It was used to designate the head of a church or monastery (who might be a bishop, abbot, or lay administrator), who was thought of as the 'heir' of its founding saint.

A prayer:
The just will be remembered forever,
he will have no fear of bad repute.[14]

We will utter Patrick's praises forever,
that together with him God may protect us.

ADDENDUM: Patrick's fast on Cruachán Aigli; from *Bethu Phátraic*[15]

Patrick went upon Cruachán Aigli on the first Saturday of Lent. The angel came
to speak with him, and said to him, 'God does not grant what you ask, for he
considers your requests to be burdensome, wilful, and overweening.' 'Is it thus that
he has determined?' said Patrick. 'It is,' said the angel. 'Then it is thus that I
determine,' said Patrick: 'I will not depart from this peak until I am dead, or until
all the requests are granted to me.'

Then Patrick remained upon the Cruachán, in ill spirits, without drinking or
eating, from the first Saturday of Lent until the Saturday before Easter, like Moses
son of Amram. For they were alike in many things: God spoke to them both out
of the fire, they both lived a hundred and twenty years, the burial places of both
of them are uncertain.

At the end of those forty nights and forty days the mountain was covered with
flocks of black birds, so that he could not distinguish heaven or earth. He recited
cursing psalms against them, but they did not go away. He became angry with
them: he rang his bell against them so that the men of Ireland heard its voice, and
threw it at them so that a piece broke off of it, so that it is called the *Bernán Brigte*
('Gapped One of Brigit'). Then Patrick wept until his face and the front of his
habit were wet. No demon came to the land of Ireland after that for seven years
and seven months and seven days and seven nights.[16] Then the angel came to
comfort Patrick, and cleaned his habit, and brought white flocks of birds to the
Cruachán which sang sweet songs to him.

'I will grant it to you,' said the angel, 'to fetch the same amount of souls from
torment as your eye can reach over the sea.' 'That does not seem much to me,'
said Patrick; 'my eye does not reach far over the sea.' 'Then you will have both sea
and land,' said the angel.

'Is there anything else granted to me besides that?' said Patrick. 'There is,' said
the angel: 'to bring seven men out of the torments of hell every Saturday forever.'
'If something is to be given me,' said Patrick, 'twelve men would be more.' 'You
will have that,' said the angel, 'and now leave the Cruachán.' 'I will not,' said
Patrick, 'since I have been injured, until I am appeased.'

14 Psalm 112:7. The psalm from which this verse is taken is itself an abecedarian one.
15 Mulchrone 1939, 71–5.   16 This encounter with the black birds seems to be the forerunner
of the famous legend of Patrick's expelling all snakes from Ireland; the latter is not attested until
a considerably later date (Breatnach 1978, 60–1).

'Is anything else granted to me?' said Patrick. 'There is,' said the angel: 'seven men delivered to you from torment every Thursday, and twelve every Saturday; and now leave the Cruachán.' 'I will not,' said Patrick, 'since I have been injured, until I am appeased.'

'Is anything else granted to me?' said Patrick. 'There is,' said the angel: 'a great sea will come over Ireland seven years before the Judgment; and now leave the Cruachán.' 'I will not,' said Patrick, 'since I have been injured, until I am appeased.'

'Is there anything else that you ask?' said the angel. 'There is,' said Patrick: 'that the Saxons not settle in Ireland, peacefully or by force, for as long as I am in heaven.' 'You will have that,' said the angel, 'and now leave the Cruachán.' 'I will not,' said Patrick, 'since I have been injured, until I am appeased.'

'Is there anything else granted to me?' said Patrick. 'There is,' said the angel: 'whoever recites your hymn at each of the offices will not have punishment or torment.' 'The hymn is long and difficult,' said Patrick. 'Whoever recites it,' said the angel, 'from "Christ has chosen him" until the end, and whoever gives anything in your name, and whoever does penance in Ireland, his soul will not go to hell; and now leave the Cruachán.' 'I will not,' said Patrick, 'since I have been injured, until I am appeased.'

'Is there anything else?' said Patrick. 'There is,' said the angel: 'on the Day of Judgment you will fetch a man out of torment for every hair in your habit.' 'Which of all the saints who labour for God,' said Patrick, 'would not bring that many to heaven? I will not accept that,' said Patrick. 'What will you accept?' said the angel. 'Not difficult,' said Patrick: 'to fetch seven men out of hell for every hair in my habit on the Day of Judgment.' 'You will have that,' said the angel, 'and now leave the Cruachán.' 'I will not,' said Patrick, 'since I have been injured, until I am appeased.'

'Is there anything else that you ask?' said the angel. 'There is,' said Patrick: 'on the day when the twelve thrones are on Mount Zion, and the four streams of fire are around the mountain, and the three households are there, the household of heaven and the household of earth and the household of hell, that it will be I myself who am judge of the men of Ireland on that day.' 'Perhaps the Lord will not agree to that,' said the angel. 'If not, then I will not agree to leave the Cruachán from now until the Day of Judgment; and if I should, I shall leave one to watch over it.'

The angel went to heaven, and Patrick went to offer mass. The angel returned at the hour of none. 'What news?' said Patrick. 'It is thus,' said the angel: 'all creation, visible and invisible, has joined the twelve apostles in petitioning [on your behalf], and they have succeeded. The Lord has said that since the apostles there has not come, and will not come, a man more wonderful, were it not for your unyieldingness. What you have requested, you will have. Ring your bell,' said the angel: 'a *glés*[17] will fall on you from heaven until it reaches your knees, and it will sanctify all the people of Ireland, both the living and the dead.' 'A blessing upon the generous King who has granted it,' said Patrick; 'I will leave the peak.'

17 Cf. p. 100 above.

'Broccán's Hymn' to Saint Brigit

Together with Patrick and Colum Cille, Brigit ranks as one of the three principal saints of Ireland. There are indications that she was originally a goddess, whose cult adapted itself to the coming of Christianity: a divinity of the same name, 'whom the poets used to worship,' figures in the early literature; and a sacred fire, watched over by a company of nuns in a manner recalling the worship of the Roman goddess Vesta, was still being maintained at her monastery of Kildare late in the twelfth century.[1] This ancient background has, however, left few if any clear traces in the legends concerning the saint herself.

Lives of Brigit have survived from many periods: we have some early Latin lives, among them that written by Cogitosus in the mid-seventh century; a life partly in Latin and partly in Old Irish, written apparently in the ninth century; and further accounts from a considerably later period. The Old Irish hymn translated below, ascribed to an early cleric named Broccán the Crooked, gives us a sort of cross-section of this extended tradition. It is based on a collection of Brigit's miracles closely resembling that used by Cogitosus; it was itself composed at some point in the Old Irish period, although scholars are disagreed as to whether it should be placed at its beginning or its end; and one of the two manuscripts in which it survives, written early in the twelfth century, provides fuller descriptions of the miracles in a commentary added in the margins.[2]

I have translated this commentary as a supplement to the hymn itself. In many cases the commentator clearly has independent knowledge of the anecdote to which the hymnodist alludes; in others he has not, and his guesswork produces a new legend. A striking example of the latter state of affairs is the story of Brigit's attempts to obtain a monastic office from Rome: here the commentator, baffled by the rare word *plea* 'region', has modified an episode in one of the early Latin lives to create the strange story of an underwater monastery.

A few features of the hymn call for special comment. In the opening quatrains it may seem rather grudging praise to assert merely that Brigit was not heretical, avaricious, quarrelsome, or the like; in fact the poet is making the specific claim that the misogynistic stereotypes found elsewhere in the early literature do not apply where Brigit is concerned. Thus the 'wisdom text' *The Instructions of Cormac* calls women 'greedy' (*santach*), 'slanderous' (*écndach*), 'stingy' (*céssachtach*), and 'mischievous' (*elc*), and compares them to serpents (*nathraig*) – all terms found in the hymn's third and fourth quatrains.[3]

1 Brief discussions of the goddess Brigit in Byrne 1973, 155–6; Mac Cana 1985, 32–4. The account of the fire at Kildare is found in the writings of Gerald of Wales (O'Meara 1951, 81–2). 2 References to the various lives of Brigit, and to the scholarship devoted to them, are given in the 'Textual Remarks' at the end of this book.   3 Meyer 1909, 28–35, lines 7, 11, 34, 52, 64, 103, 119.

The great reverence felt for Brigit by the Irish led to her being frequently likened to the Virgin Mary: one early poem already calls her 'a second Mary',[4] and later tradition anachronistically claimed that she was the midwife at the birth of the Saviour.[5] Our hymn goes a step further, stating repeatedly that Brigit is Christ's mother – a daring formulation of which it would be fascinating to know the background.

The miracles listed are for the most part of a rather humble nature, great emphasis being placed on Brigit's ability to provide enormous quantities of food; it is noteworthy too that on many occasions she uses her powers to rescue the poor and weak from the anger of their masters. Despite her divine origins, the lives portray Brigit as the daughter of a slave-woman – it is only fitting, then, that she should be so concerned with the fruits of the earth, and with the welfare of those who toiled upon it.

4 'She will be called the truly godly Brigit, because of her great miracles; she will be a second Mary, mother of the great Lord' (O'Brien 1976, 80). Unfortunately, this prophetic poem has not yet been translated. Compare the hymn *Brigit bé bithmaith* (cf. note 6 below), where the saint is called 'the branch with flowers, the mother of Jesus' (Stokes and Strachan 1901–3, 2.325).
5 Many allusions to this belief are scattered through the materials collected in Scotland by Alexander Carmichael; see especially Carmichael 1900–71, 3.155–63.

The place of this hymn's composition is Sliab Bladma, or Cluain Mór Maedóic. Its author is Broccán the Crooked. The time of its composition is the reign of Lugaid son of Loegaire as king of Ireland, and that of Ailill son of Dúnlaing as king of Leinster. This is why it was composed: [Broccán's] teacher, Ultán of Ard mBreccáin, asked him to put Brigit's miracles concisely into poetic form. For Ultán had collected all of Brigit's miracles.[6]

> Ní car Brigit buadach bith:
> siasair suide éoin i n-ailt.
> Contuil cotlud cimmeda
> ind noeb ar écnairc a mMaic.

Victorious Brigit did not love the world:
she perched in it like a bird on a cliff.
The saint slept like a prisoner,
longing for her Son.

Not much fault was found with her
with regard to lofty faith in the Trinity.
Brigit, mother of my Over-King,
was born as the best in the kingdom of heaven.

She was not slanderous (?),[7] she was not mischievous,
she was not a lover of vehement women's quarrels,
she was not a stinging speckled snake,
she did not sell God's Son for gain.

She was not greedy for treasures:
she gave without resentment, without stint.
She was not hard or stingy,
she did not love to enjoy the world's goods.

---

6 Ultán moccu Conchobuir of Ard mBreccáin (died 657 or 663) is known to have collected a body of material relating to Saint Patrick; he is also one of the authors to whom *Brigit bé bithmaith* is traditionally ascribed (Stokes and Strachan 1901–3, 2.323–6).   7 Reading *écndach* for *écnairc*.

She was not harsh toward guests;
she was kind to the unfortunate in their sickness.
She built an enclosure in the plain:
may it keep us, in our multitudes, safe for the Kingdom!

She did not tend her herds in the uplands,
but did her works in the midst of a plain.
She was a marvellous ladder whereby the tribes
could reach the kingdom of the Son of Mary.

Wondrous was Brigit's company,
wondrous the region to which she ascended.
She can meet with Christ alone,
something which is usual for assemblies.

COMMENTARY   'Wondrous the region' (*Amra plea*): That is, Placentia, a community belonging to Brigit in Italy;[8] or Plea, a community belonging to Brigit upon the Sea of Wight – and it is its office which Brigit's community celebrates. This is how it happened. Brigit sent seven men to Rome to learn the office of Peter and Paul, for God did not permit her to go there in person. When they came back to Brigit, they had not retained a single word of the office. 'The Son of the Virgin knows,' said Brigit, 'that your profit is not great, though your labour has been great.'[9] Then she sent another seven men, and the same thing happened to them as to the first seven; then she sent seven more, and her blind lad along with them, for he could memorise instantly whatever he heard. When they came to the Sea of Wight, a storm came upon them so that they let down their anchor. It caught on the tower of the chapel, and they cast lots to see who should go down. It fell to the blind lad to do so: he left [the ship] and freed the anchor, and then stayed there for a year learning the office, until the rest of the company returned from the east. Another great storm came upon them in the same place, and they let down their anchor again, so that the blind lad came up to them from below, bringing with him the office for singing the hours which was observed in that church. And he brought them a bell; and that is the 'Blind Lad's Bell' which Brigit's community possesses today, and the office which they observe is the office which the blind lad fetched from Plea.

8 There was in fact a church dedicated to Brigit in Placentia (modern Piacenza), ceded to the monastery of Bobbio in the ninth century (Gougaud 1932, 180). A legend accounting for Brigit's connection with this place appears in the introduction to the hymn *Brigit bé bithmaith* (Stokes and Strachan 1901–3, 2.323–4). For an earlier version of the present anecdote see the *Vita Prima Sanctae Brigitae*, cap. 91 (Colgan 1647, 539).   9 Brigit's words are echoed in a celebrated quatrain preserved in a manuscript of Paul's epistles: *Techt do Róim:/ mór saítho, becc torbai./ In Rí chondaigi i foss,/ maní mbera latt, ní fogbai.* 'Going to Rome: great the trouble, small the gain. The King whom you seek here you will not find, unless you bring him with you' (Stokes and Strachan 1901–3, 2.296).

Blessed the hour in which Mac Caille placed
a veil over the head of Saint Brigit:
in all her deeds it was manifest
that her prayers were heard in heaven:

'God to whom I pray for help in every trouble,
in every way of which my lips are capable:
deeper than seas, greater than reckoning,
Three, One, more wondrous than can be told.'

COMMENTARY   'Blessed the hour': That is, when Brigit wished to be consecrated as a penitent, she went with seven nuns to Cruachán Brí Éle in the territory
of the Uí Fhailgi, for she had heard that Bishop Mel was there. But when they
arrived they did not find the bishop, for he had gone into the territory of the Uí
Néill to the north. Next day she went, with Mac Caille as her guide, northward
across the bog of Faichnech, and God brought it about that the bog was a plain of
lovely flowers.

When they drew near to the place in which Bishop Mel was, Brigit told Mac
Caille that he should put a veil on her head, for she would not go to the clerics with
her head unveiled: that is the veil which is commemorated [in this verse]. When
she had come into the house in which Bishop Mel was, a fiery pillar blazed up
from her head as high as the rooftree of the church. Bishop Mel saw that and said,
'Who are these nuns?' Mac Caille answered, 'This is the famous nun from Leinster,
that is, Brigit.' 'She is welcome,' said Bishop Mel; 'it is I who foretold [what she
would be] when she was in her mother's womb.'

(For once when Bishop Mel had gone to the house of Dubthach, he saw that his
wife was sad. 'What ails the good woman?' he had asked. 'I have reason,' she had
said: 'the slave-woman who is washing your feet is dearer to Dubthach than I am.'
'That is fitting,' Bishop Mel had said, 'for your offspring will serve the offspring
of the slave.')

'Why have the nuns come hither?' asked Bishop Mel. 'To be consecrated as
penitents,' said Mac Caille. 'I will do that,' said Bishop Mel. Then orders were
conferred upon her; and Bishop Mel consecrated Brigit as a bishop, though she
had only wished to be consecrated as a penitent. And it is then that Mac Caille
placed a veil on Brigit's head, as the learned maintain. This is why, ever since,
Brigit's successor is entitled to the rank and dignity of a bishop. While that rank
was being conferred upon her, she stood holding the pedestal which supported the
altar; and the church in which that pedestal was was destroyed by fire seven times,
but [the pedestal] was never burnt.

Others say that the church in which Brigit was consecrated was in the territory
of the Fir Thulach, or in Bishop Mel's church of Ard nAchaid. After their conse-
cration, Bishop Mel preached the eight beatitudes of the Gospel to the eight nuns,

and each of them chose a beatitude; Brigit chose the beatitude of charity. Then she said that she would never eat food unless she heard preaching beforehand; and Nad Fraích, a man of the Fir Thuirbe, was her lector from that time forth.

> His enclosure pleased the sage, famous Coemgen,
> whom the wind conveyed [thither] through a storm of snow,
> to Glendalough, where crosses were endured
> until peace came to him after suffering.[10]

COMMENTARY 'the sage': i.e., the elder.... Coemgen was standing for seven years in Glendalough with nothing but a board beneath him, and without sleep all that time, as they say. And he was performing a cross-vigil,[11] as they say, so that birds made their nests in his hands. 'the wind conveyed': i.e., the wind of snow conveyed him through a storm so that he arrived (?).

> Saint Brigit was not somnolent;
> she was not cool in her love for God.
> The saint neither purchased nor pursued
> the wealth of this world.

> All the miracles that the King
> has performed for Saint Brigit:
> if they were done for anyone [else],
> where does the person live who has heard of it?

> When the first yield of milk was sent
> with the first butter in a basket,
> it did not hinder her generosity to her guests –
> their devotion to her was not lessened.

COMMENTARY 'The first yield of milk': Once an angel came to Brigit, and sent her to release her mother, who was [in service] to a druid, Mac Midrui. His mother was from Connacht, and his father was one of the men of Munster; at that time he resided in Mag Fenamna, in ... Cliach.[12] When Brigit arrived her mother

---

10 This quatrain, which has nothing to do with Brigit, was evidently inserted in the poem at some point after its composition. The scribe of the other copy of the hymn tries to explain its presence by saying that Brigit and Coemgen were alike in their practise of rigorous vigils.   11 A form of austerity frequently mentioned in Irish sources: it involved standing for extended periods with the arms extended straight out from the body on either side.   12 Here, as elsewhere in the Franciscan manuscript, bits of the commentary are lost due to the effects of time or mutilation by the binder. All such gaps are marked with dots in the translation, unless the context or another version of the story gives a good idea of what may have been lost; in such cases the supplementary phrases are enclosed in angle brackets.

was in the cow-yard, suffering from a disease of the eye. She went to her mother, accompanied by the druid's charioteer, and began to dispense food[13] in her stead, and freely distributed what was there as alms.

The druid heard of this. The charioteer came to the house. 'How are things in the cow-yard?' asked the druid. 'I am satisfied, for one,' said the charioteer, 'and the calves are fat, and the guests are content.' It displeased the druid and his wife that Brigit was dispensing alms. They came bringing a big basket, hoping to get the upper hand of Brigit and to enslave her if she could not provide plenty of butter. She had only as much as came from one and a half [churnings]. Then she recited this quatrain:

> My larder
> is the larder of the white Lord:
> a larder which my King has blessed,
> a larder with something in it.

And she said moreover:

> May my friend the Son of Mary come
> to bless my larder.
> He who is Lord as far as the ends of the earth:
> may he bring abundance.

And a third time she said:

> O my Over-King,
> who can do all things,
> bless, O God – a cry without prohibition –
> this larder with your right hand.

She divided what she had churned ... according to the number of the Trinity, then fetched half a churning's worth from the larder. 'A fine load for a big basket!' said the druid's wife. 'Fill your basket,' said Brigit, 'and God will add something to it'.... [14]

> After that, her portion of bacon:
> one evening – it was a lofty triumph –
> although the dog had had his fill of it,
> the guest was not sorrowful.

---

13 *Cuicnecht* evidently derives from *cucann* 'kitchen'; but Brigit is in a cow-yard or byre. Another version of the story says that Brigit took over the 'churning' (*maistred*), and gave away the butter (Stokes 1890, 38); this makes better sense in context.   14 Here the remaining text is lost; other versions of the story however describe how Brigit miraculously filled the basket, leading the druid to present her with the cattle and set her mother free (Stokes 1890, 187, 320).

On the day that she reaped, the reaping was good:
no fault was found with my faithful one.
It was always dry in her field
[although] it was raining throughout the world.

COMMENTARY 'On the day': This miracle was performed in Tír na mBennacht ('land of the blessings'), in the meadows of the Boyne beside Clonard; or else at Domnach Mór beside Kildare: rain in every other place, and dryness in the field of Brigit.

Bishops came to her:
it was no small risk that she ran,
had she not been able – for the King helped her –
to milk the cows three times.

COMMENTARY 'Bishops': That is, seven bishops came from Uí Briúin Chualann – more specifically, from Tulach na nEpscop – to visit Brigit in Kildare. Brigit asked Bláthnat her cook if she had any food. 'No,' she said. Brigit felt great shame at not having any food for them; but the angel told Bláthnat to bring the cows north of Kildare to Loch Lemnachta ('lake of milk') to be milked, even though they had been milked twice before. The cows were brought there, and were milked until the milk overflowed the pails. And if all the men of Leinster had fetched their pails to them they would have filled them – whence the lake took its name.

On a rainy day she herded
sheep in the middle of a plain.
Afterward she hung her cloak
in the house, on a beam of the sun.

COMMENTARY 'She herded': Brendan was at sea for four years, seeking the Land of Promise; throughout that time a monster was following him, [swimming] behind the boat. Once another monster came to kill it, and the [first] monster prayed for protection against the other one to Brendan and to all the saints of Ireland; and it was not protected until it invoked Brigit. Then Brendan said that he would not stay any longer upon the sea, until he had learned for what reason Brigit rather than anyone else could perform that miracle. Brendan set out to visit Brigit, and this was revealed to her. At that time Brigit was tending sheep in Cuirrech Life; she came and met Brendan at Domnach Mór to the west of Kildare, and they greeted each other.

At Lecc Brénainn ('Brendan's stone') next day, when it grew hot, Brigit hung her wet cloak upon the sunbeams; and it remained upon them. Brendan told his servant to hang his own cloak upon them, and it fell from them twice; the third time Brendan grew angry, and hung it upon them himself, and then it remained there.

Brigit asked her cook how much food she had. She told her that she had only an eighth of [a measure of] barley. It was taken twice to the mill of Ráith Chathaír, east of Kildare, and it could not be ground; for Ailill son of Dúnlaing, king of Leinster, was in Ráith Chathaír at that time. Brigit's messenger went a third time, and was thrown into the mill-race together with his sack. It is then that Brigit declared of Ráith Chathaír that there would be no fire nor smoke nor people therein forever; and the whole mill sank beneath the earth. Then the messenger drew the sack forth from the pool ... and the other half of malt.[15] From that a feast was made for Brendan and for Brigit and for her community, and they spent thirty days consuming it together, and each of them heard the other's confession.

First of all Brendan said that since he had entered the religious life he had never walked further than seven furrows without thinking of God. 'That is good,' said Brigit; 'thanks be to God!' Brigit however said that, [having once set] her mind upon God, she had never let it stray from him. Brendan marvelled at that. 'It is only right, then,' said Brendan, 'that you should excel us in every way.' Then he told her what he had heard from the monsters in the sea, and what they had done thereafter.

> The fierce lad who prayed
> to Brigit in the name of her King:
> he took seven wethers from her,
> [but] that number did not lessen her flock.

COMMENTARY   'The fierce lad': This miracle was performed at Ráith Derthaige in the territory of the Uí Fhailgi. A robber came to Brigit seven times, and each time got from her a wether from the flock of Dubthach's wife. When Brigit was reproached for this, she said, 'Look to your sheep, to see whether they are all still there.' Then Dubthach and his wife looked, and found that they were all there without any missing.

> If I relate the good things which she did,
> [I do so] from my own knowledge.
> One of her wonders was the bath [in which she was]:
> she blessed it around her, [and] it became red ale.

COMMENTARY   'One of her wonders': i.e., a good thing. This miracle was performed in Kildare. A poor man was obliged to provide the king of Leinster with ale, and could not do so until he came to Brigit. When he arrived Brigit was

15 No gap appears in the manuscript at this point, but some words have evidently been omitted in the course of the text's transmission.

bathing; when the poor man asked her to help him Brigit made the sign of the Cross over the bath in which she was, and transformed it into ale. It was given to the man after that, and he gave it to the king.

> She blessed the nun suffering from dropsy:
> she was healed, without poison or disease.
> Greater than any other marvel
> was her making salt from a stone.

COMMENTARY   'Without poison or disease': That is, there was a nun suffering from dropsy in Cluain Moescna. Brigit happened to come to the church, and [the nun] came up to Brigit afterwards; and then she was cleansed.

   'Salt': That is, this miracle was performed in Cuirrech Life. A man passed Brigit carrying salt on his back. 'What are you carrying?' said Brigit. 'Stones,' said he. 'That will it be,' said Brigit; and that was fulfilled. He stopped, and came past Brigit a second time. She said to him, 'What is on your back?' 'Salt,' said he. 'That will it be,' said Brigit; and that came true.

> I cannot count, I do not enumerate
> what the holy being has performed:
> she blessed the faceless man[16]
> so that his two eyes appeared.

COMMENTARY   'She blessed the faceless man': This miracle was performed in Cluain Chorcaige in the territory of the Uí Fhailgi. A leper was brought to Brigit, whom she told to pluck a clump of rushes which was beside him from the place in which it was. He plucked it forth then, and a spring of water came from that place: she sprinkled it upon his face so that he was healed.

> A dumb girl was brought
> to Brigit, her miracle was unique:
> her hand did not go from [the girl's] hand
> until she could converse clearly.

COMMENTARY   'A dumb girl': This miracle was performed in <Clonard>.[17] A dumb girl was brought to Brigit; Brigit took the girl's hand in her own, and did not release the girl's hand from her hand until she could speak plainly.

---

16 Cf. p. 148, note 4 above.   17 The manuscript has only *Cluain I* ... , and no other version of the story supplies a place-name; the mention of Clonard or *Cluain Iraird* in the account of the miraculously averted rainfall above, however, suggests that the same locale may be intended here.

A wonder was the bacon which she blessed:
the power of God was its security.
It was with the dog for a full month,
and the dog did not injure it.

COMMENTARY 'A wonder': A flitch of bacon was offered to her. This happened
in Cell Fhinnenn in Fine Gall, and her followers forgot to take it with them to
Kildare; so it was there for a month, with a dog guarding it. And it did not allow
any other animal to sully it. And it did not <meddle with it; but it guarded it> as
if it had [already] eaten its fill.

It was greater than any other wonder
when she requested a morsel from the company.
The colour of her veil was not ruined:
[when still] hot it was hurled into her bosom.

COMMENTARY 'From the company': That is, a poor man asked Brigit for a
morsel of the food which was in the pot; and the food therein was not [yet] cooked
at all, until he asked her followers <to give him something. One of them> threw
the morsel at the man in anger, and it struck Brigit's bosom, and did not spoil her
clothing.

Well did it befall (?)
the leper who made a request of her:
she blessed the best of the calves;
the best of the cows loved it.

COMMENTARY 'The leper': Perhaps it was Patrick's leper who came to Brigit
to ask for a cow; and he would only take the best cow in Brigit's cow-yard, and the
best calf, whether or not it was her own calf. So Brigit blessed the best calf in the
byre, and the cow loved it; and <she gave it> to the leper after that.

Then she drove her chariot
northward to Brí Cobthaig Choíl:
the calf and the leper were in the chariot,
with the cow following the calf.[18]

The oxen with which they set out (?)[19] –
it was well that someone should drive them back.

18 Nothing coherent can be reconstructed from the remaining fragments of the commentary on this
quatrain. 19 A conjectural rendering of the verb *do-ascnai*, which generally means 'approaches'.

The river rose against them:
in the morning they came home.

COMMENTARY   'The oxen': That is, a friend came to Brigit at Árad Mór (?) in
Cuirrech Life, and desired Brigit to promise [that she would spend] the night at
his house. While she was gone her plough-team was stolen, and fetched as far as
the river Liffey. The river rose against them, so that the thieves put their clothes
on the horns of the oxen as they were crossing. The oxen parted from them and
came back to Kildare to Brigit, bringing the thieves' garments with them.

Her horse cast off the end of its harness
as they raced downhill.
The yoke was not lopsided:
God's Son reached forth his kingly hand.

COMMENTARY   'Cast off': This happened at … between Forrach Pátraic and
Cell Chuilinn. Brigit and Nad Fraích were in a single chariot <going> northward
from Kildare. Nad Fraích was preaching God's word to them then, and let go of
the horses; one of the horses <freed> its neck from [the harness of] the chariot, so
that it was eating grass … Ailill son of Dúnlaing, the king of Leinster, saw that
<as he was going?> to Maistiu … , and set his own neck under the yoke. Brigit
said to him, 'Because of the humility which you have shown, the kingship of
Leinster will belong to you and to your descendants forever.'

A wild boar visited her herd;
the beast[20] drove them northward.
Brigit blessed it with her crozier;
[thereafter] it took up its abode with her swine.

COMMENTARY   'A wild boar visited': That is, there was a wild boar in a certain
wood north of Kildare, which would not allow other pigs to approach it. Brigit
blessed the forest with her crozier at Ros na Ferta in Kildare, north of the bell-
tower, so that it was tame (?) toward them after that; it was their leader always.

A tribute of fat pigs was granted to her:
across Mag Fea – it was a wonder –
wolves drove them to her
so that they came to Uachtar Gabra.

---

20 *Os* generally means 'ox' or 'stag', but here seems to be used in a more general sense.

COMMENTARY 'A tribute of fat pigs': That is, the king of Fothairt Tíre, a land in the south of the territory of the Uí Chennselaig, used to offer a fat pig to Brigit every year. A messenger came from the king of the Uí Chennselaig to ask for it.... The king of Fothairt said that he would not give it to him, nor would he give it to Brigit for fear of offending him; but he would let it go, and wherever God should send it, <there it would belong. Wolves drove it> across Mag Fea to Uachtar Gabra, the place where Brigit was.

> She gave away the wild fox
> for the sake of her wretched tenant;
> it escaped into the forest
> although the hosts pursued.

COMMENTARY 'She gave away': That is, <one of Brigit's tenants killed> the fox of the queen at Maistiu in the territory of the Uí Muiredaig, and he was to be put to death for it. Brigit happened to be at Maistiu then, and she said that <finding its replacement would be> better than killing [the man], provided that it could do the tricks which the other fox used to do. Then Brigit blessed the forest, and struck a wooden clapper, so that a fox came forth which could do the same tricks; and Brigit gave it ... to redeem the unfortunate man. When he had been released, the fox went [back] into the forest; and nothing could be done [to stop it] even if all the dogs of Leinster had gone in pursuit.

> It was clear in [all] her deeds
> that she alone was the mother of the Son of the Great King:
> she blessed the fluttering bird
> so that she held it in her hand.

COMMENTARY 'The fluttering bird': A certain man offered a silver chain to Brigit. She gave it to the little girls who accompanied her, for they were displeased that nothing was given to them. Then a leper came and asked her for something, and she gave him the chain without their knowing; and they wept when they found out. Then she said to them, 'What do you want in exchange for it?' 'We would like that little bird over there,' they said, 'for it is pretty.' Brigit blessed the bird, so that it was tame in everyone's hand. And so the name of the place in which that miracle was performed has been Tír ind Éoin ('land of the bird') ever since.

> She blessed nine brigands;
> they reddened their circlets[21] in a pool of blood.
> [As for] the man whom they attacked,
> no injury from wounding was found in him.

21 An allusion to an apparently pagan practice, attested in various saints' lives: outlaws swore to

COMMENTARY 'She blessed': Nine brothers from Leinster wished to go to ... in Leth Cuinn, for he had killed their father (?).[22] They came to Brigit to have their weapons blessed; at that time she was in Ros na Ferta in Kildare. Brigit blessed their weapons. When their weapons had been blessed they went northward, and came upon the man who had killed their father. They killed him, or so they thought, but they did not draw a single drop of blood from him. They were satisfied then; but through Brigit's grace the man had escaped.

> No one could correctly count
> all the miracles which she performed.
> A wonder: she took away Lugaid's meal,
> [but] the strong man's might did not diminish.

COMMENTARY 'The strong man's might': That is, three strong men were digging the ditch of the stronghold of Ailenn, one of the three principal strongholds of the king of Leinster; their names were Muired and Fiacc and Lugaid. Each of them used to eat enough for a hundred men. Lugaid's feeding was entrusted to the churches, and the other two were the responsibility of the laity. Then Lugaid asked Brigit to reduce his appetite without lessening his strength. Brigit did that for him, and blessed his mouth so that his appetite was no greater than anyone else's. Then he went and lifted from the ditch a stone which a hundred men had failed to lift the day before, [and placed it] on top of Ailenn.

> On another occasion, eagerly proclaimed,
> Brigit's Son brought
> a tree trunk which the host could not lift
> to her, to the place where it has been heard that it is.

COMMENTARY 'A tree trunk': A tree fell across the road in Fid Gabla, so that it was <an obstacle> to people; and the Uí Fhailgi could not lift it. Once it happened that Brigit came that way, and the Uí Fhailgi asked her to lift it from the place where it was. Then through the might of the Son of God she lifted it, so that from then on it has not been in the same place.

> The silver treasure, which could not be concealed:
> out of spite toward the champion's woman
> it was cast into the sea, as far as it could be thrown,
> but was found inside a salmon.

---

perform specific acts of violence, and wore some kind of ritual headgear until their oaths were discharged (Sharpe 1979, 82–5). **22** A conjectural emendation, suggested by context: I take the manuscript's *ar is eat romarb he* 'for it is they who had killed him' to be a corrupt abridgement of *ar is é a n-athair ro marb-side*.

COMMENTARY 'The silver treasure': The king of Leinster gave his poet a silver brooch as payment for his poetry; he took it home, and gave it to his slave-woman to keep. The poet's wife took it from her and <threw> it into the sea out of spite toward the slave.... When the poet asked his slave for the brooch <she could not produce it>; and the poet was going to kill the slave, because she no longer had the brooch. Brigit happened to come to the poet's house then, and she was grieved at the injustice committed against the slave. Then Brigit prayed to God that the brooch might be revealed to her. An angel of God came to her, and told her to cast nets into the water, that is, into the sea; and a salmon would be caught in them, and the brooch would be inside it. And that was done, and the slave was freed from her difficulty.

> A wonder of hers: the widow
> who offered her hospitality in Mag Coel.
> She burned her new weaving-beam
> in the fire when she cooked the calf.

> It was a wonder greater than any other
> which the saint performed (?):
> in the morning the beam was whole
> and the calf being suckled by its mother.

COMMENTARY 'A wonder of hers': Once Brigit came to the stronghold of the king of Brega in Mag Coel, which is in Fine Gall today. The queen turned her away; but a certain widow who lived beside the stronghold made her welcome, and killed <her calf> for her, and burned her new weaving-beam under it. And both calf and beam were whole again next morning, through Brigit's grace. When the king heard that Brigit had come, <he went> to speak with her, and came upon the widow. When the king saw her, Brigit's grace caused him to love her, and he took her as his wife; and it is said that from her descend the <Uí> Cherbaill.

> The silver treasure which the craftsman
> did not break – this was one of her wonders –
> Brigit struck it against her palm
> so that it broke into three pieces.

> The craftsman put it in the scales,
> whereupon a wonder was discovered:
> it was not found that any of the thirds
> was greater than another, even by a scruple.

COMMENTARY 'The silver treasure': That is, their father bequeathed a silver ingot to three brothers, and the craftsmen of Ireland were unable to divide it into three equal portions for them, until Brigit broke it with her palm. This miracle was performed in Kildare.

> No one can approach
> the multitude of miracles which she performed.
> She blessed a garment for Conlaed
> when it was brought to Letha.[23]

> When she was in peril
> her Son did not play her false:
> he put a garment in the basket
> of Rónchenn, in a two-wheeled chariot.

COMMENTARY 'She blessed': That is, Conlaed, Brigit's artisan, tried to go to Rome twice <in disobedience to Brigit's command>. He tried a third time <but was hindered>, for Brigit gave his cowl to a certain leper while she was watching the forge – for at her command he had gone to ring the bell, because the bell-ringer was not there. So he asked Brigit for a garment to wear to Rome, and she had no garment to give him. So she asked Rónchenn, a subdeacon who always looked after her clothes, whether she did not have a garment. 'You will,' said he, 'if you pray to God.' Then a garment was found in a basket which Rónchenn had in a two-wheeled chariot. Or else *rónchenn* is not a person's name, but it was a garment resembling the skin of a seal's head (*cenn róin*) which was found there. That garment was given to Conlaed, and thereafter he set out on his journey to Rome. Brigit said to him, 'You will neither reach there nor return.' That was true, for wolves ate him at Sciaich.

> The quantity of mead which was given to her –
> it was no difficulty, whoever gave it –
> was not found at all
> until it was found beside [her] house.

> She gave it for the sake of her tenant
> when he had need of it:
> there was no excess therein,
> nor a drop missing.

COMMENTARY 'The quantity': That is, the king of Leinster was entitled to ale from the king of the Uí Chúlduib, who was [in turn] entitled to it from one of his

23 A name used in early Irish for the European continent as a whole, or for certain specific parts of it; here it designates 'Latium' or Italy.

followers. [The latter] came to Brigit to ask for her help; for he had nothing to give, having given the ale to Brigit since the king of the Uí Chúlduib had not taken it from him. In this difficulty he came to Brigit. Then water was poured into the vats which were beside Brigit's house, and Brigit blessed the water so that it became mead; and after that the poor fellow took it away with him. And there was no mead better than that, and it was no more nor less than what the poor fellow owed.

May Brigit's prayers be with us;
may she help us against danger.
May they aid the sick who belong to her
before they go to meet the Holy Spirit.

May she aid us with a sword of fire
in battle against the black swarms [of devils];
may her holy prayers protect us
in the realm of heaven, beyond torments.

Before we go with the angels to battle,
may our flight bring us to the church.
Remembering the Lord is better than every poem:
victorious Brigit did not love the world.[24]

I invoke the patronage of Saint Brigit,
with the saints of Kildare.
May they stand between me and punishment;
let my soul not depart in vain!

The nun who used to ride across the Cuirrech
was a shield against sharp blades.
She found no match save Mary;
I invoke my Bríg.

I invoke my Bríg:
may she be a protection to our company.
May her patronage assist me;
may we all deserve deliverance.

---

24 This repetition of the poem's first line is an example of the Irish practice of marking a poem's 'closure' (*dúnad*) with some echo of its beginning. The six quatrains which follow may or may not be the work of the same author; in any case, they can be taken as a poem in their own right.

The praise of Christ is illustrious speech,
the worship of God's Son is an art full of virtue.
May everyone who has sung it or heard it
belong to God's kingdom without rejection.

May Brigit's blessing be upon
everyone who has sung it or heard it;
may the blessing of Brigit and God
be upon all of us together.

There are two nuns in heaven –
I do not fear that they will forget me.
Mary and Saint Brigit:
may we be under the safeguard of them both.

Selections from *Féilire Oengusso*

The *Féilire Oengusso* ('Martyrology of Oengus') is the most celebrated of the calendars of saints' days produced in medieval Ireland. It is written as an extended poem, with one stanza for every day of the year, supplemented by long sections at the beginning and end which deal more generally with the powers and merits of the saints, and with the nature of the *Féilire* itself.

The author, Oengus mac Oengobann, was keenly aware of the innovation which he had made in composing the *Féilire* as a poem, and he takes pains to explain its structure to his audience. He explains too that the limits which this structure imposes make it impossible to list more than a very few of the many saints to whom each day is dedicated, insisting however on the exactitude of his information, and the thoroughness of the research on which the work is based.

Why was the *Féilire* written? One of Oengus's principal aims was to provide a calendar of feasts which could be retained in the memory, and hence be generally available in a time when manuscripts, and indeed literacy, were scarce: 'It is profitable to the untaught, for whom it is a breastplate of piety; every generation recites it to make the feast-days known.' It is hard to guess now how much of the poem it would have been possible for any individual to learn by rote; but the fact that the last word in each stanza alliterates with the first word in the next, helping to keep all of them in the correct sequence, indicates that their memorisation was at least an ideal.

But other concerns were at least as important: besides providing information regarding the feasts of the saints, the *Féilire* was intended to establish a close relationship between whoever recited it and the saints themselves. In the epilogue, Oengus speaks at considerable length of the many benefits to be obtained by chanting his poem: it heals diseases and protects against dangers, wards off demons and summons angels, has the same spiritual merit as the celebration of seven masses or the recitation of the entire Psalter, and grants admission to heaven. Indeed, whoever recites the *Féilire* will become like one of the saints himself: his body will not decay after death, and the dew on his grave will cure the sick. In composing this work in their honour, Oengus himself entered into communion with the saints he celebrates: after he had gathered together everything which he could find in books, they came as a 'synod' to correct and inspire him, each contributing his or her own stanza.

As a versified calendar, the *Féilire* is a poem about time; and the relationship between time and poetry is another of Oengus's main themes. Implicit in the prologue is a contrast between secular poetry, which seeks to perpetuate the fame of kings; and the liturgical year to which Oengus has given poetic expression, in which all of time is consecrated in a cycle of perpetually recurring commemorations. The triumph of the saints is proclaimed in terms both of the church as a whole, and of Ireland in particular: Herod and Nero are dead and reviled, but the feasts of the holy men and women whom they persecuted are honoured throughout Christendom; the strongholds of Ireland's pagan kings are silent ruins, while its monasteries flourish. And it is of course the saints who possess the blessings of eternity, the timeless time of God.

Below I have translated the prologue and epilogue in their entirety, together with a version of the Middle Irish preface which was attached to the *Féilire* some centuries after it was written. To give some impression of the *Féilire* proper I have also translated twelve stanzas from the body of the poem, together with segments of later commentary describing the saints whose feasts are mentioned: taken as a whole, this body of additional material offers a fascinating and many-faceted view of how the saints were imagined in medieval Ireland.

[PREFACE]

Four things are asked concerning every work: place, time, person, and the cause of its composition.

It is worth knowing why place should be inquired after first, time second, person third, and the cause of composition last of all. Place comes first, because places are reckoned with reference to cathedrals (?) and churches – that is, the first place and honour go to them. Times however are reckoned with reference to kings and peoples, and the second place goes to them. Person comes third, because the author of every work belongs either to a church or to a people.[1] After that comes the cause, for the cause of precedence for poets in general was found to be a prostitute.[2]

Or else [this sequence] follows the lead of the philosophers: place comes first because place is corporeal; time second because it is incorporeal; person third because person consists of both corporeal and incorporeal; cause of composition after that, as we have said already.

Or else it is the same order which there was in the making of the form of the creation. Place comes first, for on Tuesday the earth was made. Time is second, for it is on Wednesday that the sun and moon were made, and it is by them that time is reckoned. Person third, for it is on Friday that man was made. Cause last of all, then, for it is on Saturday that God blessed the creation and revealed the reason for its making.

This, however, is the time when Oengus made the *Féilire*: the time of Aed Oirdnide son of Niall Frossach. For it is he who took the kingship of Ireland after Donnchad son of Domnall, and in the 'First Prologue'[3] Oengus alludes to Donnchad's death. It was to Fothad na Canóine that Oengus first showed the *Féilire*, when Aed came on an expedition to Dún Cuair on the border of Meath and Leinster. The clerics of Ireland came with him, following Condmach the heir of Patrick;[4] and it is on that occasion that they were freed from [having to go on] journeys and expeditions. For Fothad na Canóine gave the decision freeing the churches of Ireland, saying:

> The church of the living God:
> let it keep what belongs to it.
> Let it have its own rights,
> as has [always] been best.

1 That is, belongs either to the clergy or the laity. 2 The meaning of this statement is unclear to me. Cf. perhaps Boethius's *De Consolatione Philosophiae*, Prosa I, where the Muses are denounced as 'play-acting harlots'. 3 The *Féilire's* introductory and concluding poems are called its first and second 'prologues' in the preface. 4 Condmach (died 807) was the abbot of Armagh, and hence regarded as the 'successor' (*comarbae*) of its founder Patrick; cf. p. 159, note 13 above.

Every good, true monk,
with a pure conscience,
serves the church to which he belongs
just as a slave does.

Whoever is unattached, then,
obliged neither by law nor [a master's] will,
has leave to go to war
with great Aed son of Niall.

This is the correct rule,
which is neither great nor small:
let each man's slave serve him
without blemish and without flaw.

Thereupon Aed Oirdnide excused Ireland's churches and clerics from going on expeditions from that time forward. Then Fothad recited his 'Rule' and his 'Complaint';[5] and they made a compact with one another, and each blessed the other's composition, and they granted many graces to whoever should recite the *Féilire* often. Those are the graces of the *Féilire*, and they are related in the 'Second Prologue' of the *Féilire* itself.

It is also worth knowing in what metre the *Féilire* was composed. Not hard to answer: *rinnard*. How can *rinnard* be recognised? Not hard to answer: six syllables in every line, twelve in every couplet, twenty-four in every quatrain; and if there are more or less than that, it is an error. Oengus composed the *Féilire* with *recomarc*, that is, with the lines ending in disyllables, and in three varieties: 'easy' *rinnard*, with double assonance; *rinnard* with threefold assonance; and *rinnard* with fourfold assonance.... [6]

Others say concerning the place of this work's composition that it was begun in Cúil Bennchuir in Mag Reichet in the territory of the Uí Fhailgi, that most of it was written in Cluain Eidnech, and that it was finished in Tamlachta Librén. Its author was Oengus son of Oengoba son of Oíblén, of the community of Cluain Eidnech. The time was the reign of Cobthach Coel Breg.[7]

This is the cause [of its composition]. Once Oengus went to Cúil Bennchuir in Mag Reichet. He saw a grave there; and the space above that grave, between heaven and earth, was full of angels. He asked a priest of the church, 'Who is

5 On Fothad's 'Rule' see Kenney 1966, 473–4; the 'Complaint' is perhaps the poem whose text is given here.   6 Several examples follow, taken both from the *Féilire* and from the works of other poets. There seems to be no point in including these; but the reader may find it interesting to take a look at the sample quatrains given at the beginning of the two 'prologues'. Both show 'threefold assonance': *nime* and *gile* rhyme with one another, and consonate with *labrai; iarair* and *bliadain* rhyme with one another, and consonate with *firbail*.   7 A very peculiar error: Cobthach Coel Breg was traditionally believed to have lived *c.* 300 B.C.

buried in the grave yonder?' 'A poor old man who used to live here,' said the priest. 'What good did he do?' asked Oengus. 'I never saw him do anything particularly good,' said the priest. 'What did he do at all?' asked Oengus. 'He used to enumerate the saints of the world,' said the priest, 'as many as he could remember, when he lay down and when he arose – as was customary with retired warriors who had left the world.' 'My God of heaven!' said Oengus. 'Whoever put the praises of the saints into harmonious verse would have a great reward, since such great grace has come upon the retired warrior yonder.' Then Oengus began to compose the *Féilire*. He composed the middle portion in Cluain Eidnech. It was in Tamlachta however that it was finished. He composed it in the time of Mael Ruain....

['FIRST PROLOGUE']

Sén, a Chríst, mo labrai,
a Choimdiu secht nime;
rom berthar buaid léire,
a Rí gréine gile.

Consecrate my speech, Christ,
Lord of the seven heavens!
May the gift of exactitude be granted me,
King of the bright sun.

Bright Sun which illuminates
heaven with abundant holiness,
King who rules the angels,
Lord of men;

Lord of men,
righteous truly-good King:
may I have every good auspice
for praising your royal company!

It is your royal company that I praise,
for you are my Over-King:
I have made it my care
constantly to pray to them.

I pray a prayer to them;
may what I have recited protect me –
the fair folk of shining hue,
the royal company of whom I have spoken.

I have spoken of the royal company
surrounding the King above the clouds:
some ruling over radiant days,
others with showers of tears.

May it be to my advantage, for my comfort –
for I am weak and wretched –
following the commands of this King
to go the way that that multitude has gone.

They have cleared roadways
which are not smooth for fools:
before they came to the Kingdom
they suffered hardships.

They were crushed in the presence of armies,
in all their strength;
they were broken in assemblies,
they were slain before kings.

They were slashed by spearpoints,
they were torn apart,
they were burnt over fires
on glowing griddles.

They were thrown to wild beasts
by shameless brigands;
they were scourged – a hard path –
through furnaces of fire.

They were put into dungeons
and at last upon the gallows,
with multitudes deriding them
after they had been flayed with sharp blades.

Welcome be every death
whose horror is very great!
Many kings, formerly,
underwent glorious slaughter.

They have all suffered –
I have proclaimed many valiant deeds –
truly to magnify their thanks
to Jesus the son of Mary.

Woe to everyone who killed them,
who dared to wound them!
After their brief tribulation,
it is they who are blessed.

The great kings of the pagans
wail forever in the flames;
the hosts of Jesus, a splendid leap,
rejoice after their victory.

The warriors by whom they were slain,
with all their fierceness –
their splendour has perished,
their strongholds are desolate.

But they, after running their course,
have reached the Kingdom;
their churches, without weakness,
are settlements of thousands.

The soldiers who crucified them,
though their boasts were valiant,
suffer fierce torments
and their graves are not known.

Not so are the soldiers of Jesus:
they have come to a bright dwelling,
leaving their pious bodies
in tombs of shining gold.

Christ's royal company, after their wounding,
are mighty among hosts;
the kings of the world, after their pleasures –
for them truly all is over.

Herod and Pilate,
at whose hands our Lord suffered:
their boasting has ended,
their torments endure forever.

Although Jesus was crucified,
our Lord, our Champion,
he has arisen as the pure King
of all that he created.

Although ruddy, headstrong Nebuchadnezzar
was king of the world,
his splendour has departed
since he himself perished with his household.

It is not thus for old Paul the monk,
of the dark hermitage:
every glad company was consecrated
by the abundant grace of his holy name.

Although the sword struck down
John the mighty Baptist,
he has been glorified in this world
and made a king in God's Kingdom.

Herod and his queen,
by whom he was slain with much outcry,
have not inherited (it is a hard fate)
earth or cloudy heaven.

Every synod invokes
the holy name of Peter;
to a believer it does not seem fitting
to utter the name of Nero.

It is not known where Nero lies:
that is fitting, for he was not holy.
The world, with the multitude of its people,
praises Peter's humble grave.

Nero has the chief place
in the portico of torment.
The apostle Paul, a lofty pillar,
has come to the plains of heaven.

Nero's splendour is ended,
it [has receded] very far from him;
Paul's name, a lasting choice,
[still] surges higher.

Though Pilate's queen was haughty
on her heaped cushions,
her glory has perished
since she went into the earth.

Not thus is Mary the virgin,
the strong beloved fortress:
the race of Adam, a great circuit,
and the host of angels praise her.

However many and beautiful
were the sons of fierce Decius, whom we do not love,
there is not known, and has not remained,
the name of one of them upon the earth.

It is not thus with the child Quiricus:
the great tidings concerning him have been spread abroad.
Beautiful was his battle-cry,
which has filled the strongholds of the world.

Let all our mind
be upon the people of God, whom we do not conceal.
It will benefit us to make trial
of the prologue which we recite.

The world's strength is a deception
to whoever dwells therein;
there is no strength
save great love for the Son of Mary.

Though the kings of the world are great
to you who look [upon them],
a hundred hundred times loftier
are the humble hirelings of Jesus.

Though they are lower in the eyes of men,
and in the noise of their outcry,
they will be loftier than a prince's citadel,
for age upon age.

Fleeting is the sovereignty
of the wretched world in which we are;
the King who rules over the angels
is the Lord of every land.

Though the covetous prosper
in the land in which we are,
there is one who has preached to us therein
of the might of God, illustrious praise.

Though Tara's ponderous rampart has perished
with the passing of its sovereignty,
lofty Armagh endures
with a host of noble elders.

The glory of valiant Loegaire
was snuffed out, a great calamity;
Patrick's splendid illustrious name
[still] rises higher.

The Faith has increased,
it will endure until Doomsday;
the guilty pagans are borne away,
their settlements are abandoned.

Ráith Chruachan has passed away
together with Ailill, that gifted man;
fairer than that of princes is the splendour
in the city of Clonmacnoise;

The sweetly singing, perpetual choirs
surrounding Ciarán, if you should speak of it;
the victorious tumult
of great Clonmacnoise.

You have nothing more precious
than the love of God, if you perform it:
you will not regret
adoring the King of clouds.

The haughty fortress of Ailenn
has perished, with its boastful multitude;
great is victorious Brigit,
and fair her thronged church.

The fortress of Emain has melted away:
only its stones remain.
Populous Glendalough
is the Rome of the western world.

The mighty sanctuary (?) of Ferns
is a flaming radiant lantern;
the proud folk of the fortress
of Bécc son of Eógan are no more.

Why do you not recognise
all the judgments of the same King?
Bécc son of Eógan does not remain;
Aed son of Sétnae endures.[8]

The ancient fortresses of the pagans,
to which title had been gained by long habitation,
are empty and without worship
like the place where Lugaid dwelt.

8 Aed son of Sétnae, better known by his nickname Maedóc, was the founder of the prominent
monastery of Ferns in southeast Leinster. Bécc was one of the ancestors of a local dynasty, and
is indeed almost completely forgotten (O'Brien 1976, 353–4).

The little places that were settled
by twos and threes
are Romes, with assemblies
of hundreds and thousands.

Though it was far-flung and splendid,
paganism has been destroyed:
the kingdom of God the Father
has filled heaven, earth, and sea.

We behold something nearer at hand:
a blessed psalm
concerning the might of God; a vigorous discourse
today [and] at the end of the world.

Red fierce superb Donnchad,
or victorious Bran of the Barrow:
visiting their tombs
does not free me from suffering debility.

After his devotion Mael Ruain
is a great sun upon the southern plain of Meath:
at his pure grave
every heart's suffering is healed.[9]

The Lord is even-handed
when his flocks are examined:
he always brings his enemies low;
he always exalts his champions.

The crimson kings have been snuffed out,
the Domnalls have been afflicted;
the Ciaráns have been made kings,
the Crónáns have been exalted.

9 Mael Ruain of Tallaght (died 792) was one of the leaders of the revival of monastic spirituality known as the Céili Dé movement, to which Oengus belonged; he is also mentioned in the 'Second Prologue' below. For more on Mael Ruain see 'Stories of the Céili Dé' below, and O Dwyer 1981.

The great mountains of wickedness
have been brought low by spears;
yet there have [also] been made
mountains from the valleys.

Though we have as our challenge
a battle with the furious Devil,
there remains to help us
the same Christ, a lofty pillar.

Though the kings of the earth are proud
in their spotless garments,
after their flood-tide they will perish:
one after another they pass away.

The fair devoted King,
Jesus, above the wave of the flood –
blessed his birth from Mary;
he remains after them all.

The demon's power has been maimed,
with his black hideous host;
the mighty strength of our King
remains intact forever.

If we should come beneath his protection,
his share will come (?):
as he is not weak or feeble,
he will not fail therein.

May our purpose be strong:
to strive for what is fittest.
Let us all love Jesus,
for this is the highest thing.

Jesus, I pray you,
in the name of these multitudes,
that this great good may be pleasing to you –
that I may be able to number them.

Let me do your will,
King of thronging Zion:
may I be forever with your royal host
in the everlasting victorious Kingdom.

May I be beside you
in the Kingdom where you are;
may the blessing of every community
be upon your glory, Jesus!

Jesus, I take it upon me
to display your royal host
according to the order in which they went
to you in cloudy heaven.

There is not in the year, Christ,
if you would give ear to it,
a day in which a company would not arise
to you in the next world.

It is manifest, great King,
King whose princes are reckoned up:
we will name, without stammering,
the noble candles of each day.

We will search our books,
inquiring after each:
without omitting any, we will go
straight through the year.

This will be the body of our work,
a structure which will not be feeble:
as many fair verses
as there are days in the year.

That your mind may not
fall into wickedness,
every verse will swiftly name
the feast for each day.

The days of these great months,
through which runs this everlasting sun:
we will not injure the fame
of this glorious assembly.

Nones and ides,
the true sequence of the calends:
the lines will be
on your white margin.

You will follow the days
in your zealous books;
piously you will follow
the feasts according to the lines.

Unless you understand in this way
the order which is in our poems,
I proclaim publicly
that you are dull-witted among men.

Let us give further instruction
to a faulty intellect:
every verse will swiftly name
the feast for each day.

Reciting the days of the solar month
will not delay me,
lest our poem be tedious,
save for twelve fair calends.[10]

It shall not delay me to go
from one calends to the next,
save for three hundred
and sixty-five verses.[11]

---

10 That is, Oengus only names each month at its beginning, in the verse corresponding to its calends or first day.   11 Here 'calends' is given its special sense 'calends of January', i.e. the first day of the year: to go 'from one calends to the next' is to traverse the full annual cycle. Cf. the opening verses of the 'Second Prologue' below.

In searching for the feast,
with its mighty radiance,
study zealously, with keen attention,
the order of the verses.

The order of the verses
in the pious poems
is the same, following the lines,
as the order of the feasts.

The holy Lord of creation,
Christ son of the holy Mary,
Jesus, beloved pillar –
may he go before the race of men.

[SELECTED VERSES WITH COMMENTARY]

15 January:

Foráith mór ngúr ngalar,
carais mór trom tredan,
in grian bán ban Muman,
Íte Cluana Credal.

She helped many grievous illnesses,
she loved many arduous fasts:
the white sun of the women of Munster,
Íte of Cluain Chredal.

COMMENTARY 'She helped many grievous illnesses,' etc. That is, God helped Íte. Or else a great illness afflicted her: that is, it was a great illness for her that a beetle sucked her breast. It was the size of a lapdog, so that it destroyed one of her sides entirely. No one knew that she had this affliction. Once she went out, and the beetle came out of its burrow to follow her. The nuns saw it, and killed it. Then Íte returned, and when the beetle did not come in search of her she asked, 'Where has my fosterling gone?' 'Do not deprive us of heaven,' said the nuns. 'It is we who killed it, for we did not know but that it was harmful.' 'Whatever be the reason for it,' said Íte, 'because of this deed no nun will ever be my successor.[12]

12 This remark evidently serves as a rationalisation of the fact that Cluain Chredal, although it had a female patron saint, was administered by men; this contrasts with Brigit's foundation of

And I will not accept [any comfort] from my Lord until he gives me his Son in
the shape of an infant, to be fostered by me.' Then the angel who usually minis-
tered to her came to her. 'It is high time,' she said to him. And the angel said to
her: 'The thing which you ask will be granted to you.' And so Christ came to her
in the shape of an infant, so that she said:[13]

> 'My Jesus,[14]
> fostered by me in my hermitage:
> though a priest have much wealth,
> all is a lie save for my Jesus.

> 'The fosterage which I perform in my house
> is not the fosterage of a common peasant:
> Jesus, with the men of heaven,
> is next to my heart every night.

> 'My Jesus, tending to my eternal welfare,
> gives freely but is firm in his demands.
> Whoever does not pray to the King
> ruling all things, will repent of it.

> 'It is exalted angelic Jesus,
> not some disreputable priest,
> whom I foster in my hermitage:
> Jesus, son of the Hebrew woman.

> 'Though the sons of kings and over-kings
> should come into my land,
> it is not to them that I look for assurance;
> I trust rather in my Jesus.

> 'Sing as is fitting, maidens,
> to the man to whom you owe tribute:
> my Jesus is in his dwelling on high,
> even though he is in my bosom.'

Kildare, which was ruled by women throughout the pre-Norman period.   13 This beautiful
poem has repeatedly been edited and translated; the most recent and authoritative treatment is
that of Quin 1981.   14 I have made no attempt to find English equivalents for the many
diminutives in this poem. The most important of these is *Ísucán*, for which other translators have
proposed the renderings 'Jesukin', 'Jesuseen', and 'little Jesus'; I have tried to convey some of the
name's intimacy by translating 'my Jesus'.

8 February:

Auë án ind éicis,
ba im Chríst a labrae;
Fiachrae, ba fer ferdae,
abb Irarda amrae.

The poet's glorious descendant,
whose speech was concerning Christ;
Fiachrae, a manly man,
the marvellous abbot of Iraird.

COMMENTARY 'The poet's glorious descendant,' i.e. Onchú is his name, and he is in the church of Reilec Aingel in Cluain Mór Maedóic, and he belonged to the Connachta; and he was also a good poet. This is how it was with him: he collected the relics of the saints of Ireland, and would not recite in any church unless something of the relics of that church's saint were given to him; and he had a huge reliquary containing relics of the saints of Ireland.

He went, then, to Cluain Mór Maedóic, i.e. [the church of] Maedóc ua Dúnlaing of the Leinstermen, who is not the same as Maedóc of Ferns. It happened that Maedóc was still alive when he came. 'Give me some of your relics, cleric,' he said, 'so that they can be with the other relics.' 'That is difficult,' said the cleric. 'Do it even so,' said the poet. Then the cleric cut off his little finger and gave it to the poet. That was painful for the cleric, so that he said: 'What you have gathered will be here, and it is here that your own relics will be as well.' And that was fulfilled.

5 March:

Ro leblaing, ní balbdae,
a clú tar sál sairde:
Carthach rígdae Ruamach,
Ciarán sluagach Saigre.

Their fame, it is not garbled,
has leaped across the eastern sea:
royal Carthach of Rome,
Ciarán of Saigir with many followers.

COMMENTARY 'Ciarán of Saigir with many followers.' Ciarán belonged to the Dál mBirn, of the Osraige.

Faithful Ciarán,
noble inheritor,
eldest of the saints,
a jewel in [priestly] orders,
wondrous child,
champion[15] of the King,
whose seat and holy hill
is great Saigir,
Lugnae's son,
a sea of vast learning:
it is well that he takes land,
a tale that is not false.
On the day when Judgment approaches,
lucky will be everyone who is his companion.
Liadaine was asleep
in her bed, a saying which is not untrue:
when she turned her face to heaven
a star fell into her mouth.
Thence was born the wondrous child,
Ciarán of Saigir whom you mention;
hence (a saying without arrogance)
Lugnae said that he was not his son.

Liadaine daughter of Maine Cerr son of Oengus, of the descendants of Lugaid son of Íth, was the mother of Ciarán of Saigir; and he was born in Finntrácht Gléire. Angels were in attendance after his birth: he was baptised by the orders of heaven; and it is in Corcu Loígde that the Cross was first worshipped in Ireland. Ciarán took up residence in Saigir thirty years before Patrick. As Patrick said:

Seek out Uar,[16]
found a settlement upon its bank;
at the end of thirty long years
you and I will meet.

Pure will be the union with us
of the boy who will be born in Tulach Tinn.
After his time Conall will take away
many monks and stately nuns.

15 This word supplied from other manuscripts.   16 *Uar* ('Cold') is said to be the name of the spring where Ciarán founded the monastery of Saigir; the story is evidently a place-name legend,

It is then that Ciarán predicted Conall, and Fachtna of Ros Ailithir. And it is Ciarán who left to the king of Corcu Loígde the honour-price of the king of a province, and kingship and nobility to his descendants forever, because they were the first to believe in the Cross, and because they established Ciarán's church.

Ciarán of Saigir was a wonderful saint, for he had abundant property. For the fold in which he kept his cattle had ten gates, and there were ten stalls at every gate, and ten calves in every stall, and ten cows surrounding every calf; but Ciarán did not consume any tiny portion of all that they produced for as long as he lived, but distributed it to the Lord's poor and needy. Ciarán had moreover fifty tame horses, to plough and cultivate the land. And out of all that, this was his meal every night: a little mouthful of barley bread, and two *murráthach* roots, and the water of a pure spring. His clothing was of fawns' skins, with a wet cloak as an outer garment; and he always slept on a pillow of stone.

It is Cairnech the Bald, Ciarán's scribe, who wrote that marvellous text, the *Immirge Chiaráin* ('Ciarán's Wanderings'), with its many devices; and that book survives still at Saigir. May everyone who reads it grant a blessing to the soul of Cairnech the Bald.

17 April:

L*a féil Petair deochain*
drebraing martrae mbuaide,
cona chléir, cain díne,
Donnán Ega uaire.

Together with the feast of Peter the Deacon,
who ascended to the triumph of martyrdom,
is Donnán of cold Eig
with his monks, a fair company.

COMMENTARY 'Donnán of ... Eig.' Eig is the name of an island in Scotland, and that is where Donnán is, or else in Caithness; and it is there that Donnán and his community perished, fifty-five [of them].

It is Donnán who went to Colum Cille, to take him as his soul-friend. Colum Cille said to him, 'I will not be soul-friend to the folk of red martyrdom; for you will undergo red martyrdom, and your community with you,' and that was fulfilled.

Then Donnán went with his monks into the territory of the Gallgaídil,[17] and settled in a place where the sheep of the queen of the country used to be. 'Kill

which takes the injunction 'Seek out Uar' (*Saig Uar*) as the origin of *Saigir*. (This form of the line appears to be secondary, however; cf. O'Rahilly 1960, 144.)   **17** Literally 'Foreigner-Gaels'; a term applied to groups of mixed Irish and Viking ancestry, or to Irish who had adopted Viking ways.

them all,' she said. 'That is not devout,' said everyone. But men were sent after that to kill them. The cleric was offering mass then. 'Let there be peace between us until the mass is over,' said Donnán. 'So be it,' they said. And then, afterwards, all those who were there were killed.

7 May:

> Mo *Chuaróc la Breccán,*
> *dí gérait at glainiu,*
> *carsat Críst as diliu*
> *i nEchdromma dairiu.*

> Mo Chuaróc and Breccán,
> two most pure champions,
> loved Christ who is dearest
> in the oak-grove of Echdruimm.

COMMENTARY 'In the oak-grove of Echdruimm.' That is, it is in the north of Dál nAraide, on the boundary between Dál nAraide and Dál Riatai; or else the oak-grove of Echdruimm is in Muccrama in the west of Connacht. And the church's sacred tree is seen from the plain, but cannot be found when one comes into the grove to seek it; and the sound of the bell is heard, and the singing of psalms therein, and the church itself cannot be found.

9 June:

> Ron *snádat don bithlaith,*
> *i mbithbí léss lainnrech,*
> *Baíthíne ard ainglech,*
> *Colum Cille caindlech.*

> May they keep us safe for the eternal Kingdom,
> where there is flaming radiance forever:
> lofty angelic Baíthíne,
> candle-like Colum Cille.

COMMENTARY: 'Baíthíne ... Colum Cille.' That is, Baíthíne was the son of Brénainn son of Fergus son of Conall Gulban son of Niall Noígiallach, and Colum Cille was the son of Feidlimid son of [the same] Fergus; 'Crimthann' was Colum Cille's name at first. Eithne, the daughter of Dímma son of Noe son of Etine son of Cairpre Fili son of Ailill Már son of Breccán son of Fiacc son of Dáire Barrach son of Catháir Már, was the mother of Colum Cille. Colum Cille's three sisters were Cuimmíne and Mínchloth and Sinech.

He was called 'Colum' ('dove') because of his innocence; and 'Cille' ('of the church') because he used often to come from the church in which he read his psalms to meet with the children who lived nearby. This is what they used to say among themselves: 'Has our little dove come from the church?' – that is, from Tulach Dubglaisse, in Tír Lugdach, in the territory of the Cenél Conaill. ...

Moreover, Colum Cille gave great love to Christ since the days of his youth. An angel used to come to him from heaven; Axal was the name of the angel who used to come to Colum Cille, as if it were 'Auxil', from *auxilium* ('help'). This is what the angel said to him: 'Colum Cille, undertake to be a virgin.' 'I will not,' said Colum Cille, 'until I am rewarded for it.' 'What reward do you ask?' said the angel. 'I do not ask for a single reward,' said Colum Cille, 'but for four.' 'Name them,' said the angel. Colum Cille said: 'Death in repentance, and death from hunger, and death in youth; for bodies grow ugly in old age. ...'[18] 'All that and more will be given to you,' said the angel: 'you will be the chief prophet of heaven and earth.'

That was fulfilled: he went into exile, and he was young when he died, and he died of hunger; but it was voluntary hunger. And this is what caused that hunger of his: once he was walking around the graveyard on Iona when he saw an old woman gathering nettles to make a stew. 'Why do you do that, poor thing?' asked Colum Cille. 'Dear father,' she said, 'I have only one cow, and she has not yet born a calf. I am awaiting it; and this is what has sustained me for a long time now.'

Then Colum Cille decided that it would be mainly nettle stew which would sustain him from that time forth: 'Since she is in that great hunger in hope of [what she will get] from one unreliable cow, it is fitting that we should be in great hunger as we wait for God; for better, and certain, is that for which we hope – the eternal Kingdom.' And he told his servant: 'Make me nettle stew every night, without butter or milk therein.'

'It shall be done,' said the cook. And he hollowed out the stick for stirring the stew so that it was a tube; and he poured milk into the tube, and in that way stirred it into the stew. The community noticed the healthy appearance of the cleric, and talked among themselves; Colum Cille noticed that, and said, 'There will be murmuring among the folk who come after you forever.' 'Well then,' he said to the servant: 'what are you putting into my stew every day?' 'You yourself are witness,' said the boy, 'that unless it comes from the stick with which the stew is stirred I know of nothing in it save stew only.' Then [the trick] was revealed to the cleric, and he said, 'Good luck and good deeds forever to the one who holds your office.' And that has been fulfilled.

Then Baíthíne told him a remarkable dream: that he had seen three chairs in heaven, a throne of gold and a throne of silver and a throne of glass. 'That is

---

18 An indecipherable phrase occurs here in the manuscripts, referring perhaps to the fourth of Colum Cille's rewards.

obvious,' said Colum Cille. 'The throne of gold belongs to Ciarán the carpenter's son, because of his honour and his hospitality. The chair of silver is yours, Baíthíne, because of the purity and brightness of your faith. The chair of glass however is mine, for although my faith is beautiful I am carnal and often frail.'

As someone said:

> Mighty Colum, fair of form,
> a ruddy broad flaming face,
> a white body, fame without deception,
> curly hair, a grey bright eye.

> The sound of Colum Cille's voice:
> its sweetness sounded above every choir.
> As far as fifteen hundred paces
> it could be clearly heard – a great extent.

17 June:

> I*n dos óir uas críchaib,*
> *in grian án uas tuathaib,*
> *co ngreit ríg balc bráthair,*
> *cain míl Mo Ling Luachair.*

> The bush of gold above territories,
> the glorious sun above kingdoms,
> a mighty monk with the courage of a king,
> the fair warrior Mo Ling of Luachar.

COMMENTARY 'Mo Ling of Luachar.' That is, as he was leaping across a certain bog in Luachair Dedad, in Munster, a woman said: 'Well does the scholar leap (*–ling*) across the rushes (*luachair*)' – so that that is why he was called Mo Ling of Luachar. Dairchell was his name at first.

> Mo Ling sang:
> When I am among my elders,
> I am the proof that play is forbidden.
> When I am among giddy folk,
> they think that I am their junior. ...

<Once as he was praying in the church he saw a young man enter and come toward him: he wore a purple garment, and had a striking appearance. 'Well, then, cleric,' he said. 'Indeed,' said Mo Ling. 'Why do you not bless me?' said the youth. 'Who are you?' said Mo Ling. 'I am Christ the Son of God,' said he.

'I do not know about that,' said Mo Ling. 'When Christ used to come to speak with the servants of God it was not in purple or with a kingly semblance that he came, but in the semblance of the wretched: Christ used [to resemble] the sick and the lepers.'

'Do you disbelieve in me?' said the young man. 'Who do you think that this is?' 'It seems likely to me that it is the Devil,' said Mo Ling, 'come to do me harm.' 'Such disbelief will be ill for you,' said the young man.

'Well then,' said Mo Ling, 'here is your successor: the Gospel of Christ.' And he lifted up the Gospel. 'Do not raise it, cleric!' he said: 'It is as you think: I am the wretched one.'

'Why have you come?' said Mo Ling. 'So that you might bless me.' 'I will not,' said Mo Ling, 'for you do not deserve any better. What good is [my blessing] to you?' asked Mo Ling.

'It is as if you went into a vat of honey, so that you washed yourself and your clothing therein: its fragrance would be on you if you did not wash your clothes.' 'And why do you wish for that?' asked Mo Ling. 'I think that, even if your blessing does nothing else for me, its good fortune and its holiness and its fragrance will cling to my exterior.' 'You will not have it,' said Mo Ling, 'for you have not deserved it.'

'All right,' he said: 'then give me a thorough cursing.' 'What good is that to you?' asked Mo Ling. 'Not hard to answer, cleric,' he said: 'the mouth which utters a curse against me will cast its poison and its injury in your face.'

'Go,' said Mo Ling: 'you do not deserve a blessing.' 'I wish that I did,' he said; 'how may I deserve it?'

'Serving God,' said Mo Ling. 'Alas!' he said. 'I do not choose that.'

'Even a bit of study.' 'Your learning is no greater [than my own], and it does not help me.'

'Fasting then,' said Mo Ling. 'I have been fasting since the beginning of the world; I am no better for it.'

'Prostrating yourself,' said Mo Ling. 'I cannot bend forward: my knees are backward.'

'Go hence,' said Mo Ling. 'I cannot teach or save you.' It is concerning him that the Devil said:

> He is pure gold, he is the sky around the sun,
> he is a silver vessel of wine,
> he is an angel, he is holy wisdom,
> whoever does the will of the King.

> He is a bird around whom a snare closes,
> he is a leaky boat in grave danger,
> he is an empty vessel, he is a withered tree,
> whoever does not do the will of the King above.

He is a fragrant blossoming branch,
he is a vessel full of honey,
he is a jewel with its virtue,[19]
whoever does the will of the Son of God from heaven.

He is a hollow nut without value,
he is stinking decay, he is a withered tree,
he is a crabapple branch without blossom,
whoever does not do the will of the King.

Whoever does the will of the Son of God from heaven
is a blazing sun in which there is summer,
he is the seat of God in heaven,
he is a pure vessel of crystal.

He is a victorious horse crossing a level plain,
the man who seeks the kingdom of the great God:
he is a chariot in which a king is seen to ride,
which carries off the prizes with reins of gold.[20]

He is a sun which warms the holy heaven,
a man in whom the the great King is well pleased,
he is a prosperous noble temple,
he is a holy shrine covered with gold.

He is an altar on which wine is shared out,
around which many choirs sing;
he is a purified chalice full of drink,
he is bright *findruine*, he is gold.>[21]

6 July:

Mo *Ninne int shléibe,*
Cuilinn ba cain áige;
gabais buaid gel glaine,
siür Muire máire.

---

19 Probably an allusion to the belief that different precious stones had special curative properties.   20 Reading *a hallaib óir* with the Book of Leinster; the other manuscripts have *allaig náir, a halaib oir.*   21 I have taken the story of Mo Ling's conversation with the Devil (enclosed in angle brackets) from another manuscript of the *Féilire*. It also occurs separately in

Mo Ninne of the mountain
was the fair pillar of Cuilenn.
The sister of great Mary
gained the bright victory of purity.

COMMENTARY 'Mo Ninne, etc.' That is, Mo Ninne of the mountain of Cuilenn; and Sárbile was her name at first, or else Dar Ercae was her name originally. But a certain dumb poet fasted in her presence, and the first thing which he said was '*Nin, nin*' – whence the nun was called 'Mo Ninna', and he himself Ninne the poet. The nuns used to call her 'Mo Ninne', as if it were 'Mo Nanna' (?)

'Sister of ... Mary.' That is, because she was a virgin like Mary.

One hundred and eighty years, all told,
according to reckoning which is not feeble,
without folly, without wrong, without risk,
was the age of Mo Ninne.

'Mo Ninne' was given [as a name]
to the radiant pious virgin saint;
the nuns used to pronounce her name
'Mo Nanna', with grace.

Or else the nun's name
was given her from the call
which Ninne the poet uttered (he was the better for it),
he who begged her for her prayer.

I will tell you
her usual personal name:
she was called Dar Ercae in her time,
before she got her nickname.

29 August:

Aisnéid césad Iohain
Bauptaist, bith co léiri,
la noí cét, co n-óigi,
la fresgabail Héli.

Best et al. 1954-83, 5.1238-40

Tell of the suffering of John
the Baptist, a world with devotion,
together with nine hundreds, with purity,
[on the day] of the ascension of Elijah.

COMMENTARY 'Tell of the suffering of John the Baptist,' etc. That is, he is
called 'John the Baptist' because he was the first to perform baptism, or because he
baptised Christ. [It is not] really his beheading which happened here, but the
finding of his head for the second time; for he died [not] in autumn but in the
spring, before Passover, in the city of Edessa in the province of Phoenicia. And on
the following Passover, a year later, Christ died. And [this is the day of] the
ascension of the prophet Elijah, and of the passing of Elisha, and of nine hundred
martyrs with him.

The beheading of dear glorious John
was in Acirunda, in Arabia;
Sebasten, its span is written,
is the name of the village where he was buried.

If there has been struck, if there has been killed,
if an axe has struck (grim the reason!)
anyone like him, that noble jewel (?),
he will not be on the marvellous shore forever.[22]

The women of the world, except for a few,
burn in the fire of Doomsday.
It is not fitting to speak to them
after the murder of John.

It is in revenge for the death of John the Baptist, then, that the Broom will come
from Fanat to cleanse Ireland at the end of the world, as Ailerán the Wise and
Colum Cille have prophesied. It is in the hour of terce in particular that the
Broom will come from Fanat, as Colum Cille said: it will cleanse Ireland with the
zeal of two yoked horses grazing.

Ailerán said of the Broom: 'Two alehouses will be in a single enclosure, side by
side. A man going from one of them to the other will find no one alive in the
house into which he goes, and after that will find no one alive in the house from
which he has come – such will be the swiftness with which the Broom will come
from Fanat.'

22 I do not understand this verse.

Riagail said: 'This plague will be in Ireland for three days and nights more than a year. When a boat on Loch Rudraige can be clearly seen from the refectory – it is then that the Broom will come from Fanat.'

On a Tuesday in spring, after Easter: that is the day of the week in which the Broom will come to avenge the suffering of John. As Mo Ling said, describing the feast-day of John:

> On the feast-day of John will come an assault
> which will range across Ireland from the southeast:
> a savage dragon which will burn whomever it reaches,
> without communion, without mass....

23 September:

> D*o Adomnán Iäe,*
> *asa toídlech toíden,*
> *ro ír Ísu uasal*
> *soerad buan ban nGoídel.*

> To Adomnán of Iona,
> of the radiant retinue,
> noble Jesus granted
> the freeing forever of the women of the Gaels.

COMMENTARY 'To Adomnán of Iona,' etc. One day it happened that Adomnán was crossing Mag mBreg with his mother on his back, and they saw two armies contending with one another. It chanced, then, that Adomnán's mother Rónait saw a woman with an iron sickle in her hand dragging a woman from the opposing army, and the sickle was sticking in her breast. For in those days women fought in battles just the same as men.

Then Rónait sat down and said, 'You will not carry me with you from this place until women are freed forever from that sort of thing yonder, and from fighting and serving in armies.'

Then Adomnán promised that. It happened that there was thereafter a great assembly in Ireland; and Adomnán went to that assembly with the pick of the clerics of Ireland, and freed the women there.

These are the four laws of Ireland:[23] the law of Patrick, which forbids killing clerics; the law of the nun Dar Í, which forbids killing cows; the law of Adomnán, which forbids killing women; the law of Sunday, which forbids sinning then.

---

23 The word used for 'law' here is *cáin*: more precisely, it refers to a law whose authority depends not upon royal power or the traditions of a community, but upon the authority of a saint. The 'Law of Adomnán' (*Cáin Adomnáin*), promulgated in 697, was concerned with

27 October:

E*rc Domnaig móir moínig,*
Abbán abb cain cliarach,
Odrán sab soer snámach,
Colmán auë Fiachrach.

Erc of rich Domnach Mór;
Abbán, fair abbot of communities;
Odrán, a noble support, a swimmer;
Colmán descendant of Fiachrae.

COMMENTARY 'Colmán descendant of Fiachrae.' That is, in Senbotha Fola in the territory of the Uí Chennselaig. In his church are the ducks with which no one dares to meddle. For if, as the result of a mistaken cast made by night, they are put into water over a fire, the water will not boil even if all the forests in the world were burnt, until they are put back in the same pool.

24 November:

L*a Cianán Doimliac,*
caindias diar tuirinn,
macc Lénéni rolainn,
la Colmán Duib Chuilinn.

Together with Cianán of Doimliac,
a fair wheat-ear from our harvest,
are the son of keen Léiníne
and Colmán Duib Chuilinn.

COMMENTARY 'Cianán of Doimliac.' This is how Cianán's body is: uncorrupted and undecaying, in the tomb to the east of Doimliac. And this is the reason for that: Cairnech of Tuilén came once to Cianán's [monastery] of Doimliac. His hosts sought to offer him a bath, but no bottom was found in the tub. 'How unfortunate!' said Cianán. 'What?' asked Cairnech. 'That there is no bottom in the tub,' said Cianán. 'Put water in the tub,' said Cairnech, 'and let the washing take place.' It was put in, and not a drop ran out.

protecting various classes of non-combatants; in later tradition it was remembered primarily as a measure rendering women exempt from military service. The text of the *Cáin*, and a more detailed version of the legend of Adomnán's freeing of the women, are edited with translation in Meyer 1905.

'Go into the tub, Cairnech,' said Cianán. 'Let us go together,' said Cairnech. They went, then. '[Your] body is beautiful, cleric,' said Cairnech. 'It is so,' said Cianán. 'I pray to God, then,' said Cairnech, 'that it will be thus forever, without decay, until Christ comes to the great assembly of the Judgment.' And that has come true.

His hair and nails were trimmed every Maundy Thursday until the time of Adomnán. Adomnán went into the tomb to see him, and to handle the body. His eye was blinded immediately. After that he fasted concerning it, until his eye was given to him again; no one has dared to go in from then until now.

It is Patrick who wrote the law of Cianán, and Cianán wrote the law of Patrick – they made an exchange. Patrick requested that, for Cianán was the better scribe.

This is how the union was made between Cianán and Colum Cille:[24] Colum Cille stretched his arm halfway into the tomb, reaching through its south wall, and Cianán stretched his arm halfway out through that wall (?). They made their union in that way.

Cianán was the son of Sesnán son of Drónae son of Tigernach son of Findcham son of Fiacc son of Imchad Uallach son of Condlae son of Tadc son of Cian son of Ailill Aulomm.

'Colmán Duib Chuilinn.' That is, in the Renna; that is, in Dún Reichet. Or [he is called] 'Colmán Duib Chuilinn' from Cuilenn, a mountain at Belach Con Glais in Leinster and in other places. Comgall of Bangor went to the house of Colmán Duib Chuilinn's father. His wife was barren. Then the cleric asked that ink (*dub*) for writing be given to the barren woman. This was done, and Colmán was conceived thereby. Hence he is called 'Colmán son of the ink of Cuilenn.'

---

24 'Union' (*oentu*) is used in this context to denote a special compact of friendship and alliance, established between two churches or two families of churches.

['SECOND PROLOGUE']

Ón challainn co araili,
ro fersam ar n–iarair:
a Ísu, co fírbail,
fort shelbai do bliadain!

From one calend to the next (?)
we have pursued our search:
yours is your year,
blessed Jesus!

We have reckoned the vanguard
of the company of each day:
we have removed what was left over,
from one January's beginning to the next.[25]

In the most lowly body
our strength would have been but feeble,
save that what is highest guided us (?):
the lofty love of the army of Jesus.

Though the patriarchs and prophets
were Christ's companions,
their feast-days are not fully
known among men.

But it is known that no soul
from this enduring world
has reached the King's lofty heaven
save on one of these feast-days.

The full company of each day,
in the vessel of the radiant Kingdom:
after victory and triumph,
may they come to minister to us.

---

25 In other words, it has only been possible to fit the most important saint or saints for each day
into the corresponding verse.

The number which has gone each day
from earth to heaven –
you would speak no falsehood if you boasted
that it is more than thousands of thousands.

That abundance of thousands,
that mighty everlasting sea:
we have only given, out of that company,
the kings of those multitudes.

The fair assembly of each day,
whose powers are great:
may they come to me with [their] kings,
across the lands from every side!

Holy King, I pray to you –
after having laboured I have come forward (?) –
may I live in your Paradise
with the multitude which I have enumerated.

The royal company which I have numbered
(and it is but a mouthful from a great sea):
may each of them, with his pious retinue,
come to my assistance.

May they all lift me up
to my King, whose lords are reckoned;
may my sages protect me,
each with the company of his day.

The company to which I bid welcome,
with everyone whom I love:
may they protect me and my people
in mind and sense, in body and soul.

Every soul which has attained
to heaven, most exalted of journeys,
will come to what is highest:
it will have the blessing of Jesus.

May they all bless
the assembly to which they come;
may they sanctify and glorify
the high King whom they serve.

May the abundant blessing of that King,
with his fair retinues,
be above your assemblies,
and upon Mael Ruain before [all] men.

May my teacher deliver me
to Christ, dear beyond loving,
with his pure blessing,
with the ardour of his heart.

May I be guarded, Christ,
from every disgrace high or low,
in answer to my sinless prayer,
for the sake of your heroes.

The troop which we have set forth
is the pillar of Christ's kingdom;
there is much profit
in what we have searched out in books.

It is profitable to the untaught,
for whom it is a breastplate of piety;
every generation recites it
to make the feast-days known.

Though it be sages who read it,
deeply learned in history,
there is abundance of beauty therein:
they will whet its points (?).[26]

King of heaven, with its angels,
whose fame we do not hide:
every martyr whom we reckon up
has gone into [this poem's] making.

---

26 There is probably a play on words here: *rinn* can mean 'point', but can also designate the rhyming or consonating end of a line of verse; and the metre in which the *Féilire* is written is called *rinnard*. The sense may accordingly be something like 'They will appreciate its artistry'.

It is not knowledge which has produced
the zealous shining book,
but the King's angelic help,
fair candle-like Jesus.

A noble synod came to me,
in the midst of my house,
that I might correct it in their presence
in obedience to the King of heaven.

It is not cleverness which has brought it into being:
it would be a sin for us to claim it.
Each saint, in purity,
has composed his verse.

If anyone disturbs
the order of the verses
it is, I declare it here publicly,
a massacre of this multitude.

The assembly which piously
corrected this book
determined its feast-days
before they died in sanctity.

I have examined the calendar
near and far;
I have composed it with fervour,
I have given it to the saints.

They have granted their blessing
to whomever recites it:
they will come to attend upon him
at the time of his death;

And his soul will live,
after it has been carried beyond suffering,
in the Kingdom of the bright sun,
upon the summit of the seven heavens.

Whoever is not mentioned,
it is not through forgetfulness or neglect,
but rather a shortening of speech
skilfully adjusted.

Even though there were seven tongues
in my wise learned mouth,
it would take until Doomsday, greater than every noise,
if I were to enumerate them.

The pious book
is neither too long nor too wordy:
it is a commemoration of the pure saints,
skilfully made harmonious.

Though our book be harmonious
with the vigour of its verse,
it is not flattery or pride
which has milked many volumes:

The great volume of Ambrose,
Hilary's fervent treatise,
the text of Jerome,
Eusebius's martyrology;

The many books of Ireland,
a wise company:
we have studied all the calendars
of the men of the Gaels.

I assert, without blushing,
that even if you went to their tombs
you would not find that any had
a calendar more correct.

Singing it without weakness
is a protecting fortress;
it is a strong wall, without delay,
against men, against demons.

It is a prayer to God,
it is mighty strength against the Devil,
it is a psalm which invokes great power,
it is a truly accurate calendar.

Whoever shall have as his song
this enduring noble poem
will be guarded by this multitude
in the King's eternal Kingdom.

This King's excellent army,
of whom I make my boast:
this cry answers to them;[27]
I give my pledge on their behalf.

I give my pledge that he will be blessed
who recites it every day.
I promise, without falsehood,
that he will be in the eternal Kingdom;

And that his soul will live
with dear Christ the mighty Lord:
his salvation is not difficult
if it is his custom [to recite it] with groans.

If a holy man recites it
with pure tears,
many wonderful miracles
will be wrought for its sake.

If a saint recites it,
it is worth seven masses;
if a layman recites it,
it is worth the thrice fifty [psalms].

---

27 Literally, 'of whom this cry is the equal number'; the sense seems to be that the enumeration of the saints in the *Féilire* (Oengus's 'cry') is a counterpart of the saints themselves. For *nuall* 'cry' in the sense 'prayer' cf. 'Fer Fio's cry' (*nuall Fir Fhio*).

All of these feast-days are the equivalent
of a splendid celebration;
it is sanctification of his soul,
it is subjection of his will.

It is a true act of confession,
it is the equivalent of three three-day fasts;
it is the prayer of a hundred believers
wherever it is recited.

It is a relic, it is a eucharist,
it is a canticle together with the psalms,
it is protection for the faithful,
it is intercession for the dead.

Even though his heart be hard,
it awakens piety.
His glory rises up;
it carries him into the kingdom of heaven.

It is a breastplate guarding faith
from the temptations of demons;
it adorns a vigil with gold,
it heals every pestilence.

It is a prayer in [this] life
against the terror of every peril;
it sanctifies deeds,
it prolongs life.

It reveals miracles,
it exalts every settlement,
it grants the loftiest rank,
it maintains dignity.

It is fear of the Lord,
it is unswerving love of God,
it banishes demons
and summons angels.

Very wondrous are all
the miracles which we relate:
there is a blessing upon everyone
who reads them hereafter.

Provided that it was thus that he used to pray
to the fair Lord,
the worms of the earth will not touch him
nor will his corpse decay.

None will oppose his entry
into bright heaven;
after he has reached it,
healing will come from the dew upon his grave.

In remembering their feast-days,
may constancy in praying to them protect me:
it is not toil in vain
that we have reckoned them all.

Close is our friendship
with the royal multitude which I have reckoned:
after numbering their feast-days
I will enumerate their companies:

The company of the archangels of heaven,
with noble blessed Michael,
with the nine orders of the gracious King,
of the city of the mighty King;

The company of the ancients[28] surrounding Noah,
across the expanses of the salt seas:
the companion of the noble radiant King,
the rebirth of the world;

Isaiah's company of seers,
the fair prophet of whom we sing;
we pray to the patriarchs
with wonderful Abraham;

28 The Irish word *rerach* can mean either 'ancient one' in a broad sense or can, as here, refer
more specifically to the patriarchs who lived before the Flood.

The company of the apostles surrounding Peter,
with the disciples of Jesus:
fearless preeminent Paul,
the loftiest chief of learning;

The company of martyrs with Stephen,
the pure golden bush;
the anchorites surrounding Paul the Old;
the company of holy virgins surrounding Mary;

The company of the holy bishops of Rome,
a glorious community surrounding Peter;
the bishops of Jerusalem
with noble James;

The company of the bishops of Antioch
with Peter, their first flame;
the bishops of Alexandria
with ruddy royal Mark;

The holy company of Honoratus,
the famous warrior leading hosts;
the learned company which was ennobled
along with triumphant Benedict;

George's famous company,
no puny thing to gaze upon;
every boy who was martyred
by Herod in Bethlehem;

The company of priests who suffered
the torment of the cross for the sake of Christ:
may they help me every day
together with Aaron, the rod of sages;

The company of monks surrounding Anthony,
whose ways lead among mysteries;
a lofty company of the saints of the world
with Martin, the soldier of battle;

The company of the high saints of Ireland
with Patrick, who is highest;
Colum Cille
with the companies of the saints of Scotland;

One last mighty company
which completes the fair chain:
Saint Brigit, after victories,
with the virgins of Ireland.

May all these companies,
together with noble high kings,
come to my aid: a white shining host,
a mighty army of saints.

Every saint who was, is, and will be
until the mighty separation on the Day of Judgment:
may they be a help to me,
companions of devoted Christ!

May they be a help to me
in heaven and on earth;
may they come in their multitudes
to the aid of my soul.

For as long as my soul
and my injured body suffer,
may the royal multitude
to which I have prayed be a help to me.

I have prayed to the royal company
concerning whom the search was made:
truly blessed Jesus,
it is to you that I pray now.

High King who is not hidden,
Christ whose follower[29] I am:
after [my] enumeration of these companies
have mercy on me.

---

29 The word *céile* can be translated 'friend', 'companion', 'follower', 'client', or 'servant'. In this
context it also alludes to the ascetic revival movement of the *Céili Dé* ('Servants of God'), to
which Oengus belonged; cf. the introductory remarks to 'Stories of the Céili Dé' below.

Have mercy on me,
royal abundant Lord,
Jesus whom I love,
great God to whom I pray.

Great God to whom I pray,
hear my sad groan!
May I, after this struggle,
be with this host forever.

The great host which I enumerate
has died every kind of death:
to you, Christ who is noblest,
I invoke their sufferings.

I invoke their innocent blood
upon the roads,
I invoke their limbs,
and the spears [thrust] through their flanks.

I invoke their groans,
their keen sighs;
that you may take pity on me, Christ,
I invoke their feast-days.

Against the world's violence
(and great is its power)
I invoke their yearning
as they stand around you in white garments.

I invoke their spirits
in your beautiful royal Kingdom;
to you – for they should be known –
I invoke their relics.

So that you may not refuse
every prayer which I utter,
I invoke their tears
upon their white faces.

I invoke your heavenly Kingdom,
vast and mighty,
[filled] from centre to edge
with holy troops of angels.

I invoke every sacrifice
which has been offered under showers:
your dear body, beneath the clouds,
upon holy altars.

I invoke the shout of victory
cried out by every son of piety:
a shower of cold blood
through his own side.

Your humanity, your divinity:
together with your beautiful Holy Spirit,
I invoke your bond
with the heavenly Father.

Together with your saints, I invoke to you
all that I have said:
may I possess in your Kingdom
all that for which I have cried out.

In every struggle in which
my proud, spirited mind has been overcome
by my shrewd body,
your household has prayed.

Jesus, give ear
to your weak, puny outcast:
I think it better to part from the world
than to remain in it.

May my suffering be healed
as recompense for my prayer.
My Friend is not grudging:
I invoke all things [in praying] to you.

Hail, choir of heaven!
May one of you give heed to me.
It troubles me greatly
that I am not in your company.

Great grief afflicts me
here beneath the fair starry heaven:
it is good to be in your company,
but your absence is heavy for me.

You can help me,
for your compassion is great:
heal my heart
for the sake of Mary's Son.

I am tightly confined
in a narrow body of skin.
Great are my faults,
[but] you can help me.

If you possess charity,
with its proper reckoning,
there would be here for you, in the depths,
a wretch to whom it could be shown.

If you can admonish,
it is the right time for you to come:
here there is one who is most forlorn,
a weakling of the tribe of Jesus.

Although there is no danger for you
before the face of the King of clouds,
I am a sorry weakling
without help for my tears.

Holy company of the seven heavens,
since your compassion is great,
heal my heart
for the sake of Mary's Son.

For the sake of the King
to whom this cry is made,
help this poor wretch
in his affliction!

Though all these prayers
seem miserable to the brethren,
it is to you, Christ,
that I have prayed in this hour.

I pray another prayer
for the sake of the men of the world,
Lord of princes,
King who gives judgments.

Perhaps the whole of this prayer
is not pleasing to men:
after our time, lest it be [a cause of] anger,
let the prayer be changed.

The prayer which I have prayed
seeks no harm for men:
I think it better to part from wickedness
than to remain therein.

Hearken, Jesus,
Christ whose servant I am:
grant all that there is
in the prayer of every son of piety.

Lord, the prayer of every son of piety
is not a useless thing:
grant them what they ask,
if it be proper.

If what they ask be proper,
King who rules the earth,
deliver their bodies,
sanctify their souls.

Through you, the soul
of every son of life has been sanctified:
the race of noblest Adam
has been delivered, Jesus.

Deliver me, Jesus,
my body and my soul,
from every evil which there is,
[every evil] which assails the earth.

Deliver me, Jesus,
fair Lord of covenants,
as you delivered Elijah
and Enoch from the world.

Deliver me, Jesus,
from every evil upon the earth,
as you delivered Noah
son of Lamech from the Flood.

Deliver me, Jesus,
King of pure radiance,
as you delivered Abraham
from the hands of the Chaldaeans.

Deliver me, Jesus,
gracious King of mysteries,
as you delivered Lot
from the sin of the cities.

Deliver me, Jesus,
lofty wondrous King,
as you delivered Jonah
from the belly of the great sea-monster.

Deliver me, Jesus,
in your heaven full of graces,
as you delivered Isaac
from his father's hands.

Deliver me, Jesus,
when you come with your saints,
as you delivered Thecla
from the jaws of the beast.

Deliver me, Jesus,
for your mother's sake,
as you delivered Jacob
from his brother's hands.

Deliver me, Jesus,
from every evil unloved thing (?),
as you delivered John
from the venom of the serpent.

Deliver me, Jesus,
from woeful hell,
as you delivered David
from the fury of Goliath's sword.

Deliver me, Jesus,
you who have delivered all,
[as you delivered] Susannah, with her honour,
when she was slandered.

Deliver me, Jesus,
for the sake of your word,
as you delivered Nineveh
at the time of plague.

Deliver me, Jesus –
I know that you will not deny me –
as you delivered the people of Israel
from Mount Gilboa.

Deliver me, Jesus,
most holy Lord,
as you delivered Daniel
from the lions' den.

Deliver me, Jesus,
glorious gracious King,
as you delivered Moses
from the hand of Pharaoh.

Deliver me, Jesus –
you have wrought great miracles –
as you delivered the three youths
from the furnace of fire.

Deliver me, Jesus,
King of every kindred,
as you delivered Tobias
from the affliction of blindness.[30]

Deliver me, Jesus,
for the sake of your martyrs,
[as you delivered] Paul and Peter, before the kings,
from the penalty of imprisonment.

Deliver me, Jesus,
from the ravages of every sickness,
as you delivered Job
from the torments of demons.

Deliver me, Jesus –
may it not be neglected, Christ –
as you delivered David
when Saul was accusing him.

Deliver me, Jesus,
for the sake of your mother's kin,
as you delivered Joseph
from the hands of his brothers.

Deliver me, Jesus,
blessed King,
[as you delivered] holy Israel
from the slavery of Egypt.

30 Thus the text; in the Biblical account however it is not Tobias who is blind, but his father
Tobit.

Deliver me, Jesus,
for it is with you that I have made my alliance,
as you delivered Peter
from the waves of the sea.

Deliver me, Jesus,
from fierce ravenous hell,
as you delivered John
from the flaming cauldron.

Deliver me, Jesus,
King above the princes,
as you delivered Samson
when he escaped from the city.

Deliver, Jesus,
my soul from every vengeance,
as you delivered Martin
from the priest of the idol.

Deliver me, Jesus,
for the sake of your followers,
as you delivered Patrick
from poison in Tara.

Deliver me, Jesus,
for I am your servant,
as you delivered Coemgen
from the falling mountain.

Deliver me, Jesus:
your miracles are everlasting.
Lord whom I invoke,
I look to your coming.

When [your] bounty shall reach me (?),
whether it be in Easter or Lent,
may the royal multitude which I have enumerated
comfort and protect me.

IV THE HOLY LIFE

Aipgitir Chrábaid: 'The Alphabet of Devotion'

Most of the manuscripts in which this text appears ascribe it to Colmán mac Beógnai, nephew of Colum Cille of Iona and abbot of Lynally in County Offaly, who died in the year 611. If this attribution is correct, it is one of the oldest documents in the Irish language which has come down to us. Various statements in the *Aipgitir* itself point to its having been composed at a very early period: thus paganism is still spoken of as a threat; a single word (*crésine*) signifies both 'the religious life' and 'Christianity', again suggesting a society in which not everyone was Christian; and the characterisation of the man who is 'at a distance' from Christianity seems to describe a wealthy pagan who, although he serves as a patron to Christian converts, postpones his own baptism.

This historical dimension, however intriguing and important, is far from exhausting the *Aipgitir's* interest for us. It is a collection of precepts and maxims, arranged in sequences of varying length, which reflect a keen perception of the ethics and psychology of the contemplative life. Drawing on the monastic treatises of John Cassian (died 435), on the sapiential books of the Old Testament, and probably on native wisdom literature as well, the author distils his teachings into phrases of two or three words each – statements whose crystalline economy of expression demands slow and meditative reading. The *Aipgitir* is laid out as a series of parallelisms and contrasts, which clarify and develop fundamental concepts as they unfold. Its subtlety and acuteness repay careful study: much experience of human nature lies behind such deceptively simple passages as the list of complementary virtues with which the text begins, the list of vices which can masquerade as virtues on p. 237, and the discussion of truth on pp. 237–9.

Although much of the *Aipgitir's* teaching is applicable to any Christian, or indeed to anyone seeking to live a spiritual life, its audience was evidently a monastic one: the text speaks of rising at the summons of the bell, obedience to the prior, and communal life with the brethren. It is conceived, like much Irish didactic literature, as a series of instructions given by a master to his disciple: hence the frequent use of the second person singular ('What does that bring about for you?'; 'How should you speak the truth?'; 'You should not ask; you should not refuse').

With its repeated references to the decay or destruction of desires, and the joys of heaven, the *Aipgitir* is markedly otherworldly in its orientation; the author also stresses, however, that a virtuous life will have 'hundredfold' rewards here on earth. These rewards take the form of good reputation, rather than the physical pleasures to which the laity might aspire: a saintly monk will have a seat with the elders of the community, 'honour upon earth', and freedom from mockery and slander.[1]

1 This may be one of the ideas drawn from Cassian's *Collationes*; thus Ó Néill 1987, 207. References in the *Aipgitir* to property and to the receiving of gifts seem to be later additions (cf. note 9 below).

The *Aipgitir* appears to have been written roughly a century and a half prior to the ascetic revival associated with such figures as Mael Ruain of Tallaght, some account of which is given in the 'Stories of the Céili Dé' below. It evidently exercised a potent influence on that movement, and in fact one copy is inserted in the collection of material from which those anecdotes are drawn.[2] The *Aipgitir's* enunciation of general principles, and the attention given in the stories to their enactment in practice, complement one another to provide a rich and nuanced picture of the Irish monastic ideal; it has been suggested that the *Aipgitir* 'very probably served as an initiation to be used by the director of the young, to be fleshed out in more detail for them by explanations and examples on the lines of the Tallaght documents.'[3]

In the lucid conciseness of its pregnant, interlocking teachings, the *Aipgitir Chrábaid* often approaches the diction of poetry – and indeed some of its sections, with their rhythmic cadences and chains of alliteration, resemble the conservative accentual verse found in Irish legal treatises and heroic sagas. It was clearly intended to sink deep into the memories of those who heard it and, once absorbed, to guide them from within.

2 Gwynn and Purton 1911, 161.   3 O Dwyer 1981, 182.

Faith together with works,
eagerness together with steadfastness,
tranquillity together with zeal,
chastity together with humility,
fasting together with moderation,
poverty together with generosity,
silence together with conversation,
division together with equality,[4]
patience without resentment,
detachment together with nearness,[5]
fervour without harshness,
mildness together with fairness,
confidence without carelessness,
fear without despair,
poverty without arrogance,
confession without excuses,
teaching together with fulfilling,[6]
climbing without falling,
being low toward the lofty,
being smooth toward the harsh,
work without grumbling,
guilelessness together with prudence,
humility without laxity,
religion without hypocrisy –
    all these things are contained in holiness.

It is when full of charity that one is holy.
    He walks in charity.
Every evil fears him;
    every good loves him.
He has honour upon earth;
    he has glory in heaven.

---

4 That is, recognition of the various strengths, weaknesses, and offices of individuals, but avoidance of elitism or privilege. 5 That is, the ability to be free of attachment while still living among the things of the world, and one's fellow mortals. 6 That is, practising what one preaches.

Love God:
>   everyone will love you.
Fear God:
>   everyone will fear you.

This is the rule of the clergy: devotion subject to moderation according to God's will. He who learns it and practises it will be rewarded hundreds of times on earth, and will possess the kingdom of heaven.

Everyone should call upon and beseech the Lord of heaven and earth to stir up fear and love of Him within his heart; for until the fear of God enters his heart, one is but lukewarm (?).
When fear is weak, repentance is weak.
When repentance is weak, religion is weak.
For he who does not fear God will not love Him.
He who does not love him will not fulfil His commandments.
He who does not fulfil his commandments will not possess eternal life in heaven.
For in fear, love is found.[7]
In love, holy action is found.
In holy action is found eternal life in heaven.

Love of the living God
>   washes the soul,
>   contents the mind,
>   magnifies rewards,
>   casts out vices,
>   renders the earth hateful,[8]
>   washes and binds the thoughts.
What does the love of God accomplish in a person?
>   It kills his desires,
>   it cleanses his heart,
>   it protects him,
>   it swallows up his vices,
>   it earns rewards,
>   it prolongs his life,
>   it washes his soul.

---

7 Literally, 'fear contains love'.   8 Literally, 'rots the earth'.

There are four redemptions of the soul:
 fear and repentance,
 love and hope.
Two of them protect it on earth,
 the two others bear it up to heaven.
Fear is an obstacle to the sins which are ahead;
 repentance dissolves the sins which have gone before.
Love of the Creator, and hope for His kingdom:
 it is they that bear it up to heaven.
Anyone, then, who fears God,
 and loves Him,
 and does His will and keeps His commandments,
will have honour among men here
 and blessedness with God beyond.

WHAT A MAN SHOULD LEARN

What should a man learn?

Not hard to answer:
 constancy in holiness,
 shortness of words,
 gentle brotherliness,
 smoothness in giving,
 fulfilling the rule without urging,
 rising early before dawn,
 walking in obedience to God,
 clemency in pardoning,
 watching over the sick,
 zeal in prayer,
 fasting with the brethren (?),
 compassion for a neighbour,
 bringing pride low,
 simplicity of heart,
 shattering desire,
 trampling nature,
 patience in the face of hardship.

What does that bring about for you?

Not hard to answer:
    an invitation from the elders,
    a comfortable seat,
    an unexpected gift from someone,
    gain without struggle,
    many hundredfolds,
    friendship with the brethren,
    eternal life in heaven.

What should be avoided by a holy person?

Not hard to answer:
    recurrent anger,
    vanity without skill, without property,[9]
    boldness toward a superior,
    slowness in answer to the bell,
    conspiring with false witnesses,
    too much travel,
    mocking the brethren,
    impure words,
    sharpness in answering,
    holding out against the prior,
    resisting reproof,
    quarreling with the monks,
    asking questions often.

What does all that bring about for you?

Not hard to answer:
    separation from the elders,
    toil without sparing,
    scant reward,
    being held suspect by others,
    fasting without benefit,
    giving honour to the Dark One,
    blackening the patron saint,
    exile from heaven.

9 Rank in early Ireland was based on the possession either of material wealth (usually reckoned in cattle), or of a craft or skill; as it stands, the line appears to reflect these two criteria. Probably,

It is proper that we not let the vices beguile [us] in the guise of the virtues.[10]

> For laxity can beguile [us] in the guise of compassion,
> severity in the guise of righteousness,
> pride in the guise of uprightness,
> unholy fear –
>> which does not protect righteousness,
>> which does not denounce wrong –
>>> in the guise of humility,
> meanness and avarice in the guise of moderation,
> arrogance in the guise of chastity,
> presumptuousness in the guise of abstinence,
> wastefulness and prodigality in the guise of generosity,
> intemperate anger in the guise of spiritual fervour,
> feebleness and effeminacy in the guise of tranquillity,
> hardness and calculation in the guise of steadiness,
> haste (?) and flightiness in the guise of genius,
> partiality (?) and instability in the guise of flexibility,
> laziness and indolence in the guise of detachment,
> hesitation in the guise of prudence.

> He who lives in unity with the universal church,
>> and reposes in the hope of heaven,
>> and fulfils the commandments as they have been commanded,
> will have hundrefold rewards on earth
>> and eternal life in heaven.

ON KNOWING THE TRUTH[11]

> If anyone desires to know the truth,
>> he should correctly know what hides it, what reveals it.
> Truth hides itself from everyone who despises it;
>> it reveals itself to everyone who fulfils it.

however, this was not the original reading. The sequence in which the phrase occurs is bound together by linking alliteration: the words *cen folad* 'without property' break this pattern, and are evidently a secondary addition. Other phrases in the text also look like insertions: in the immediately preceding section, omission of 'an unexpected gift from someone' and 'many hundredfolds' yields linking alliteration throughout.   10 Literally, 'in the place of the virtues'.
11 Here as elsewhere in the *Aipgitir* the section-heading is in Latin, while the text which follows is in Irish. *Veritas* in the heading unequivocally means 'truth'; its Irish equivalent in what follows

Four things cover up the truth:
    love and fear,
    indulgence and poverty.

As long as a person is unrighteous, he cannot properly proclaim the
    truth.
Three things seize upon him then:
    boastfulness and pride and anger.
If anyone yields to him,
    it awakens boastfulness in him.
If anyone resists him,
    it awakens anger and pride in him.
For many yearn for the truth; save for a few holy folk, however, they
    are wrathful and savage in their search for it.

Two things are to be guarded against in yearning for the truth: anger
    and lukewarmness (?). For whichever befalls it, it is an injury to the
    truth.

With respect to yearning for the truth, it is fitting that its require-
    ments be striven for:
    fervour without anger,
    humility without negligence.

In what manner should the truth be proclaimed?
    With humility, without indulgence;
    for the truth is not indulgent.
The humble person, however:
    he who is not truly humble is not righteous;
    he who is not righteous is not truly wise.
For there is not room for both true wisdom and unrighteousness in a
    person:
    thick is the veil between them.
His righteousness is nearer to encountering wisdom
    than his wisdom is to encountering righteousness:
for a person is truly wise when he is righteous.

How should you speak the truth?
    Without bitterness, without indulgence,
    with patience, with gentleness.

Moderation and wisdom and true holiness:
>one attains to them together.
When does one attain to them?
>When his truth is without fault.
When is his truth without fault?
>It is when his heart is as it should be that truth is therein, as if
>>it was not born from man.[12]

ON THE SOUL'S VIRTUES[13]

The fifteen virtues of the soul:
>the virtue of faith,
>the virtue of gentleness,
>the virtue of humility,
>the virtue of patience,
>the virtue of mortification,
>the virtue of obedience,
>the virtue of charity,
>the virtue of truth,
>the virtue of mercy,
>the virtue of generosity,
>the virtue of forbearance,
>the virtue of brotherliness (?),
>the virtue of moderation,
>the virtue of holiness,
>the virtue of almsgiving.
Any one of these virtues which one practises in addition to another,[14]
>it will reduce his trial in the fire,
>it will magnify his advocacy in heaven.

When is one capable of bearing witness on behalf of the souls of others?
>When he is capable first of bearing witness on behalf of his own.
When is he capable of correcting others?
>When he can first correct himself.

is however *firinne*, meaning both 'truth' and 'righteousness'. In translating, I have used the English word which seems most appropriate to each individual instance. 12 This somewhat obscure phrase seems to mean that when the heart is cleansed of its human failings it is filled with divine illumination. Cf. the discussion of the 'vessel of the Holy Spirit', p. 245 below. 13 Latin *virtus* is rendered below by *nert*, an Irish word whose usual sense is 'strength, power'. 14 Apparently an allusion to the doctrine, most fully exemplified in the first section above, that virtues should be practised in complementary pairs.

When a person converts his own soul to life, how many souls could
   he convert?
      The people of the whole world: provided that they are open to
         correction, he could convert them to life so that they would
         belong to the kingdom of heaven.
      It is their own resistance to correction, and their wickedness,
         and their inconstancy, which exile them from the kingdom of
         heaven.

The body shelters the soul.
The soul shelters the mind.
The mind shelters the heart.
The heart shelters faith.
Faith shelters God.
God shelters man.

As a lamp brings forth its light in a dark house,
      so truth rises in the midst of faith in a person's heart.
When it rises there, it casts out four darknesses:
      the darkness of paganism,
      the darkness of ignorance,
      the darkness of doubt,
      the darkness of sin,
so that there is not room for any of them there.

Three come to Christianity:
      one of them is within it,
      another is beside it,
      another is at a distance from it.
But they are not equal:
      the one who is within it is better than the one who is beside it;
      the one who is beside it is better than the one who is at a dis-
         tance from it.
The one who is within it is he who pays three things each day,
      so that he may obtain the life of his soul:
      any good of which he has heard,
      and any good thing which he has seen,
         he has loved and believed in and fulfilled it.
The one who is beside it is he who renounces the world with his lips
      and affirms it in his heart.

He frets (?) over fasting and prayer.
>He has not declared war upon avarice and stinginess.
One of his hands is stretched to heaven (?),
>the other to earth.
The one who is at a distance from it is he who maintains Christians
>with his wealth,[15]
>but does not practise their customs for as long as he lives;
>he thinks it easier to do so at some other time.

The three enemies of the soul:
>the world,
>and the Devil,
>and a sinful teacher.

Three things which drive out the spirit of instability, and make the
>mind steadfast:
>vigil,
>and prayer,
>and labour.

The four foundations of piety:
>patience to withstand every desire,
>forbearance to withstand every wrong,
>asking pardon for every deception,
>forgiving every sin.

Four teachings for which we should strive, even if we do not fulfil them:
>devotion to God,
>gentleness to men,
>good will to every person,
>expecting death each day.

Four things which do not befall anyone who loves God:
>he is not ridiculed,
>he is not threatened,
>slander does not strike him,
>he is not thought ill of by any.

---

15 The phrase 'with his wealth' follows 'customs' in the manuscripts, but seems to give better sense here. Wealthy pagans supporting Irish Christians are mentioned in the early text *Synodus Episcoporum* (Bieler 1975, 56–9 §§13, 24).

He is thought well of by all;
    he thinks well of all.

The four guarantees of the sons of life:
    decay of desires,
    fear of punishments,
    love of hardships,
    belief in rewards.
If the desires did not decay,
    they would not be relinquished.
If the punishments were not feared,
    they would not be guarded against.
If the hardships were not loved,
    they would not be endured.
If the rewards were not believed in,
    they would not be gained.

The four bonds of sinners:
    their eyes closing to the world,
    the earth closing over their bodies,
    the kingdom of heaven being closed to their souls,
    hell closing upon them.

The four oppressions of sinners:
    it oppresses them that they do not give up their desires;
    it oppresses them that their torments will not pass;
    it oppresses them that they did not repent [until] it was too late;
    it oppresses them that they have no dwelling in the Kingdom.

Four things which warfare[16] brings upon one:
    it compresses boundaries,
    it increases enmities,
    it shortens life,
    it lengthens punishments.

16 The Irish word *fiannas* can mean any kind of violence, whether perpetrated by a king's warriors or by outlaws; from the reference to changing territorial boundaries it appears that it specifically designates military activity here.

Four things through which the kingdom of God may be sought:
    steadfastness and detachment from the world,
    devotion and constancy.

A man's four heavens[17] in this world:
    youth and wealth,
    health and friendship.
A man's four hells in this world:
    disease and old age,
    poverty and friendlessness.

Three things through which the Devil is made visible in a man:
    through face,
    through step,
    through speech.
And through these three God is recognised in a man.

A man pronounces three renunciations in the three waves which go
        over him at baptism:
    he renounces the world with its splendours;
    he renounces the Devil with his traps;
    he renounces the desires of the flesh.
This is what changes a man
    from a son of death to a son of life,
    from a son of darkness to a son of light.
If he breaks these three vows,
    [made] in the three waves which go over him,
he cannot enter the kingdom of God unless he pass again through
        three fluids:
    the fluid of the tears of repentance,
    the fluid of blood shed in penance,
    the fluid of the sweat of toil.

What is best in religion?
    Simplicity and sincerity.
A lazy religiosity,
    which avoids much hardship,
will have much trial in the fire,
    will have little reward in heaven.

17 Literally, 'kingdoms', understanding 'kingdom' (*flaith*) to mean 'kingdom of heaven'.

An active religiosity,
  which avoids much comfort,
will have little trial in the fire,
  will have a great reward in heaven.

What is best in a mind?
  Breadth and lowliness;
  for every good thing can find room in a broad and lowly mind.
What is worst in a mind?
  Narrowness and confinement[18] and tightness;
  for no good thing can find room in a mind which is narrow,
    confined, and tight.

Desire and youth, death and old age:
  it is better to guard against them from afar.

You should not ask; you should not refuse;
  you should protect; you should bestow.

He who does not denounce, agrees.
He who does not forbid, commands.
He who is silent, conceals.
He who shares the deed[19] will share the punishment.

THE THREE PRINCIPAL COMMANDMENTS

If anyone desires the commandments, let him go to the crossroad
    where they all pass.
Let him take charity and humility and patience into his heart.
For thus the commandments will not go from him, but he will have
    them all in their wholeness.

THE MOST PRUDENT MAN

Who is most prudent?
  He who praises before death what he fears after death.

18 Hull translates the otherwise unattested *cróche* as 'bloodthirstiness (?)', taking it to be an abstract noun ultimately based on *crú* 'blood, gore'; the context however suggests a derivation from *cró* 'pen, enclosure'. 19 More literally perhaps 'shares the service': the verb *con-mancha*, otherwise unattested, seems to mean something like 'jointly performs (monastic) service'.

You do well in correcting.
> You do not do well in rebuking.
> The mind rises up against rebuke.
It is lowly toward correction.

Wisdom without learning is better than learning without wisdom.

Who is closest to God?
> The one who meditates concerning Him.
Whom does Christ help?
> The one who does good.
In whom does the Holy Spirit abide?
> In the one who is pure, without sin.
> One is a vessel of the Holy Spirit when the virtues come in place
>   of the vices.

Desire of God grows in one
> when worldly desire decays.

We had better be mindful of the five meetings to which we shall come:
> a meeting with groaning,
> a meeting with death,
> a meeting with God's household,
> a meeting with demons,
> a meeting with resurrection on the Day of Judgment.

The end. Amen.

Stories of the Céili Dé

The eighth century saw a monastic revival in Ireland, an attempt to recover the austere way of life and fervent devotion to prayer attributed to the saints of earlier times. Many clerics and religious houses were connected with this movement, which is generally known as that of the *Céili Dé* (anglicised as 'Culdees') or 'Servants of God'; but the figure most closely associated with its rise is Mael Ruain (died 792), founder of the monastery of Tallaght. Various documents have survived which describe the practices of the Céili Dé, affording a vivid picture of Irish monastic life in this period; below I give selections from one of these, apparently the work of a follower of Mael Ruain's disciple Mael Díthruib.

Unlike much early Irish religious writing, these little stories are distinguished by their realism and practicality: even when an angel descends from heaven, as in the story of the assembly of Mag Léna, he does so in order to discourage rigid idealism. By the standards of most moderns, the life-style described is forbiddingly harsh; but it is an asceticism which takes careful account of the body's frailties. In sections of the text which I have not included here, it is repeatedly emphasised that no single dietary regimen can be appropriate for everyone, and special provision is made for the old and sick. The story of the abbot of Iona who revived his monks by feeding them butter without their knowledge illustrates the same compassionate flexibility; and excessive austerity is condemned in such stories as the account of Colcu of Slane.

Although the discipline and purification of the body are primary concerns of the text, it is in some respects notably relaxed in the view which it takes of the moral implications of physical impulses. To feel desire is not itself a sin – merely the result of an excess of fluid in the body, and one which can be corrected by a change of diet. When a hermit has a sexual dream it is his reaction to it, not the experience itself, which is significant in the eyes of God. Most striking of all, perhaps, is the story of the monk who sinned with a woman whom he encountered on the road: in the end he is rebuked not for the act itself, but for brooding on his own remorse rather than accepting the advice of his superiors.

Mael Ruain, Mael Díthruib, Duiblittir, and the rest sought to establish enclosed communities in which the search for perfection could be pursued with a minimum of distractions and temptations: their aim was not to reform the church as a whole, but to create enclaves of purity within it. In many cases in fact they were supported by the wealth of the less rigorous 'old churches', to which they felt entitled as the spiritual heirs of the founder saints. And so a proselytising spirit is markedly lacking in the zeal of the Céili Dé, who often indeed were reluctant to take responsibility for the spiritual welfare of outsiders. What appears in some of the stories as an almost callous indifference can be seen in other cases as an open-minded generosity of spirit. Although Mael Ruain did not himself approve of listening to music, he sent food to the piper hermit Cornán; and we are told that the latter was considered to be 'a man of grace'.

The movement's growth surely suffered greatly from the incursions of the Vikings, whose attacks on Ireland began at the eighth century's close: Tallaght itself, and the Céili Dé community of Finglas, were both adjacent to the Viking settlement at Dublin. The revival's most lasting and pervasive legacy has been in the field of literature, for at the hands of the Céili Dé the use of the Irish language for religious purposes was greatly developed and extended. Oengus mac Oengobann, whose *Féilire* is a particularly imposing example of the union of sacred subject matter and vernacular artistry, blesses Mael Ruain as his teacher, calling him 'a great sun upon the southern plain of Meath'.

A retired warrior was living with a son of life. He said that he did not know why he spent so much time reciting the *Beati*[1] and the canticle of Mary (that is, the *Magnificat*).

'That is not hard to answer,' he said. 'A man standing at the foot of the gallows would pour out praise and supplication to the king, so that he might be freed. In the same way we pour out supplication in the *Beati* to the King of heaven, so that we may be freed. And it is fitting that the diadem which came forth from the head of Mary the virgin, after she had conceived by the Holy Spirit through the message of the angel, should be set as a crown upon that hymn, in which are praise of God and supplication to him.'

Mael Díthruib of Terryglass asked Helair of Loch Cré whether, if the way of life of the folk of the old churches were not [devout] enough, he should accept any of the church's produce from them. Helair said that he should take it, 'for it does not pollute you, provided that you have no share in ordaining them or disciplining them; for though they may be polluted themselves, they do not pollute the produce of the patron saint. For that belongs more properly to us than to them.' The only bread which used to be given to him, on his island, was the bread of Ros Cré. Helair said, 'It is Mo Chua's bread which is given to us.'[2]

No drop of beer was drunk in Tallaght during Mael Ruain's life. As for his community, when they went elsewhere they would not drink a drop of beer in the region of Cualu, whomever they might meet; but they were told that they could drink when they journeyed far off. No scrap of meat was eaten in Tallaght during his life, except for a stag or a wild pig. It was guests <who ate>[3] such meat as was there.

Duiblittir came to Mael Ruain, to urge upon him that these austerities should be relaxed for his community on the three principal holy days, even if there were no relaxation afterward or beforehand.

---

1 Psalm 118, *Beati immaculati in uia*. On this psalm's sanctity in early Ireland see p. 143, note 4 and p. 147, note 3 above.   2 Mo Chua, or Crónán, was the founder and patron saint of Ros Cré; Helair, in the adjacent island monastery of Loch Cré, argues that by maintaining the ideals of the founder he has a better right to be Mo Chua's heir than have the monks of Ros Cré themselves. 3 Manuscript illegible at this point.

Mael Ruain said, 'For as long as I am in authority, and for as long as my rule is observed in this place, the ale of forgetfulness of God will not be drunk here.'

'Well,' said Duiblittir, 'my community drink it, and they will be in heaven along with yours.'

Mael Ruain said, 'Anyone in the community who listens to me, and keeps my rule, will not need to be purified by the fire of Doomsday, nor to attend the Judgment, for they will be pure already. Perhaps though there will be something in your community which the fire of Doomsday can cleanse.'

There was a bishop of the Déisi in Finglas, whose name was Cainchomrac. He was the soul-friend of Duiblittir. One day the two of them left the garden in advance of the brethren, crossing over into the green. There was a poor old woman in the green, begging Duiblittir to let her sleep in the nuns' house.[4]

The old woman's prayers to God exasperated him. 'Go back the way you came,' he said, 'and ill luck be upon your face!'

At that, Cainchomrac at once prostrated himself upon the ground. 'What is this?' asked Duiblittir. 'Grave is the deed which you have dared,' said Cainchomrac: 'denouncing the unfortunate woman.'

At once he too prostrated himself. 'I will do your will in this matter,' said Duiblittir. 'This is my will,' said Cainchomrac: 'let her go into the nuns' house, and let a cow and a cloak be given to her. And now we will devise the penance which it is proper for you to perform.' 'So be it,' said Duiblittir.

Mael Ruain did not recommend listening to music.[5] A piper named Cornán lived in the south of Leinster; he was a hermit. They called him Cornán of Glenn Essa, a man of grace; Mael Ruain used to send him offerings. Once he said to Mael Ruain's community, 'If only I could play music for the cleric!' Afterward, Mael Ruain said, 'Say to Cornán: "These ears are not inclined to the music of the earth, so that they may be inclined to the music of heaven".'

Mael Díthruib asked Mael Ruain if it was enough to recite fifty psalms, if it happened that one gave instruction together with them. Mael Ruain said that, in his opinion, what there was in the whole Psalter was not beyond

4 This sentence is somewhat ambiguous: the word *caillech* can mean both 'old woman' and 'nun', and seems to be used in both senses here.   5 The manuscript has 'stories'; but 'music' gives better sense in context, and appears in the version of this anecdote in the later *Teaching of Mael Ruain* (Gwynn 1927, 31 §50).

[anyone's] ability. 'For that is the additional task of all of us. Thus we have a man for the sickle, and for the flail, and for the measuring-rod, and for the ditch: the three fifties are the additional task of each of them, and none of them goes to the table until he has done his additional task.'

Nothing which one does for the sake of the dead is not helpful: vigils, fasting, requiems, almsgiving, frequent blessings. Maedóc's whole community spent an entire year on bread and water, to deliver the soul of Brandub mac Echach. Children ought to do penance for the sake of their dead parents, etc.

The daughter of the king in the lands to the east offered land to Fursa. This is what she said to Fursa: 'What kind of man are you?' 'I am,' he said, 'like an old blacksmith, with his anvil on his back.' 'The anvil of faith?' she said. 'Constancy in holiness,' he said. 'If God should give you a block on which your anvil could be set, would you remain with it?' 'It is likely,' he said. Then she offered him the place in which he was.

[Mael Díthruib] considers that anyone who undertakes some good deed in his own mind should make a vow to perform it, and should announce whatever he has undertaken; for what one does only in thought does not please God greatly.

This is what Mo Cholmóc ua Litáin had to say regarding constant preparation to do a thing. A layman came to ask him for soul-friendship. 'What kind of life do you lead?' asked Mo Cholmóc. 'Do you still live in union with your wife?' 'No,' he said; 'it is three years since we had intercourse together.' 'Have you made a vow?' asked Mo Cholmóc. 'No,' he said. Then Mo Cholmóc said, 'That is too long to be parted from the Devil without coming to God. For one enters God's household when one takes a vow.'

With regard to soul-friendship, some think that it is sufficient if they merely make confession, even if they do not do penance afterwards. [Mael Díthruib] does not recommend this. He does however think that it is good to give them such advice as will be profitable to them, even if one does not ask them to confess.

Helair received many at first, but in the end dismissed them all; for he saw that they were not fervent in their penance, and that they concealed things when making confession. After that, he ended by receiving no one in soul-friendship; he used however to allow some of the perfect to seek his advice.

As for Mael Ruain, in the end he had no difficulty in turning folk away; he had not even much desire to receive Mael Díthruib. He said, 'Did you ask permission back there, before coming here?' 'Yes,' said Mael Díthruib. 'Even artisans,' said Mael Ruain, 'blacksmiths and carpenters and the rest, do not take it kindly if one of their community goes to someone else.' 'I have anticipated you,' said Mael Díthruib; 'I have obtained leave and permission.' Then he prostrated himself in submission to Mael Ruain.

'You will have a year with us in which to be purified afresh,' said Mael Ruain: 'three times forty nights on bread and water, except for a mouthful of milk on Sundays.' And he was allowed to mix a little whey in the water, but only during the summer Lent.[6] Until that time he had been subject to the soul-friendship of Échtguide.

Mael Ruain said to him, 'When you hear of someone's death, the fire which you think it worst to be burned by is the one to which you will go.'

Mael Díthruib said to Mael Ruain, 'For a long time I have longed for four things. First, I have longed for whatever holy writings have come into Ireland, to read them and to cast my eyes upon them. And I have longed for the house of the most perfect sages in the land, that I might serve those sages and earn their blessing. And that I might get my fill of conversing with you; and that I might earn the blessing of your whole community, both those with whom we used to speak and those with whom we did not.'

'Our teacher Fer Dá Chrích said this to us,' said Mael Ruain, 'with regard to continually preparing for something: "Let those of their dearest wishes which are good be granted to the sons of life, so that their rewards may be granted to them even as those wishes merit".'

There was a hermit in Cluain Dubáin. His exertions were great: he used to prostrate himself a hundred times at matins, and a hundred times at each of the offices, and a hundred times at nocturns – seven hundred altogether. Mael Ruain was told of that. 'My word declares,' said Mael Ruain, 'that there will come a time for him before his death when he will not be able to make even a single prostration.' That was fulfilled: his legs were afflicted so that he could not perform any vigils for a long while before he died, because of the excessive number which he used to perform before that.

This is what Mael Ruain said to the bishop Sechnasach, from Cell Guilbín – his mother had asked him to take care of her, but did not wish to turn aside from sinning. Sechnasach asked Mael Ruain, 'How shall I behave in this dilemma?' He said, 'If you cannot bring her to life, let her not carry you to death; but if she changes her ways, you should care for her.' But if anyone

6 The forty days following Pentecost.

given to carnal things is truly poor, then it is right to take care of him, as one would take care of any poor person.

This is what he thinks proper with respect to the regular preparation of food for sick folk who are doing penance: vivifying and mortifying them by turns, lest prolonged austerity bring about their deaths. And if that is done, it should be done without their knowledge: the servant who attends upon them should be told to give them some condiment in porridge or on bread. (But giving it to them in porridge works best.)

Once the abbot who was in Iona saw that the recluses looked poorly. Then he went to the cook, and that day he made the porridge himself. He added a third more water to each portion that day, and boiled the water until a third of it had boiled away; he put a lump of butter on each portion and boiled it on the water, and then added the meal. He did this every day. Then they noticed that their appearance had changed, and did not know the reason; for they saw that they had the same amount, without change. When a good appearance, and vitality, had returned to them, he mortified them again, reviving them once more in this way whenever they began to die.

Those whose desires are stirred up, whether through hearing confessions, or simply from thinking, or on account of youth, should practice rigorous abstinence to put them down; for what has caused this is too much blood in the body. Then, when the blood subsides, the desire and the appetite subside as well.

Mo Laisse of Devenish had a sister named Copar. Desire was a great burden for the girl; for desire is a third again as strong in women as in men. He regulated her routine and her diet for a year, assigning her a fixed portion.

At the end of the year she came to him, and confessed that desire still remained in her. He was sewing when she came. He thrust the needle three times into her palm, so that three streams of blood came from her hand. Then he said, 'It is natural that it should be difficult for a body to control itself, when these great floods are in it.'[7] Then he reduced her ration again.

She persisted thus until the end of a year, and still her desire continued. Then he thrust the needle three times into her hand, and three streams of blood came from it.

---

7 Use here of the word *tólae* 'flood, flood-tide, abundance' probably involves a punning allusion to *tol* 'desire'.

He reduced her food for another year, and then thrust in the needle. But now not a drop of blood came out of her. Then he said to her, 'Continue now with this portion until your death.'

A merchant travelling around Munster in Samthann's time used to take her greetings to the sons of life of that region. She summoned him to her, and exhorted him not to add to nor to take away even a single word in her utterances, or in the utterances of anyone to whom he was sent. 'Tell Mael Ruain for me,' she said (or else it was Fer Dá Chrích; and that is likelier, for Mael Ruain was younger than Samthann),[8] 'that of all the clerics of the south he is especially dear to me. And another thing: ask him whether he receives the confessions of women, and whether he will be my soul-friend.'

The merchant relayed these things to him. But when he told him that he was especially dear to Samthann, he got up at once and raised his two arms in a cross-vigil,[9] and gave thanks to God. And when he asked him whether women could seek his counsel, and whether he would be her soul-friend, he blushed as far down as his chest, and prostrated himself thrice, and was silent for a long time. Then he said, 'Tell her that she should ask herself.'

Afterwards the merchant told all these things to Samthann, and she said, 'I think that something will come of that lad.' Then she took her brooch from her mantle, and thrust it into her cheek so that it stuck in the bone, and then pulled it out. But not even a single drop of blood came forth. The merchant began wailing and lamenting as he watched. After that she took the wound between two fingers, and squeezed it for a long time, and not a drop came out. At last a small small droplet appeared, after the long squeezing. It was a little drop of water, with a bit of yellow in it to change its colour. She put that tiny secretion on her fingernail. 'As long,' she said, 'as there is this much juice in his body, let him not have company or fellowship with women.'

It is forbidden to eat a meal in a house in which there is a corpse, even though it be that of a saint; rather there should be recital of psalms there, and prayer. Even the cleric administering the sacrament to a sick man must leave at once, lest he die in his presence. For if he should be in the house at the moment of death, he is not permitted to offer mass until a bishop consecrates him.

8 According to the annals Samthann died in 739, Mael Ruain in 792. Fer Dá Chrích has been mentioned above as Mael Ruain's teacher. 9 Cf. p. 167, note 11 above.

It happened once to Diarmait, and to Blathmac mac Flainn, that Cú Roí was in their hands when he died. They were going to celebrate mass without being consecrated, until Colcu stopped them. The authority for this is Leviticus;[10] and Diarmait, abbot of Iona, was with him then.

Once a certain monk went on a journey to Finnio mac Fiatach. He met a woman on the road, and she asked him to lie with her; in the end she laid hands on him, and they made a tryst and slept together. Afterwards he did not wipe the tear from his cheek, but went at once to Finnio and confessed his sin. Finnio said: 'This will be no great matter. The Devil has caused it, to take you away from us, and to plant you among the laity, and to bring you into a house of penance, so that you should be shamed before everyone. But it will do him no good: you will not go into a house of penance, and he will not carry you off among layfolk. You will take communion, and will follow the same rule through each fast.'

After that Satan came and tempted him again, saying, 'The advice which Finnio gives to you will not purify you much. This is what you should do: go to Comgall, so that he can pass judgment on you.' Then he went, and made his confession to him; and Comgall said, 'Welcome is your coming! This will be no great matter' – and Comgall said the same words to him which Finnio had said.

As he was leaving Bangor, Colum Cille's boat came to land, and Satan urged him to go to Colum Cille. 'You will get no healing from Finnio and Comgall,' he said; 'this is what you should do: go to Colum Cille.' He went then, and made his confession to him.

Colum Cille said to him, 'You have crucified Christ four times: once, by your own sin; a second time with respect to Finnio, because you did not believe that he spoke through the Holy Spirit; a third time with Comgall; a fourth time with me. I pronounce upon you,' said Colum Cille, 'fifteen years' penance for despising a true limb of Christ, that is, Finnio.'

A demon accompanies a garment which has been obtained from layfolk, until it has been washed; and shaking it or beating it is no precaution, but only washing it.

There was a hermit in Clonmacnoise named Laisrén. He was entirely bare and free of attachments, with nothing on his conscience; but he was weak from illness. Each of the students in turn used to take him home. A certain student took him home one night, and put a blanket under him;

10 Leviticus 21:4.

and Laisrén slept upon the blanket. He had a carnal dream; and he had never had one from the time when he was born until that night.

He got up, and began wailing and lamenting. He began to perform a vigil, and recited the hundred and fifty psalms in that vigil. Then a stupor came over him, and an angel came to him and said, 'Do not be sorrowful. What you have felt tonight, you will not feel again for as long as you live. This is what caused it: the blanket on which you slept was the blanket of a couple, and it has not been washed since being with that couple; a demon has accompanied it because it was not washed.' For a demon accompanies (?) any blanket taken from lustful folk, for as long as it is not washed, etc.

I have heard from Crunnmael that Mael Ruain only fasted three times after founding Tallaght; it was against Artrí mac Faelmuire, because of the quarrel which there was between him and the monks of Tallaght. After the first fast the king's leg broke in two. After the second fast he fell into the fire, so that it burnt him from top to bottom. After the third fast the king died.

This is the authority for regularly consuming gruel.

There was a great assembly of the saints of Ireland in Mag Léna. This is what gathered them together: anxiety because penitents were dying on a diet of bread and water; and that had agreed with (?) the elders who had lived before them. They fasted against God with regard to this.[11]

An angel came to them, and said, 'Do not be surprised that bread and water do not nourish the penitents today. The fruits and plants of the earth have been laid waste, so that today there is not enough strength or virtue in them to nourish anyone. The deceit and sin and injustice of men have robbed the earth and its fruits of their strength and virtue. When men lived in accordance with God's will, the plants of the earth had their proper strength: water was not less nourishing then than milk today.'

Then the angel told them to mix some meal with their butter in order to make gruel, so that the penitents should not die in their hands because bread and water did not nourish them.

---

11 In early Irish law, fasting was used to put pressure on those whose status was too high to allow of their being subjected to more direct forms of coercion (Kelly 1988, 182–3). Mael Ruain's fast against a king in the preceding paragraph, although its supernatural effects make it more than merely a legal procedure, is in essence an example of this practice. By a natural extension of the same principle, saints fast against God in the religious literature; cf. the episode from *Bethu Phátraic*, which I have given as as an addendum to the hymn *Audite omnes* above.

There was a certain hermit from Slane, from the north, named Colcu; he was a relative of Mo Chutu. He bound himself to a discipline of extreme abstinence. Cattle and property were given him by the community [of Slane]; he was much given to distributing them to the poor. He wanted to abandon it all and go to Mael Ruain, for it weighed upon his conscience to be eating the produce of a community in which not everyone who fetched him food was sufficiently pure. The elders told his cook to accompany him to Mael Ruain.

Mael Ruain asked him the reason for the sickliness of his appearance, and he did not confess it. Then the cook came, and showed Mael Ruain the portion on which he subsisted; and he was greatly disturbed. 'You have done violence to yourself!'[12] said Mael Ruain. 'I will submit to your will in this matter,' he said.

'First of all,' said Mael Ruain, 'there is no room for you in this place, where matters are ordered properly, for as long as you are in this condition. Those who are here do their proper work; they can eat their assigned portion. But you have no place among them, for you do no work; you cannot eat your portion.'

Then he prostrated himself, submitting entirely to Mael Ruain. 'This is my will,' he said. 'So that your life be not cut short, add something to that meagre portion, even though doing so seems loathsome to you, and you do not wish it. And then let there be given to you,' said Mael Ruain, 'some of the patron saint's produce. Even though everyone [who fetches it] is impure, it is pure for one who is holy. Let it be displayed in the midst of your house; for the produce of the patron saints belongs more properly to you than to them.[13] But it is not forbidden to you, for your conscience's sake, to distribute to the poor the fruits of the patron's land.'

The Gospel helps and aids the souls for whom it is elevated, even as it helps the living; and for that reason it should be elevated for the dead.

Once there arose a struggle in Clonmacnoise, on account of rivalry for the abbacy. Then Adomnán installed a stranger[14] in their midst. When Adomnán was in Iona they harassed the stranger, and took the abbacy away from him. Thereupon he sent his followers to Adomnán, to complain concerning them;

---

12 Literally, 'You have perpetrated kin-slaying upon yourself!' The murder of a relative (*fingal*) was one of the most heinous crimes in early Irish law (Kelly 1988, 127–8); to denounce self-destructive asceticism as if it were a kind of kin-slaying ingeniously appeals to Colcu's most deeply-rooted values.   13 Cf. the discussion of this question by Helair and Mael Díthruib above.   14 The word *deórad* can have the technical sense of a voluntary exile, who has abandoned his own country in order to serve God; this may perhaps be the meaning here.

and he told them that they should neither eat nor unfasten their shoes until they could speak with him.

Adomnán said that they should eat that night; and they ate, and the next day they did not come to him until the hour of terce. Then Adomnán raised his hand, holding the Gospel, and in the same instant fire burned the monks of Clonmacnoise. It did not permit any of them to sit or to lie down until they had taken the stranger back.

Adomnán told the messengers to return home, and when they arrived they found their companion already installed as abbot. The messengers asked the exact hour in which he had been made abbot, and it was the same in which Adomnán had lifted up the Gospel beyond the sea.

Afterwards he was asked about the speed of that miracle. He answered, 'Do not be surprised. The sign of the Cross, acting through the Gospel, passes through all of creation, as far up as heaven, in the blinking of an eye. And with the same swiftness it reaches the depths of torment, and the rising and setting of the sun, and the south and north of the world – all in the same blink of an eye. And it overcomes every difficulty.'

In Lent Mael Díthruib subsisted on bread and water for as long as he lived, for the sake of his father's soul; for he always prayed for him during Lent.

There was a layman in Mugdorna; he and his wife lived in lawful matrimony under the soul-friendship of Echu ua Tuathail, and they had ten sons. Then his enemies murdered him, and when they saw this all the laity said, 'What did it profit him to do good deeds?'

At once Echu went to Duiblittir, and told him what had happened. Duiblittir said that a half or a third of his property should be distributed to the poor; and that one of his sons should offer his body and soul to God; and that that son should do for his father's sake the penance which he would have done himself, scanty rations and vigils and toil, for seven years; and that his wife should do penance both for his sake and for her own for the same period. All that was done; and seven years after that day his son and his wife came to receive communion.

On that night, after seven years, he appeared to Duiblittir; and <great>[15] was his beauty, and he wore radiant garments. Then he blessed Duiblittir for the help which he had given him, and said to him, 'Tonight the Lord has had mercy on me, and has brought me out of hell into the kingdom of

15 Manuscript illegible.

heaven.' Duiblittir said to him, 'Who are you?' 'I am a wretch, of whom Echu was mindful.' On the same night he appeared to Echu, and to his son and wife, and blessed them, and spoke the same words to them.

V THE LAST THINGS

Fís Adomnáin: The Vision of Adomnán

A desire to know the soul's fate after death is one of the most potent and universal of human needs; and every culture – from the ancient Egyptians, with their elaborate travelogues of the afterlife, down to our own society, with its literature of the 'near-death experience' – has undertaken to gratify this curiosity in its own way. Medieval Europe produced many accounts of the next world, the most celebrated being Dante's *Divine Comedy*.[1]

This vision literature drew upon source material of two kinds, which influenced one another increasingly as the genre evolved. Authors of descriptions of heaven and hell made extensive use of earlier such descriptions, taking their own places in a textual tradition extending back to Jewish and Christian apocrypha and beyond. But this tradition was repeatedly enriched by narratives of contemporary visions, the actual experiences of individuals who had entered extraordinary states of awareness as a result of ascetic practices or serious illness.[2]

Fís Adomnáin, by contrast, reads like a creative adaptation of earlier written sources: its vividness seems to be that of imagination, rather than of experience. One of the clearest examples of the author's use of literary models is also one of the most interesting. The descriptions of heaven and of hell are separated by an account of how souls are cleansed by experiencing a series of trials as they ascend through the seven heavens, after which the damned are made to pass through the bodies of twelve infernal monsters: these ideas are echoed in Anglo-Saxon texts, and go back ultimately to the teachings of the Egyptian Gnostics.[3]

Adomnán, abbot of Iona from 679 to 704, is best known as the author of a biography of his famous predecessor Colum Cille, and for the promulgation of a law to protect non-combatants against violence:[4] no early source speaks of him as a visionary, and the account of his otherworldly experiences translated here was written centuries after his death. Several anecdotes, however, describe both Adomnán and Colum Cille as receiving visitations and revelations from angels, demons, and other supernatural entities: the *Fís*'s association with the figure of Adomnán evidently reflects an extensive tradition that the two greatest abbots of Iona had been privy to the mysteries of the beyond.

The account is fitted into the framework of a sermon, opening with an exposition of two verses from Psalm 146 which speak of God as rewarding the righteous and

---

1 Another vision tale extremely popular throughout medieval Europe was the *Vision of Tnugdal*, written around 1150 by an Irish monk living in Germany (Picard and de Pontfarcy 1989). 2 A famous example of the latter is the Irish monk and missionary Fursa (died 649). On his career in England and on the Continent, see Kenney 1966, 500–3; Bede's account of his vision is given in Colgrave and Mynors 1969, 270–5. A brief anecdote concerning him is included in 'Stories of the Céili Dé', p. 250 above. 3 Stevenson 1983; Carey 1994a, 24–6. For another view, see Bauckham 1993. 4 Herbert 1988, 47–56; cf. p. 207, note 23 above.

punishing sinners, and concluding with an exhortation to the congregation to be mindful of the next world and to pray for God's mercy. The author emphasises the homiletic value of what he has to say by claiming that even the apostles preached on this theme, and goes on to describe the prophet Elijah giving a sermon of the same sort to the souls of the blessed in Paradise. Many types of text were presented as sermons in medieval Ireland: nearly all Irish saints' lives take this form, and in *In Tenga Bithnua* a description of the cosmos has been adapted to serve as a meditation for the Easter vigil.

THE BEGINNING OF 'THE VISION OF ADOMNÁN'

'Great is our Lord, and great his power; and his wisdom has no number' (Psalm 146:5). The Lord is lofty and wondrous; and great and amazing are his strength and might; and there is no bound nor number to the abundance of his wisdom, nor of his great knowledge. 'The Lord raises up the meek, but casts sinners down to the earth' (ibid., verse 6). The Lord, then, raises up to himself in heaven those who are loving and compassionate and gentle and kind; but he assails and overthrows, [casting them down] to earth and hell, the unprofitable assembly of the sons of malediction.

The Holy Spirit, the Spirit from whom come every comfort and every counsel to the church of the Old and New Testaments, is the Spirit who has illuminated the gifts and mysteries of the divine laws for the Christian church throughout the whole world, the Spirit who inspired these words uttered by the royal prophet, David son of Jesse, so that he said:

'Great is our Lord.' Great and vast is our Lord, the Lord Jesus Christ. 'No one can offer him fitting praise,'[5] that is, no one is able to praise him in a way that befits him. 'Greater than every praise is the power by which he established the nature of things, and sustains the heavy mass of the earth,' for he exceeds every praise with regard to his might and his coeternal power, for he created the nature of the creatures, and holds up the weight and heaviness of the earth without stirring.

'And his wisdom has no number; that is, the Father knows the quality of all things.' Abundant is the knowledge and learning of the Lord; that is to say, although the creatures are many and various, there is nothing in them which is not plain to him.

'The Lord raises up the meek – that is, the humble, those not contending against the law – to the image of God.' The Lord accepts into his household those of good will and compassion; they are the company who always keep within themselves the likeness and image of God, and do not go against the Father's law.

'But casts down sinners – that is, only those opposed to the gentle, that is, the savage, and those who lack the meekness to gain an understanding of the

5 Like the passages enclosed in quotation marks above, this phrase is in Latin in the manuscript; but it is not a quotation from the psalm. The author seems to have used a Latin commentary on the Psalter, paraphrasing both the Biblical text and some of the commentator's remarks. Text and commentary both continue to be cited in what follows.

Scriptures.' He diminishes and overthrows sinners, especially those who are opposed to the meek, the ones whose pitilessness and mercilessness keep them from having an inner knowledge of the Holy Scripture.

'Down to the earth; that is, as far as the wisdom of earthly things, or as far as the senses of the flesh.' He casts them down to the earth, in other words, down to worldly wisdom, or to the senses.

'If, therefore, it is certain that the meek, that is, the gentle, will possess the good things of the Lord in the land of the living, what then will those sinners have – the savage ones, the ones who are not the meek but are opposed to them – apart from eternal torments according to their kinds?' If, then, abundant heavenly rewards are ordained for the gentle and the compassionate, what else will there be for the savage and unbelieving and pitiless but a raging multitude of eternal punishments according to their various kinds?

There are many of the saints, and of the righteous, and of the disciples of the Lord Jesus Christ, to whom the mysteries and secrets of the household of heaven and the golden rewards of the righteous have been revealed in such a fashion, and to whom the various torments of hell have been revealed also, together with the ones who suffer them. For to Peter was revealed the four-sided vessel which was let down from heaven to earth (Acts 10:11), with four cords coming from it, sweeter to listen to than any music. And Paul was raised up to the third heaven, so that he heard the ineffable words of the angels and the wondrous conversation of the household of heaven (2 Corinthians 12:2–4). On the day of Mary's death, moreover, the twelve apostles were taken to see the torments and the woeful sufferings of the unrighteous, when the Lord called upon the angels of the west to open the earth before them, so that they beheld and contemplated hell with its many torments, as he himself had foretold to them a little while before he suffered.[6]

After that, moreover, what is preached here was revealed to Adomnán grandson of Tinne, the chief scholar of the west of the world, when his soul parted from his body on the feast of John the Baptist, and was borne to heaven with the angels of heaven, and to hell with its rabble army. When Adomnán's soul parted from his body, he immediately saw the angel which had attended upon him for as long as he was in the flesh; and first of all he took him to visit the kingdom of heaven.

6 An allusion to the apocryphal text *The Passing of Mary*. On the Irish versions see McNamara 1975, 122–3; a translation appears in Herbert and McNamara 1989, 119–31.

The first land to which they came was the land of the saints. That is a fruitful radiant country: there are various wonderful assemblies there clothed in chasubles of white linen, wearing bright white cowls upon their heads. The saints of the east of the world are in one assembly, in the east of the land of the saints. The saints of the west of the world are in the west of the same country. The saints of the north and south of the world are in two huge assemblies in the south and north. Every saint in the land of the saints is equally close to the sound of the music and the sight of the enclosure in which the nine orders of heaven are, arranged in grades and according to rank.

At times the saints sing wonderful music in praise of God; at other times they fall silent, because of the music of the household of heaven. For the saints have no want of anything save to listen to that music before which they fall silent, and to contemplate the light which they behold, and to take their fill of the fragrance which is in that land.

There is a wonderful kingdom facing them on the southeast. A crystalline veil separates them from it, with a golden portico against it to the south, and through it they see the shapes and shadows of the household of heaven. But there is no obscurity between the household of heaven and the saints: they are manifest and present to them on that side always. There is a fiery ring around that company: everyone passes into it and out of it, and it does no harm to any of them.

The twelve apostles and the Virgin Mary are in a gathering apart, surrounding the mighty Lord. The patriarchs and prophets and disciples of Jesus Christ are next to the apostles. There are holy virgins on Mary's right, with a small interval separating them. Infants and youths surround them on every side, and the music of the birds of the household of heaven entertains them always. Splendid swift companies of the angels which watch over souls are perpetually serving and ministering to those assemblies, in the presence of the King. No one in the world could describe or give an account of those assemblies as they really are. The companies and assemblies which we have described in the land of the saints will remain in that glory until the great gathering of Doom, when on the Day of Judgment the true Judge will set them in the places where they will be forever, gazing upon God's face with no veil between them.

Although the brightness and radiance in the land of the saints is great and vast, as we have related, the brilliance in the plain of the household of heaven, around the Lord's own throne, is a thousand times greater. This is how that throne is: it is a skilfully-fashioned chair held up by four pillars of precious stone. And if one had no entertainment save the harmonious singing together of those pillars, he would have enough of glory and delight.

But [besides this] there are three noble birds upon the chair, in the King's presence, and it is their perpetual gift to have their minds fixed on their Creator throughout the ages. They celebrate the eight offices, praising and glorifying the Lord together with the choir of archangels. The birds and the archangels begin the song, and thereafter the whole household of heaven answers them, both saints and holy virgins.

There is a vast arch above the Anointed in his royal chair, like a well-wrought helmet or a kingly diadem: if human eyes beheld it, they would melt at once. There are three circles in a great ring between that and the host, and what they are cannot be made known by any description. Six thousand warriors in the forms of horses and birds surround the fiery chair, burning forever and without end.

As for the mighty Lord who is upon that throne, none can describe him unless he should do it himself, or should tell it to the orders of heaven. For no one else could relate his fieriness and his energy, his love and his great radiance, his splendour, his beauty, his constancy, his firmness, and the multitude of his angels and his archangels singing songs for him. His very many ministers pass to him and from him, with concise answers to each company in turn: his mildness and great mercy to some, his sternness and harshness to others.

If anyone were to gaze upon him all around, from the east and from the west, from the south and from the north, he would find his lordly face on every side, seven times brighter than the sun. But he would not see him in a human form, with head or foot; but a red fiery mass burning throughout the world, and everyone trembling before it in fear. Heaven and earth are full of his glory, and radiance like that of a royal star surrounds him on all sides. Each of the choirs which sing hymns around him sings three thousand different songs, and each of those songs is as sweet as all the multitudinous music of the world.

This is how the stronghold is which contains that throne: seven crystalline walls of varied colours surround it, each wall higher than the last. Its floor and lowest foundation is of bright crystal, with the appearance of the sun.

A very gentle, very merciful company inhabits that stronghold, lacking no good thing. For none ever enters or dwells in that stronghold except for saints,[7] or pilgrims, or those who make zealous repentance to God. It is

7 'Holy virgins' in another manuscript.

difficult to know the way in which they are arranged or ordered, for none of them turns his back or side to another, but the ineffable power of the Lord has disposed and established them face to face in their ranks, in their equally-lofty crowns, in a great ring around the throne, splendidly, beautifully, their faces all turned to God.

There is a screen of crystal between each pair of choirs, splendidly adorned with silver and gold. There are three precious stones which make a gentle sound, which make sweet music, between each pair of principal assemblies, their tops burning like lanterns. Seven thousand angels in the form of mighty candles light and illuminate the stronghold on every side; seven thousand more stand in its very centre, burning throughout the ages around the royal seat. If the men of the world, however many they may be, were gathered in one place, the fragrance of the top of just one of those candles would suffice to nourish them.

All of the people of the world who do not reach that stronghold in their lives, but are destined to dwell there after the judgment of Doomsday, exist in a fleeting, unstable state: their dwelling places are in high places and in hills, in marshes and in bogs, until Doomsday comes. This is how those hosts and assemblies are: the guardian angel of each single soul is serving and ministering to it.

A veil of fire and a veil of ice are before them in the principal gateway of the stronghold, knocking and crashing against one another throughout long ages; the sound and noise of those veils is heard throughout the world. If the race of Adam were to hear that noise, trembling and intolerable terror would seize them all because of it. Sinners are woeful and distressed at that sound. On the side [facing] the household of heaven, however, only a little of that harsh din is heard, and it is as sweet as any music.

Vast and strange to tell of is the ordering of that stronghold; all that we have related of its varied ranks and its wonders is only a small part of its greatness.

It is difficult for the soul to reach the throne of the Creator, after being the companion and neighbour of the flesh with its slumber and luxury and comfort, unless it has angels to guide it; for there are very many hardships on the ladder of the seven heavens, and none of them is easier than the others. There are six protective doorways set before the human race on the way to heaven. A watchman and doorkeeper from the household of heaven has been set to guard each of the doorways.

The archangel Michael was set in the doorway of the nearest heaven, together with two virgins with iron rods in their bosoms to scourge and beat the sinners: so that it is there that sinners encounter the first reproof and the first suffering on the path which they tread.

. The archangel Uriel is the guardian of the second heaven, together with two virgins with fiery whips in their hands: with these they scourge the faces and eyes of the sons of death. A flaming fiery stream has been placed before the doorway; Abersetus is the name of the angel who watches over that stream and guards it. The stream tests the souls of the saints, and cleanses them from whatever sin still clings to them, so that they attain to the purity and brightness of the radiance of the stars. A delightful well has been placed there, mild and fragrant, to wash and cleanse the souls of the righteous; but it pursues and burns the souls of sinners, and does not remove any [guilt] from them – they obtain in it only an increase of torment. Then the sinners rise up with sorrow and great grief, the righteous however with joy and rejoicing, to the doorway of the third heaven.

A furnace of fire is there, perpetually burning. Its flames reach to a height of twelve thousand cubits. The souls of the righteous pass through that furnace in the twinkling of an eye; but the souls of sinners are kept there until the end of twelve years, when the guardian angel bears them to the fourth doorway.

The entrance of the fourth heaven is girded about by a fiery stream, like the stream [described] above. A wall of flaming lead encircles it, and the extent of those flames is reckoned at twelve thousand cubits. The souls of the righteous step across it as if it were not there at all; the souls of sinners are fixed there for the space of twelve years, in wretchedness and great suffering, until the guardian angel bears them to the doorway of the fifth heaven.

There is a fiery stream there also, but it is different from the other streams: for in the midst of that stream there is a remarkable whirlpool, which spins the souls of sinners around, and holds them until the end of sixteen years. The souls of the righteous, however, cross it without delay. When it is time for the sinners to be released thence, the angel strikes the stream with a hard rod with the nature of a lion (?),[8] so that he raises the souls up on the end of the rod.

Then Michael bears the souls to the doorway of the sixth heaven; and no torment or suffering is allotted to souls in that doorway, but it is bright with the light and brilliance of precious stones. Then Michael comes to the

8 This is the only evident meaning of the phrase *co n-aicniud leomain*. Other manuscripts have *co n-aicniud lecdu* 'with a stony nature': this may be the original reading, or else a later revision by a scribe who found 'the nature of a lion' as puzzling as we do.

Angel of the Trinity, and they both bring the soul forward into the presence of the Creator.

Great and indescribable then is the rejoicing of the household of heaven, and of the Lord himself, at the coming of that soul if it is innocent and righteous. But if the soul is unrighteous and imperfect, then it experiences the severity and harshness of the mighty Lord. He says to the angels of heaven: 'Hand this soul, greatly sinning, over to the angel of Tartarus; and let him plunge it into hell' – [that is,] 'Drag this faithless soul away with you, angels of heaven, and entrust it into the hand of Lucifer to be drowned and smothered in the depths of hell forever.'[9]

Then, dreadfully and horrifically, the wretched soul is cut off from the presence of the kingdom of heaven and the countenance of God, and is cut off too from the protection of the archangels by whom it has been brought to heaven. Then it utters the groan which is heavier than every groan, as it goes into the Devil's presence after beholding the beauty of the household of heaven. Then the twelve fiery dragons swallow it, one after the other, until the lowest dragon releases it into the Devil's mouth. There it finds fulfilment of evil and lack of every good thing, in the presence of the household of hell forever.

When the guardian angel had shown Adomnán's soul these visions of the kingdom of heaven, and of the first experiences of every soul after departing from its body, he took it thereafter to visit the deepest hell, with all the multitude of its torments and sufferings.

The first land to which they came was a black, dark country, bare and scorched, [but] with no torments at all therein. Just beyond that there is a valley full of fire. There is a flame in it, which flares forth beyond its borders on every side: it is black below, red in the middle and on top. There are eight beasts in it, with eyes like fiery ingots.

A great bridge stretches across the valley from one edge to the other, high in the middle but low at the ends. There are three companies undertaking to set out across that bridge, but not all of them reach the other side. For one of the companies the bridge is broad from start to finish, so that they cross the fiery valley entirely unscathed and without fear. For another of the companies which sets out upon it the bridge is narrow at first but broad thereafter, so that in that way they get across the valley. For the last of the companies, however, the bridge is broad at first but later narrow

9 The first version of God's words here is in Latin, the second an Irish paraphrase (cf. Dumville 1977–8, 66).

and cramped, so that they fall from its midst into that perilous valley, into the jaws of the eight smouldering beasts who have their dwelling there.

Those for whom that path was easy are the virgins, and penitents, and those who have undergone red martyrdom for God.[10] Those for whom the path was narrow at first and broad thereafter are the folk who are driven by force to do the will of God, [but] turn that constraint into delight in performing the Lord's service. But those for whom the bridge was broad at first and narrow later are the sinners, who hear the teaching of God's word and do not fulfil it.

There are vast multitudes suffering torment beyond that cooler country.[11] Time and again the torment ebbs away from them, and then goes over them once more. Those who are in that torment are the ones whose good balances their evil. On the day of Doom judgment will be made between the two, and their good will consume their evil on that day: they will be borne thereafter to the haven of life, to be before God's face forever.

There is another vast assembly near that company, in terrible torment. This is their condition: they are chained to fiery pillars. There is a fiery wall around them which reaches to their chins. There are fiery chains around their waists in the form of serpents. Their faces burn as they are tortured. Those who endure this heavy punishment are the ones who have killed their kin, and devastated God's church – that is, pitiless superiors of religious communities who have been given charge of the relics of the saints so as to collect gifts and tithes for God, but they take that wealth as their own possession rather than bestowing it upon the Lord's guests and the poor.

Great multitudes stand there perpetually, in black pools which reach to their belts. They wear short icy cowls. They never pause nor rest, but their belts burn them with cold and heat. Armies of demons surround them on every side, with fiery bludgeons in their hands with which they beat them about the head, ceaselessly accusing them. All of those unfortunates face the north, and together with all of their other sufferings a harsh biting wind blows into their faces. Red fiery showers pour down on them each day. They cannot avoid them, but endure them perpetually with lamentation and sorrow and grief.

10 'Red martyrdom' designates martyrdom as the term is understood in modern English: the voluntary acceptance of violent death for God's sake. In early Ireland 'martyrdom' could also refer to other forms of renunciation; on the triple classification of 'red', 'white', and 'blue' martyrdom see Stancliffe 1982. 'White martyrdom' was voluntary exile: this may be the reason why pilgrims rather than martyrs appear in the enumeration of the three companies dwelling in the heavenly stronghold at p. 266 above. 11 That is, the 'black, dark country', cooler than the region about to be described.

There are others with streams of fire in the orifices of their faces, others again with nails driven through their tongues, still others with nails driven into their heads. Those who endure that torment are the folk given to grasping and refusal, lacking charity and the love of God; thieves and perjurors and traitors and slanderers and ravagers and raiders, unjust judges and troublemakers, witches and satirists, relapsed brigands and scholars who teach heresy.

There is another company there, on islands in the midst of that sea of fire. A silver wall surrounds them, made of the garments and the alms which they have given away. Those are the folk who offer charity without stint, but in other respects lead lax lives, concerned <with fleshly things>,[12] until the day of their death; their alms help them in the midst of the sea of fire until Doom, and after Doom they are conveyed to the haven of life.

There is another company there, wearing red fiery chasubles. Their quakings and their cries are heard throughout the firmament. An innumerable throng of demons is stifling them, holding stinking half-raw hounds which they egg on to devour them. Red fiery wheels are burning perpetually around their necks. By turns they are caught up to the firmament and then dashed down into the depths of hell. Infants and boys are at all times wounding and slashing them from every side. Those who are in that torment are priests who have violated their vows, and those whose faith is cold, and liars who mislead and deceive the multitudes and take it upon themselves to perform for them feats and miracles which they cannot accomplish.

Another great company is there: eastward and westward they go without pause over the fiery stones, battling against hordes of demons. Too many <to be counted>[13] are the showers of red-flaming arrows which the demons pour upon them, and they fleeing without stop or pause until they reach the black rivers and black lakes, to quench the arrows therein. Mournful and wretched are the wailings which the sinners utter in those waters, for it is an increase of torment which they obtain there. Those who are in that torment are dishonest artisans and comb-makers and merchants, the unjust judges of the Jews and faithless kings, crooked sinful superiors of communities, adulterous women and the go-betweens who seduce them into wickedness, and satirists.

There is a wall of fire beyond the land of torments, seven times more fearsome and harsh than the land of torments itself. But souls will not dwell there until Doomsday: it belongs to the demons alone until the Day of Judgment.

---

12 Words in angle brackets supplied from other manuscripts. 13 Words in angle brackets supplied from other manuscripts.

Woe to whoever is in those torments, dwelling together with the Devil's household! Woe to whoever does not beware of that household! Woe to whoever has as his lord the wild headlong Devil! Woe to those whose black swift lord is the base, sharp, savage Devil: wretched desperate lamentation, great misery without rest, perpetual cold and hunger are theirs. Woe to whoever hears the moaning and lamentation of the souls in their misery, pleading with the Lord concerning the swift approach of Doomsday, that they may learn whether they will get any lessening of their punishment at the Judgment – for until Doom they get no rest save for three hours every Sunday. Woe to the one for whom that land is his allotted place forever!

This is how that place is: there are hollow thorny mountains there, bare burnt plains, black fiery valleys, red harsh hills, deep stinking pools, great brambly bogs, filthy ever-dark pathways, sharp prickly grasses, slippery fiery sharp keen cutting stones, swift searing bitter rough wintry winds, red fiery showers, bitter perpetual sharp rough burning wounding snows. It is darker than a winter's night, colder than eternal snow, hotter than great fires, more bitter than poison. Putrid monster-filled lakes, cold rough wintry islands, stinking smouldering pits. It is a harsh sandy country: smooth and slippery; red and marshy; black, dark, and smoky; rocky, hilly, and fiercely burning; crooked and frozen with ice, with hail like fiery rocks. There are broad fiery stones on the surface of that plain, scorched and burnt: just one of those stones would burn up the whole world. There are great poisonous putrid seas, with terrible storms, with dragons with fiery manes, with various other monsters in that sea, with four different kinds of fire: black burnt smoky fire, red wretched leaping tearing bitter fire, green terrible sharp harsh cutting fire, ruddy bitter vast fire with streams of poison. There are huge mountains of fire there. There are great red pointed iron nails there, all of them equally close, equally thick, equally sharp, equally long, with a drop of poison on the point of each nail, so that the poison of just one of those nails would drown and burn the men of the whole world.

The vast incomparable host of the demons cries out around the luckless soul, when they drag it with them into the depths of hell: they have red fiery whips in their hands, and half-raw stinking hounds with them which they egg on against the souls of the sinners: they ply the fiery whips upon them, so that they cry out and shriek and shout and wail bitterly and grievously. And the stars of heaven, and the constellations, and the firmament, and all creation, are full of the great lamentation which the souls of sinners make beneath the hands and fists of those undying enemies, that is, the Devil with his rabble multitude. After that they bear them away with them into the fiery hills and the black dark deep vast smoky gloomy mournful ruinous nethermost valleys of hell, upon the bare burnt stones and the streams of various fires of which we have spoken.

For there are four great streams across its expanse: a red-sided stream of fire, a stream of perpetually-red snow with slabs of ice, a stream of deadly poison, a stream of black dark bitter water; and the furious hosts of the demons bathe themselves in them after their game and pasttime of torturing the souls. When the saintly hosts of the household of heaven chant the harmonious recitation of the eight offices serenely and joyfully to the great Lord, then the souls of the sinners utter wretched sorrowful cries as they are battered unceasingly by the throngs of demons.

Those are the torments and weighty sufferings which his guardian angel revealed to the soul of Adomnán after visiting the kingdom of heaven. Then the soul was borne in the blinking of an eye through the golden portico and through the crystalline veil to the land of the saints: that was the first country to which it had been brought when it left its body. But when it thought to linger and remain in that country, it heard through the veil the voice of the angel summoning it, so that it was returned again to the body from which it had been parted, and related in assemblies and gatherings of laity and clergy the rewards of the household of heaven and the punishments of hell, as the guardian angel had revealed them to it.

That is what Adomnán was accustomed to preach for as long as he lived. That is what he preached at the great assembly of the men of Ireland, when he imposed the Law of Adomnán upon the Gaels, and when women were freed by Adomnán, and by Fínnechta Fledach son of Dúnchad son of Aed Sláine king of Ireland, and by the men of Ireland as well. For both men and women used to go into battles and combats, until the Law of Adomnán was imposed.[14] Patrick son of Calpurnius was accustomed to preach on the same theme, telling those who believed in the Lord of the rewards of heaven and the punishments of hell. Peter and Paul and the other holy apostles did likewise most frequently; and that is the theme on which Sylvester the abbot of Rome preached to Constantine son of Helena, the king of the world, at the great assembly at which he offered Rome to Peter and to Paul.[15]

That is what Elijah is accustomed to preach to the souls of the righteous, beneath the tree of life in Paradise. When Elijah opens his book to

14 On the 'Law of Adomnán' (*Cáin Adomnáin*) see page 207, note 23 above.   15 An allusion to the widespread legend, only disproved in the Renaissance, that the emperor Constantine (died 337) gave Rome to Pope Sylvester I (reigned 314–335) as a permanent possession of the Church.

preach, the souls of the righteous come to him from every side in the shapes of white birds. At first he relates to them the rewards of the righteous, the delightfulness and the pleasures of the kingdom of heaven; and they are joyful then. But then he relates to them the punishments and sufferings of hell, and the calamities of Doomsday; and then sorrow and grief are plainly to be seen upon him and upon Enoch, whence they are called 'the two sorrows of the kingdom of heaven'.[16] Then Elijah sets aside the book from which he has preached; and the birds raise a great cry of lamentation, and press their wings against their bodies so that streams of blood flow from them, for fear of the torments of hell and of Doomsday.

When the souls of the righteous and the saints, for whom a lasting habitation has been appointed in the kingdom of heaven, make that lament, then it is even more fitting that the folk of the world should do so, even to the extent of shedding tears of blood in fear of Doomsday. There will be many evils and great sufferings on that day, namely Doomsday: it is then that the Lord will give his own reward to every single person in the world, punishments to sinners and rewards to the righteous. <Sinners>[17] will be cast into the depths of eternal punishment, and the fetter of God's word will close upon them, the condemnation of the Judge of Doomsday. But the saints and the righteous, those who have shown charity and mercy, will be conveyed to God's right hand, to dwell there forever. Then they will be in that great glory: in the union of divinity and humanity in the Son of God; in the union, loftier than every union, of the holy Trinity, Father and Son and Holy Spirit. Let us beseech God's mercy through the prayers of Adomnán, etc.

16 There is a brief text entitled 'The Two Sorrows of the Kingdom of Heaven' (*Dá Brón Flatha Nime*), in which this scene is more fully described. A translation is provided in Herbert and McNamara 1989, 19–21; further discussion in McNamara 1975, 24–7.   17 This word supplied from other manuscripts.

Textual Remarks

ALTUS PROSATOR

The *Altus* survives in three Irish manuscripts: Leabhar Breac, and the two manuscripts of the Liber Hymnorum kept in Trinity College Dublin and in the Franciscan Library in Killiney. Of these, the Leabhar Breac and Trinity copies are extensively glossed, but the latter lacks stanzas XIV–XXI due to the loss of a leaf; Leabhar Breac has only stanzas I–VIII. In the translation below I give the preface and glosses as they appear in the Trinity copy, supplying the missing stanzas from the other manuscripts, and headings for those stanzas from the Franciscan copy; for the text of the hymn itself, I have on several occasions used preferable readings found in other manuscripts. I have tried to give only those glosses which comment on the hymn's actual content, not those which deal merely with lexical questions; but sometimes this distinction is an elusive one, and in doubtful cases I have preferred to err on the side of inclusivity. At some points additional comments in the margins are of greater interest than the interlinear glosses, and I have accordingly given these instead. For the original text, with full variants, the reader is referred to Bernard and Atkinson 1898, 1.62–83; further references in Lapidge and Sharpe 1985, 148 §580. A new translation, with commentary which is particularly helpful in pointing out the *Altus*'s use of the Bible and of the writings of John Cassian, appears in Clancy and Márkus 1995, 39–68.

The fundamental source for Colum Cille's life is the *Vita Columbae* written by Adomnán, his kinsman and successor as abbot of Iona, about a hundred years after his death (Anderson and Anderson 1991, Sharpe 1995); on the history and hagiographic traditions of the network of monasteries which he founded see Herbert 1988.

ON THE MIRACLES OF HOLY SCRIPTURE

On the Miracles was a well-known and influential book: shortly after the time of its composition it was already being cited by the author of a treatise on time-reckoning (Ó Cróinín 1983, 81 n. 2), and in a book of cosmology which came to be ascribed to Isidore of Seville (Díaz y Díaz 1972, 19; cf. above pp. 55 n. 3, 61 n. 8) For a few instances of its use by Old and Middle Irish writers see the notes above at pp. 52 n. 2, 55 n. 3, 65 n. 10.

No new printed edition has appeared since the Benedictines of St.-Maur included *On the Miracles* in the monumental edition of Augustine which they published in the years 1679–1700; this was reprinted in Migne 1844–64, 35.2149–2202, which I have used as the basis of my own translation. Valuable discussions of the text appear in Esposito 1919, Grosjean 1955, and Smyth 1996; for further references see Lapidge and Sharpe 1985, 79 §291.

IN TENGA BITHNUA

My translation is based on the most conservative version, surviving in the Book of Lismore; but I have also taken account of the readings of other manuscripts. The only previous full translation is that of Stokes 1905b; a more recent rendering of much of the text appears in Herbert and McNamara 1989, 109–18. I am currently at work on a full critical edition, with commentary and textual notes.

In Tenga Bithnua was probably composed in the ninth century; it remained very popular in Ireland down almost to the present day, with manuscript copies still being produced in the 1800s. In the intervening period further recensions evolved, adding some fresh material and attempting to smooth away many of the obscurities of the original (Dottin 1900, 1903, 1907; Nic Énrí and Mac Niocaill 1971); and bits of the text are reflected in many other medieval Irish works. One of the most striking pieces of evidence of its widespread appeal is found in a twelfth-century English manuscript, where a few paragraphs of *In Tenga* have been translated into Latin – an almost unique instance of the influence of vernacular Irish literature elsewhere in Europe (Kitson 1984, 127–30).

SALTAIR NA RANN

The *Saltair* has never been translated in its entirety, although the Irish text was printed over a century ago (Stokes 1883). Parts of Cantos I and II are translated in Hull 1912, 3–19. In 1952 W.W. Heist published a translation of Cantos CLIII–CLXII in his extended study of the signs preceding Doomsday. The *Saltair's* account of the events surrounding the fall of Adam and Eve (Cantos IV–XII), probably the most vivid and fully developed section of the work, was edited with translation by David Greene and Fergus Kelly in 1976; Brian Murdoch contributed a volume of commentary examining the relationship between the story in the *Saltair* and such apocrypha as the *Vita Adae et Evae* and the *Apocalypsis Mosis*. Most recently, Gearóid Mac Eoin has given a translation of Canto CLII, a moving expression of man's inability to penetrate the mysteries of God's creation, as an appendix to his article 'Observations on *Saltair na Rann*' (1982). The present translation is based on the text in Oxford, Bodleian MS Rawlinson B 502, as edited by Stokes; I have also consulted the independent copy of the *Saltair's* opening cantos in Dublin, Royal Irish Academy MS 24.P.27.

It was for a long time universally accepted that *Saltair na Rann* was written in the year 988, a date supplied by a series of synchronisms in the body of the work. The significance of this passage has however been questioned (Mac Eoin 1960), leading the late James Carney to propose that the *Saltair* was in fact composed in the ninth century (1983, 207–16) – a view which has itself not found general acceptance. The full text only survives in a single manuscript; but prose adaptations, the earliest of which appears to go back to the eleventh century, are widely attested (Dillon 1958, Carey 1986a; cf. McNamara 1975, 16–20).

TWO LORICAE

In including these two prayers in this collection I have gone against my usual policy of selecting only texts which can be shown to have enjoyed a wide currency among the medieval Irish themselves. The *Faeth Fiada* is found in three manuscripts, and seems to be cited in the Middle Irish introduction to the *Altus Prosator* (see p. 32, n. 7 above), but it does not appear to have enjoyed anything like the popularity of the *Altus*, of *Audite omnes amantes*, or of the *Amra Coluim Chille*; while *Nuall Fir Fhio* survives only as an example in a metrical treatise. The former however has been so widely admired and discussed in our own time that it seems worthwhile to make a fresh attempt to situate it in its proper context, and *Nuall Fir Fhio* provides valuable assistance in such an undertaking.

Both have been often translated, most recently in Greene and O'Connor 1967, 27–35.

The *Faeth Fiada* occurs in the Trinity College copy of Liber Hymnorum (written c.1100), and in two manuscripts of the fourteenth and fifteenth centuries (London, British Library MS Egerton 93; Oxford, Bodleian MS Rawlinson B 512). The most authoritative discussion of its eighth-century date is that of Binchy 1966; the prose preface, like the others in Liber Hymnorum, probably belongs to the late tenth or early eleventh century. The present text and translation are based on the edition in Stokes and Strachan 1901–3, 2.354–8; cf. Bernard and Atkinson 1898, 1.133–6, 2.49–51. For the prayer itself, I offer an eclectic text with normalised spelling.

Nuall Fir Fhio survives in the second of the Middle Irish metrical treatises edited by Rudolf Thurneysen (1891, 53–4 §98); the first critical edition with translation was that of Meyer 1914, whose treatment of the text I have for the most part followed. There is also an Italian translation (Campanile 1966, 160–5); further valuable observations have been made by Calvert Watkins (1976, 271).

PSEUDO-HISTORICAL PROLOGUE

The tale survives in three legal manuscripts, edited in Binchy 1978, 2.339–44, 3.874–7, and 5.1650–7; there is also a version which appears to be independent of the *Senchas Már* text tradition (Plummer 1884; Stokes 1887, 2.562–7). The bulk of the present translation is a slightly modified version of that which accompanies my critical edition of the text (Carey 1994b); the rendering of Dubthach's judgment is based on one which has appeared separately (Carey 1990, 13–15). The legend underwent a good deal of editing and indeed reinterpretation during the Middle Irish period, and allusions elsewhere in the literature attest to its influence in this developed form (Carey 1994b, 2; also Meyer 1911, 62–3).

Various scholars have analysed the text in very different ways; for three contrasting views see Binchy 1975–6, McCone 1986, and Carey 1990.

AUDITE OMNES AMANTES

Audite omnes has been repeatedly edited and translated; the most recent translation, with insightful discussion, is that of Orchard 1993. My own translation of hymn, preface, and glosses is based on the early fifteenth-century manuscript Leabhar Breac (Bernard and Atkinson 1898, 1.3–13). The Leabhar Breac preface contains much material additional to what is found in older manuscripts; to give the reader a sense of how texts grew and were enriched in the course of transmission, I have enclosed these secondary sections in angle brackets. Further references in Lapidge and Sharpe 1985, 146 §573.

'BROCCÁN'S HYMN'

The nature of this hymn's dependence on the earliest Latin lives of Brigit is discussed most extensively by Ó Briain (1978, 112–19); his views have however been challenged in this as in other respects by Sharpe (1982, 104). At all events, there is no doubt that the hymn did draw for its narrative material on a source or sources identical with, or closely similar to, the so-called *Vita Prima Sanctae Brigitae* and the life by Cogitosus (known also as the *Vita Secunda*).

The most recent discussions of the interrelationships of the early Latin lives are those of Sharpe 1982 and McCone 1982; a translation of Cogitosus's life appears in Connolly and Picard 1987. There is also a Latin metrical life, dating from the eighth or early ninth century (Kissane 1977); a prose ninth-century life, written partly in Latin and partly in Old Irish (Ó hAodha 1978); and other accounts of the saint written in Irish of a significantly later date (Stokes 1890, 182–98; Hogan 1894, 65–86). There is considerable disagreement regarding the date of the hymn translated in this collection, with estimates ranging from the seventh century to the ninth (Binchy 1979–80, 46; Carney 1983, 182–3). The hymn survives only in the two manuscripts of the Liber Hymnorum; I have based my translation on the text as it is printed in Stokes and Strachan 1901–3, 2.327–49. The marginal commentary appears only in the copy of the Liber Hymnorum kept in the Franciscan Library at Killiney.

FÉILIRE OENGUSSO

Féilire Oengusso was probably composed in the early ninth century (Ó Riain 1990); its preface and commentary were added considerably later. It exists in several manuscripts, and its popularity is further reflected by quotations from it in other works. There have been two editions, both by Whitley Stokes: the first (1880) presents the versions of four manuscripts in parallel columns, while the second (1905a) attempts to establish a critical text.

For the Middle Irish additions I have drawn upon a single manuscript, Leabhar Breac; the only exception which I have allowed myself has been in the case of Mo Ling, where Leabhar Breac lacks the evocative account of the saint's encounter with Satan. In selecting stanzas for individual days, my original intention was to give one for each month; since Leabhar Breac however contains almost no commentary for December, I decided instead to include the feasts of two important saints in June. In rendering the *Féilire* itself I have also adopted several Leabhar Breac readings not included in Stokes's normalised text, when these are supported by one or more of the other manuscripts.

AIPGITIR CHRÁBAID

This translation is based on the edition by Vernam Hull (1968); another rendering, which also takes Hull's text as its point of departure, is that of Clancy and Márkus 1995, 195–207. In preparing his edition Hull abandoned his earlier view (1956; following Thurneysen 1936, 114) that Colmán mac Beógnai can be accepted as the *Aipgitir*'s author, proposing instead that the text was written 'in the first half of the eighth century.' This second position has been accepted by Peter O Dwyer (1981, 177), but persuasively rebutted by Pádraig Ó Néill (1987). The *Aipgitir* exercised a prolonged and widespread appeal: Hull based his edition on nineteen versions from thirteen manuscripts, ranging in date from the fourteenth to the seventeenth century; and echoes of its phrasing occur in texts of many periods (e.g. Fursa's remark, p. 250; Stokes 1880a, 252–3).

STORIES OF THE CÉILI DÉ

The document from which I have drawn the excerpts presented here was edited in its entirety, with translation, by E.J. Gwynn and W.J. Purton (1911); it has no title or colophon in the only manuscript in which it survives, and was designated 'The Monastery of Tallaght' by the editors. Much of the text is taken up with detailed dietary rules and liturgical instructions; I have translated only those sections which contain some narrative element. An extended discussion of this work, and of our other sources of information on the Céili Dé, is provided in O Dwyer 1981.

Although the text only occurs in a single manuscript, it is so valuable as a collection of illustrative anecdotes that its inclusion here seems justified. Many of the same stories occur in a later text called *The Teaching of Mael Ruain* (Gwynn 1927, 2–63: §§32, 35, 39–41, 50, 65, 68, 71, 74–7, 81, 103), and the account of Maedóc's fast for the soul of Brandub mac Echach is retold in *The Rule of the Céili*

Dé (ibid. 77 §45); the anecdotes concerning the assembly at Mag Léna, the monk who sought penance three times, and the haunted blanket also appear as separate pieces elsewhere (Scarre 1907, Bergin 1905).

FÍS ADOMNÁIN

The language of the *Fís* has been variously assigned to the tenth or to the eleventh century. The text survives in four manuscripts; and parts of it have been incorporated into two monastic voyage tales (Stokes 1890, 115–16, 260–1; id. 1905c, 140–59). Previous English translations have been based on Lebor na hUidre, the oldest of the manuscripts containing it (Stokes 1870; Boswell 1908, 28–47; Jackson 1951, 317–25; Herbert and McNamara 1989, 137–48). The present rendering however is based primarily on the version in Leabhar Breac: a later manuscript, but one which comes closer to preserving the text in its original form (thus Dumville 1977–8, 65–6). I have used the edition of Ernst Windisch (1880).

Bibliography

Ahlqvist, Anders 1982, *The Early Irish Linguist* (Helsinki).

Anderson, Alan Orr, and Marjorie Ogilvie Anderson 1991, *Adomnán's Life of Columba*, revised edition (Oxford).

Atkinson, Robert 1883, *The Passions and Homilies from Leabhar Breac* (Dublin).

Bauckham, Richard 1993, 'The Apocalypse of the Seven Heavens: the Latin version', *Apocrypha* 4.141–75.

Bergin, Osborn 1905, 'A fragment of Old Irish', *Ériu* 2.221–5.

Bernard, J.H., and R. Atkinson 1898, *The Irish Liber Hymnorum*, 2 vols. (London).

Best, R.I. 1952, 'Some Irish charms', *Ériu* 16.27–32.

—— et al. 1954–83, *The Book of Leinster*, 6 vols. (Dublin).

Bieler, Ludwig 1952, *Libri Epistolarum Sancti Patricii Episcopi*, 2 vols. (Dublin).

—— 1962, *The Irish Penitentials* (Dublin).

—— 1963, *Ireland Harbinger of the Middle Ages* (London).

—— 1971, *Four Latin Lives of Saint Patrick* (Dublin).

—— 1975, *The Irish Penitentials* (Dublin).

—— 1979, *The Patrician Texts in the Book of Armagh* (Dublin).

Binchy, D. A. 1962, 'The Old-Irish table of penitential commutations', *Ériu* 19.47–72.

—— 1966, 'Varia III: 3. *Atomriug*, 4. The date of the so-called "Hymn of Patrick"', *Ériu* 20.232–7.

—— 1975–6, 'The Pseudo-historical Prologue to the *Senchas Már*', *Studia Celtica* 10/11.15–28.

—— 1978, *Corpus Iuris Hibernici*, 6 vols. (Dublin).

—— 1979–80, '"Bergin's Law"', *Studia Celtica* 14/15.31–53.

Boswell, C.S. 1908, *An Irish Precursor of Dante* (London).

Breatnach, Pádraig 1978, 'Medieval traditions from West Munster', *Studia Hibernica* 17/18.58–70.

Breen, Aidan 1990, 'Iduma', *Celtica* 21.40–50.

Brown, Alan 1975, 'Bede, a hisperic etymology and early sea poetry', *Medieval Studies* 37.419–32.

Byrne, F.J. 1973, *Irish Kings and High-Kings* (London).

Campanile, Enrico 1966, 'Mittelirische Verslehren II, 96–98', *Studi e Saggi Linguistici* 6.157–65.

Canny, Nicholas 1989, 'Early modern Ireland, c. 1500–1700', in R.F. Foster, ed., *The Oxford Illustrated History of Ireland*, 104–60 (Oxford).

Carey, John 1985, 'Cosmology in *Saltair na Rann*', *Celtica* 17.33–52.

—— 1986, 'The heavenly city in *Saltair na Rann*', *Celtica* 18.87–104.

—— 1986a, 'A tract on the creation', *Éigse* 21.1–9.

—— 1987, 'The Irish vision of the Chinese', *Ériu* 38.73–9.

—— 1987a, 'Angelology in *Saltair na Rann*', *Celtica* 19.1–8.

—— 1988, 'Three notes', *Celtica* 20.123–29.

—— 1989, 'Ireland and the Antipodes: the heterodoxy of Virgil of Salzburg', *Speculum* 64.1–10.

—— 1990, 'The two laws in Dubthach's judgment', *Cambridge Medieval Celtic Studies* 19.1–18.

—— 1994, 'The uses of tradition in *Serglige Con Culainn*', in J.P. Mallory and G. Stockman, eds., *Ulidia: Proceedings of the First International Conference on the Ulster Cycle of Tales*, 77–84 (Belfast).

—— 1994a, 'The sun's night journey: a pharaonic image in medieval Ireland', *Journal of the Warburg and Courtauld Institutes* 57.14–34.

—— 1994b, 'An edition of the Pseudo-historical Prologue to the *Senchas Már*', *Ériu* 45.1–32.

Carmichael, Alexander 1900–71, *Ortha nan Gaidheal: Carmina Gadelica*, 6 vols. (Edinburgh).

Carney, James 1964, *The Poems of Blathmac son of Cú Brettan* (Dublin).

—— 1983, 'The dating of early Irish verse texts, 500–1100', *Éigse* 19.177–216.

Charles-Edwards, Thomas 1976, 'The social background of Irish *peregrinatio*', *Celtica* 11.43–59.

Clancy, Thomas Owen, and Gilbert Márkus 1995, *Iona: The Earliest Poetry of a Celtic Monastery* (Edinburgh).

Colgan, John 1647, *Trias Thaumaturga* (Louvain, reprinted Dublin 1997).

Colgrave, Bertram, and R.A.B. Mynors 1969, *Bede's Ecclesiastical History of the English People* (Oxford).

Connolly, Seán, and Jean-Michel Picard 1987, 'Cogitosus's *Life of St. Brigit*', *Journal of the Royal Society of Antiquaries of Ireland* 117.5–27.

Cunningham, Terence P. 1970, *Church Reorganization*, A History of Irish Catholicism, vol. 5 part 7 (Dublin).

Díaz y Díaz, Manuel C. 1972, *Liber de ordine creaturarum: Un anónimo irlandés del siglo VII* (Santiago de Compostela).

Dillon, Myles 1958, 'Scéal Saltrach na Rann', *Celtica* 4.1–43.

Dottin, Georges 1900, 'Les deux chagrins du royaume du ciel,' *Revue celtique* 21.349–87.

—— 1903, 'Le *Teanga Bithnua* du manuscrit de Rennes,' *Revue celtique* 24.365–403.

—— 1907, 'Une rédaction moderne du *Teanga Bithnua*,' *Revue celtique* 28.277–307.

—— 1919–20, 'Un traité irlandais du moyen-age: La langue toujours nouvelle,' *Annales de Bretagne* 34.190–207, 278–97.

Dumville, David 1973, 'Biblical apocrypha and the early Irish: a preliminary investigation', *Proceedings of the Royal Irish Academy* 73C.229–338.

—— 1977–8, 'Towards an interpretation of *Fís Adamnán*', *Studia Celtica* 12/13.62–77.

Dumville, David, et al. 1993, *Saint Patrick A.D. 493–1993* (Woodbridge).

Dutton, Paul Edward 1992, 'John Scottus Eriugena', in Jeremiah Hackett, ed., *Medieval Philosophers, Dictionary of Literary Biography* vol. 115, 168–84 (Detroit and London).

Edwards, H.J. 1917, *Caesar: The Gallic War* (London).

Esposito, Mario 1919, 'On the pseudo-Augustinian treatise *De mirabilibus sacrae Scripturae*, written in Ireland in the year 655', *Proceedings of the Royal Irish Academy* 35C.189–207.

Gougaud, Louis 1911–12, 'Étude sur les loricae celtiques et sur les prières qui s'en rapprochent', *Bulletin d'ancienne littérature et d'archéologie chrétiennes* 1.265–81; 2.33–41, 101–27.

—— 1932, *Christianity in Celtic Lands*, trans. Maud Joynt (London, reprinted Dublin 1993).

Greene, David, and Fergus Kelly 1976, *The Irish Adam and Eve Story from Saltair na Rann*. Volume I: Text and Translation (Dublin).

Greene, David, and Frank O'Connor 1967, *A Golden Treasury of Irish Poetry, A.D. 600 to 1200* (London).

Grosjean, Paul 1955, 'Sur quelques exégètes irlandais du VIIe siècle', *Sacris Erudiri* 7.67–98.

Gwynn, Aubrey 1968, *The Twelfth Century Reform*, A History of Irish Catholicism, vol. 2 part 1 (Dublin).

Gwynn, Aubrey, and R. Neville Hadcock 1970, *Medieval Religious Houses: Ireland* (London).

Gwynn, E.J. 1927, *The Rule of Tallaght*, *Hermathena* no. 44, second supplementary volume (Dublin).

Gwynn, E.J., and W.J. Purton 1911, 'The Monastery of Tallaght', *Proceedings of the Royal Irish Academy* 29C.115–79.

Heist, W.W. 1952, *The Fifteen Signs Before Doomsday* (East Lansing, Michigan).

Herbert, Máire 1988, *Iona, Kells, and Derry* (Oxford, reprinted Dublin 1996).

Herbert, Máire, and Martin McNamara 1989, *Irish Biblical Apocrypha: Selected Texts in Translation* (Edinburgh).

Herren, Michael W. 1987, *The Hisperica Famina II: Related Poems* (Toronto).

Hillgarth, J.N. 1984, 'Ireland and Spain in the seventh century', *Peritia* 3.1–16.

Hogan, Edmund 1894, *The Latin Lives of the Saints*, Todd Lecture Series vol. 5 (Dublin).

Howlett, D.R. 1994, *The Book of Letters of Saint Patrick the Bishop* (Dublin).

Hughes, Kathleen 1966, *The Church in Early Irish Society* (London).

Hull, Eleanor 1912, *The Poem-Book of the Gael* (London).

Hull, Vernam 1956, 'The date of *Aipgitir Crábaid*', *Zeitschrift für celtische Philologie* 25.88–90.

—— 1968, '*Apgitir Chrábaid*: The Alphabet of Piety', *Celtica* 8.44–89.

Jackson, Kenneth Hurlstone 1951, *A Celtic Miscellany* (London).

Jones, H.L. 1917–32, *The Geography of Strabo*, 8 vols. (London).

Kelly, Fergus 1973, 'A poem in praise of Columb Cille', *Ériu* 24.1–34.

—— 1975, '*Tiughraind Bhécáin*', *Ériu* 26.66–98.

—— 1988, *A Guide to Early Irish Law* (Dublin).

Kenney, James 1966, *The Sources for the Early History of Ireland: Ecclesiastical*, with notes by Ludwig Bieler (New York, reprinted Dublin 1993).

Kissane, D.N. 1977, '*Vita Metrica Sanctae Brigidae*: a critical edition', *Proceedings of the Royal Irish Academy* 77C.57–192.

Kitson, Peter 1984, 'The jewels and bird *hiruath* of the "Ever-new Tongue"', *Ériu* 35.113–36.

Lapidge, Michael 1977, 'The authorship of the adonic verses *Ad Fidolium* attributed to Columbanus', *Studi medievali* 3rd series 18.815–80.

Lapidge, Michael, and Richard Sharpe 1985, *A Bibliography of Celtic-Latin Literature 400–1200* (Dublin).

Mac Airt, Seán, and Gearóid Mac Niocaill 1983, *The Annals of Ulster (to A.D. 1131)* (Dublin).

Macalister, R.A.S. 1938–56, *Lebor Gabála Érenn: The Book of the Taking of Ireland*, 5 vols. (London).

Mac Cana, Proinsias 1974, 'The rise of the later schools of *filidheacht*', *Ériu* 25.126–46.

—— 1979, '*Regnum* and *sacerdotium*: notes on Irish tradition', *Proceedings of the British Academy* 65.443–75.

—— 1985, *Celtic Mythology* (New York).

Mac Eoin, Gearóid 1960, 'The date and authorship of *Saltair na Rann*', *Zeitschrift für celtische Philologie* 28.51–67.

—— 1982, 'Observations on *Saltair na Rann*', *Zeitschrift für celtische Philologie* 39.1–28.

Mac Neill, Eoin 1930–2, '"De Origine Scoticae Linguae"', *Ériu* 11.112–29.

McCone, Kim 1982, 'Brigit in the seventh century: a saint with three lives?', *Peritia* 1.107–45.

—— 1986, 'Dubthach maccu Lugair and a matter of life and death in the Pseudo-historical Prologue to the *Senchas Már*', *Peritia* 5.1–35.

—— 1990, *Pagan Past and Christian Present in Early Irish Literature* (Maynooth).

McNamara, Martin 1975, *The Apocrypha in the Irish Church* (Dublin).

McNeill, John T., and Helena M. Gamer 1938, *Medieval Handbooks of Penance* (New York).

Meid, Wolfgang 1992, *Gaulish Inscriptions* (Budapest).

Meroney, Howard 1945, 'Irish in the Old English charms', *Speculum* 20.172–82.

Meyer, Kuno 1899, 'The vision of Laisrén', *Otia Merseiana* 1.113–19.

—— 1905, *Cáin Adamnáin* (Oxford).

—— 1909, *The Instructions of King Cormac mac Airt*, Todd Lecture Series vol. 15 (Dublin).

—— 1911, *Betha Colmáin maic Lúacháin* (Dublin).

—— 1916, 'Ein altirischer Heilsegen', *Sitzungsberichte der preussischen Akademie der Wissenschaften*, Phil.-hist. Klasse, 420–2.

—— 1919, 'An Old Irish prayer for long life', in *A Miscellany Presented to John Macdonald Mackay, LL.D.*, 226–32 (Liverpool).

Meyer, Kuno, and Alfred Nutt 1899, 'The colloquy of Colum Cille and the youth at Carn Eolairg', *Zeitschrift für celtische Philologie* 2.313–20.

Meyer, Robert T. 1978, *Bernard of Clairvaux: The Life and Death of Saint Malachy the Irishman* (Kalamazoo).

Migne, J.P. 1844–64, *Patrologia Latina* (general editor), 221 vols. (Paris).

Mooney, Canice 1967, *The First Impact of the Reformation*, A History of Irish Catholicism, vol. 3 part 2 (Dublin).

—— 1969, *The Church in Gaelic Ireland: Thirteenth to Fifteenth Centuries*, A History of Irish Catholicism, vol. 2 part 5 (Dublin).

Mooney, Desmond 1990, 'Popular religion and clerical influence in pre-famine Meath', in R.V. Comerford et al., eds., *Religion, Conflict and Coexistence in Ireland*, 188–218 (Dublin).

Muir, Bernard J. 1983, 'Two Latin hymns by Colum Cille (St Columba)', *Revue du Moyen Age Latin* 39.205–16.

Mulchrone, Kathleen 1939, *Bethu Phátraic* (Dublin).

Murdoch, Brian 1976, *The Irish Adam and Eve Story from Saltair na Rann*. Volume II: Commentary (Dublin).

Murphy, Gerard 1956, *Early Irish Lyrics* (Oxford).

Nic Énrí, Úna, and Gearóid Mac Niocaill 1971, 'The second recension of the Evernew Tongue,' *Celtica* 9.1–59.

Ó Briain, Felim 1978, 'Brigitana', *Zeitschrift für celtische Philologie* 36.112–37.

O'Brien, M.A. 1976, *Corpus Genealogiarum Hiberniae*, vol. 1 (Dublin).

Ó Cróinín, Dáibhí 1983, 'Early Irish annals from Easter tables: a case restated', *Peritia* 2.74–86.

O'Curry, Eugene 1861, *Lectures on the Manuscript Materials of Ancient Irish History* (Dublin, reprinted Dublin, 1995).

O Dwyer, Peter 1981, *Céli Dé: Spiritual Reform in Ireland 750–900* (Dublin).

Ó Fiaich, Tomás 1969, 'The church of Armagh under lay control', *Seanchas Ardmhacha* 5.75–127.

O'Grady, Standish Hayes 1892, *Silva Gadelica*, 2 vols. (London).

Ó hAodha, Donncha 1978, *Bethu Brigte* (Dublin).

O'Meara, John J. 1951, *Giraldus Cambrensis: The History and Topography of Ireland* (Mountrath).

—— 1988, *Eriugena* (Oxford).

Ó Muraíle, Nollaig 1983, 'Notes on the history of Doire na bhFlann', in Michael Ryan, ed., *The Derrynaflan Hoard I: A Preliminary Account*, 54–61 (Dublin).

Ó Néill, Pádraig 1987, 'The date and authorship of *Apgitir Chrábaid*: some internal evidence', in Próinséas Ní Chatháin and Michael Richter, eds., *Irland und die Christenheit: Bibelstudien und Mission*, 203–15 (Stuttgart).

O'Rahilly, Cecile 1960, 'Notulae quaedam', *Celtica* 5.143–4.

—— 1976, *Táin Bó Cúailnge: Recension I* (Dublin).

Orchard, Andy 1993, '"Audite omnes amantes": a hymn in Patrick's praise', in Dumville et al., 153–73.

Ó Riain, Pádraig 1990, 'The Tallaght martyrologies, redated', *Cambridge Medieval Celtic Studies* 20.21–38.

Oskamp, Hans P. A. 1974, 'Echtra Condla', *Études celtiques* 14.207–28.

—— 1977–9, 'The Irish material in the St. Paul Irish codex', *Éigse* 17.385–91.

Petrie, George 1837, 'On the history and antiquities of Tara hill', *Transactions of the Royal Irish Academy* 18.25–232.

Picard, Jean-Michel, and Yolande de Pontfarcy 1989, *The Vision of Tnugdal* (Dublin).

Plummer, Charles 1884, 'The Conversion of Loegaire, and his Death', *Revue celtique* 6.162–72.

Quin, E.G. 1981, 'The early Irish poem *Ísucán*', *Cambridge Medieval Celtic Studies* 1.39–52.

Russell, Paul 1988, 'The sounds of a silence: the growth of Cormac's Glossary', *Cambridge Medieval Celtic Studies* 15.1–30.

Scarre, Annie F. 1907, 'Bithbin Menadaige', *Anecdota from Irish Manuscripts* 1.75.

Selmer, Carl 1959, *Navigatio Sancti Brendani Abbatis* (Notre Dame, reprinted Dublin, 1989).

Sharpe, Richard 1979, 'Hiberno-Latin *laicus*, Irish *láech* and the Devil's men', *Ériu* 30.75–92.

—— 1982, '*Vitae S. Brigitae*: the oldest texts', *Peritia* 1.81–106.

—— 1984, 'Armagh and Rome in the seventh century', in Próinséas Ní Chatháin and Michael Richter, eds., *Irland und Europa/Ireland and Europe*, 58–72 (Stuttgart).

—— 1995, *Adomnán of Iona: Life of St Columba* (Harmondsworth).

Sheldon-Williams, I.P., and John J. O'Meara 1987, *Eriugena: Periphyseon (The Division of Nature)* (Montréal and Washington).

Silke, John J. 1976, 'The Irish abroad in the age of the Counter-Reformation, 1534–1691', in T.W. Moody et al., eds., *Early Modern Ireland 1534–1691*, A New History of Ireland, vol. 3, 587–633 (Oxford).

Simms, Katherine 1994, 'An eaglais agus filí na scol', *Léachtaí Cholm Cille* 24.21–36.

Sims-Williams, Patrick 1986, 'The visionary Celt: the construction of an ethnic preconception', *Cambridge Medieval Celtic Studies* 11.71–96.

Smyth, Marina 1986, 'The physical world in seventh-century Hiberno-Latin texts', *Peritia* 5.201–34.

—— 1996, *Understanding the Universe in Seventh-Century Ireland* (Woodbridge).

Stancliffe, Clare 1982, 'Red, white and blue martyrdom', in D. Whitelock et al., eds., *Ireland in Early Mediaeval Europe*, 21–46 (Cambridge).

Stevenson, Jane 1983, 'Ascent through the heavens, from Egypt to Ireland', *Cambridge Medieval Celtic Studies* 5.21–35.

Stokes, Whitley 1870, *Fis Adamnáin* (Simla).

—— 1873–5, 'The Klosterneuburg incantation', *Revue celtique* 2.112–15.

—— 1880, *On the Calendar of Oengus* (Dublin).

—— 1880a, 'Tidings of Doomsday', *Revue celtique* 245–57.

—— 1883, *Saltair na Rann* (Oxford).

—— 1887, *The Tripartite Life of Patrick*, 2 vols. (London)

—— 1890, *Lives of Saints from the Book of Lismore* (Oxford).

—— 1899, 'The Bodleian Amra Choluimb Chille', *Revue celtique* 20.31–55, 132–83, 248–89, 400–37.

—— 1900, 'Acallamh na Senórach', *Irische Texte* 4.1.

—— 1905, 'The Colloquy of the Two Sages', *Revue celtique* 26.4–64.

—— 1905a, *Félire Óengusso Céli Dé* (London).

—— 1905b, 'The Evernew Tongue', *Ériu* 2.96–162.

—— 1905c, 'The Adventure of St. Columba's Clerics', *Revue celtique* 26.130–70.

—— and John Strachan 1901–3, *Thesaurus Palaeohibernicus*, 2 vols. (Cambridge, reprinted Dublin 1975)

Thurneysen, Rudolf 1891, 'Mittelirische Verslehren', *Irische Texte* 3.1.1–182.

—— 1932, 'Colmán mac Lénéni und Senchán Torpéist', *Zeitschrift für celtische Philologie* 19.193–207.

—— 1936, 'Irisches', *Zeitschrift für vergleichende Sprachforschung* 63.114–17.

Toynbee, Arnold J. 1961, *A Study of History*, 12 vols. (Oxford).

Walker, G.S.M. 1970, *Sancti Columbani Opera* (Dublin).

Walsh, Maura, and Dáibhí Ó Cróinín 1988, *Cummian's Letter De Controversia Paschali and the De Ratione Conputandi* (Toronto).

Watkins, Calvert 1976, 'The etymology of Irish *dúan*', *Celtica* 11.270–7.

Watt, J.A. 1987, 'Gaelic polity and cultural identity', in Art Cosgrove, ed., *Medieval Ireland 1169–1534*, A New History of Ireland, vol. 2, 314–51 (Oxford).

Windisch, Ernst 1880, 'Fís Adamnáin', *Irische Texte* 1.165–96.

Wright, Charles D. 1993, *The Irish Tradition in Old English Literature* (Cambridge).

Index

Aaron 218
Abbán of Cell Abbáin 208
abbot 16, 31, 128, 197, 208, 246, 252–4,
    256–7, 273
  God as Abbot 124
abecedarian hymns 29, 147, 151
Abersetus, angel 268
Abian, mountains of 77
Abijah, class of Jewish priest 61
Abiron 69
Abraham 65, 71, 217, 224
abyss
  cosmic 41
  infernal 35
Acallam na Senórach 9–11, 17
Acheron, river 40
Acirunda 206
Adam 36, 43, 72, 76, 85, 88, 93
  descendants of 45, 55, 77, 79, 90–1, 94,
      112, 114, 118–20, 188, 224, 267
  fall of 37–8, 66–7, 72, 81, 90–1, 94,
      142, 276
  see also sin, original
adamant, a stone 84
Adiutor laborantium 31
Adna son of Othar 144
Adomnán of Iona 29, 97, 207, 209,
    256–7, 261, 264, 269, 273–5
  law of 207, 261, 273
Aed Oirdnide son of Niall Frossach 182–3
Aed son of Ainmire 31
Aed son of Sétnae, *see* Maedóc of Ferns
Aedán son of Gabrán 31
Africa 89
Ailenn 175, 190
Ailerán the Wise 206
Ailill son of Dúnlaing 164, 170, 173
Ailill son of Mata 190
Aipgitir Chrábaid 231–45, 279
air 69, 79, 99, 101, 108, 118
  body made from 67, 71
  inhabited by demons 35, 38
  lower 60–1

Alab, a tree 85
Alexandria 218
Alien, stream of 84
allegory 54, 60
almsgiving 73, 164, 167–8, 172, 174, 177,
    199, 239, 249–50, 256–7, 270–1
  see also generosity
alphabet 29, 31–2, 147, 149, 151
Altus Prosator 29–50, 75, 128, 147, 275,
    277
Amairgen Glúngel 144
Ambrose of Milan 156, 214
Amra Coluim Chille 13, 29, 277
Ananias 74
anchorites, *see* hermits
ancients, antediluvian 217
Angel of the Trinity 269
angelic language 75, 78–80, 95
  specimens of 78, 80–2, 86–7, 89–91
angels 53–5, 60–1, 66, 79–80, 85, 87–9,
    91, 93–5, 97, 119–24, 151, 178, 198,
    265–7
  as messengers 50, 57, 61, 64–5, 73,
      94, 120, 150, 167, 176, 246, 248,
      255, 261
  emissions of 82
  guardian 150–1, 160–1, 196, 201, 264–5,
      267–9, 273
  humans may act as 153, 203
  invoking 32, 127, 131, 180, 216
  nine orders of 33–4, 80, 93, 95, 115,
      118–19, 123–4, 217, 265
  praise of God by, *see* singing of
  rebel angels 29, 34–5, 54, 124
  singing of 9–10, 36–7, 47, 63, 78, 81–3,
      95, 108–9, 113–16, 120–1, 124,
      150, 188, 265–6
Angels, as angelic order 34, 115, 119–23
Anglo-Normans 11, 17
anmchara, *see* soul-friend
Anthony of Egypt 218
Antioch 218
Apocalypse of Philip 75

Apocalypsis Mosis 276
apocrypha 10, 22, 29, 97, 261, 276
apostles 48, 66, 68, 73–4, 131, 151, 153,
    159, 161, 218, 262, 264–5, 273
appearances, illusory 58, 67, 71, 73, 128,
    135
Arabia 206
Arachel, archangel 123
Árad Mór 173
archangels 45–6, 49, 81, 108–9, 123, 131,
    217, 266–9
Archangels, as angelic order 34, 115, 119–
    23
Ard nAchaid 166
Ark of the Covenant 60
Armagh 11, 16, 19, 147, 150, 189
Armenia 90
Artrí mac Faelmuire 255
Assian, spring of 83
Assyrians 90
astrologers 65
Audite omnes amantes 29–30, 147–61, 277–8
Augustine of Hippo 51, 97, 159, 275
Augustinians 11, 16
Augustinus Hibernicus 51
Aulol, lands of 84
autumn 41, 78
Axal, angel 201

Babichel, archangel 123
Babylon 54, 93
Baíthín(e) son of Brénainn 31, 200–2
Balaam 65
Bangor 209, 254
baptism 11, 66–7, 141–2, 148–9, 155–6,
    206, 243
Barachel, archangel 123
barbarians 152
Barrow, river 191
beasts
    creation of 36, 107
    four living creatures 47–8
    varieties of 91
Beati immaculati in uia (Psalm 118) 143,
    147, 248
beatitudes, the eight 166–7
Bécc son of Eógan 190

Bede 31, 39, 157
beetle, monstrous 195
Belach Con Glais 209
bells 160–1, 165, 200, 231, 236
Benedict of Nursia 24, 218
benefits
    obtained by reciting sacred texts 20,
        30, 32, 50, 128, 130, 147, 150–1,
        161, 180, 214–17
    of virtuous living 231, 233–7, 241–2
Benén 130, 135, 143
Benignus, *see* Benén
Bera, devotee of Patrick 150
Bernán Brigte 160
Bernard of Clairvaux 16
Bethlehem 63–5, 94, 218
Bethu Phátraic 135, 147, 160
Bible 10, 23, 29, 75, 97, 147, 275
    citations:
        Genesis 1:1 36, 77, 80; 1:3 33; 1:7
            81; 1:22 70; 1:26 90; 2:2 52;
            2:8 43; 3:14 37–8, 54; 3:19 55
        Exodus 3:6–10 56; 16:15 154; 21:2
            148; 24:15–16 44
        Leviticus 21:4 254
        Numbers 11:7 60; 24:17 65
        Deuteronomy 8:3 61; 15:12 148;
            32:1 151
        1 Kings 17:21 71
        Job 9:9 46; 9:10 52; 26:5 39;
            26:7 41; 26:8 40; 38:32 46
        Psalm 3:8 129, 135, 138; 22:6 63;
            49:1 151; 77:25 60; 85:13 42;
            103:4 57; 103:5 41; 109:3 66;
            110:10 35; 134:7 38; 146:5–6
            263; 148 127; 148:7–8 61
        Ecclesiastes 1:9–10 58
        Sirach 18:1 81
        Isaiah 6:1 33; 14:12 34; 14:13–14
            54; 66:1 66
        Ezekiel 33:12 50
        Daniel 3:52–80 127; 7:9 33
        Zephaniah 1:14–16 44
        Matthew 3:2 55; 3:17 66; 4:4 61;
            4:7 38; 4:10 38; 4:17 55; 5:15
            155; 5:16 152; 10:9 73; 10:16
            31; 10:20 141; 16:18 152; 16:27

Matthew *(contd)* 45, 48; 19:28 159; 22:30 55; 24:28 153; 24:29 47; 25:34 95; 25:41 42, 54
Mark 9:47 42
Luke 2:14 78; 4:4 61; 9:23 156; 10:18 54; 16:22 42
John 5:17 52; 8:44 54; 10:15 156; 11:4 71; 14:2 48
Acts 3:6 73; 3:19 55; 10:11 264; 20:9–10 72
Romans 9:3 156
1 Corinthians 1:19 35; 13:9 23; 15:44 73; 15:58 152
2 Corinthians 5:10 45; 12:2–4 264
Galatians 4:19 60
Ephesians 6:11–17 127
Philippians 2:9–10 42
1 Thessalonians 4:15 45; 4:17 69; 5:8 127
Hebrews 2:16 55; 10:27 48; 11:39–40 72
Revelation 1:5 71; 1:20 65; 2:7 43; 4:4 47; 5:1, 3, 5 42; 5:13 42; 6:15–16 47; 9:1 34; 10:7 45; 12:3–4 35; 16:18 44; 22:2 43
birds
  creation of 36, 107
  diabolical 160
  extraordinary 86–90
  heavenly 109, 117–18, 160, 265–6
  souls appear as 50, 58, 274
  varieties of 91
bishops 77–8, 143, 147, 166, 169, 218, 249, 251, 253
blasphemy 23, 86–7
Blathmac mac Flainn 254
Bláthnat, a stone on Iona 31
Bláthnat, Brigit's cook 169
blessings 11, 49–50, 70, 135, 138, 141, 161, 168–75, 177–9, 183, 193, 203, 211–13, 217, 250–1, 257–8
'Blind Lad's Bell' 165
blood 59, 79
body 55, 68, 72, 79, 93, 141, 219, 222, 240, 242, 267
  angelic 141
  of air 67, 71

prayers for 130, 133, 211, 224
resurrection 69, 73
spiritual 73
undecaying 208–9, 217
see also flesh
Boethius 182
Book of Kells 75
Book of Leinster 204
Book of Lismore 276
Boyne, river 11, 18, 169
Bran son of Muiredach 191
Brandub mac Echach 250, 279
'breastplate', *see lorica*
Breccán of Echdruimm 200
Brega 176
Brendan of Clonfert 169–70
Bretha Nemed 144
Brí Cobthaig Choíl 172
Brian son of Cennétig 49
Bríg, another name for Brigit 178
Bríg, devotee of Patrick 150
Bríg Ambue, Judgments of 144
Brigit of Kildare 160, 162–79, 190, 219, 278
  as mother of Christ 163–4, 174–5, 177
Britain 11–12, 14, 29, 31
Britons 14, 148
Brittany 13, 148
Broccán, Patrick's scribe 9
Broccán the Crooked 162, 164
'Broccán's Hymn' 162–79, 278
Broom from Fanat 206–7
Bruide son of Melchú 31
Bush, river 137

Caílte son of Rónán 9
Cain son of Adam 93
Cainchomrac, bishop 249
Cairnech of Tuilén 143, 208–9
Cairnech the Bald 199
calendars 13, 180–227
  see also time
Calpurnius, father of Patrick 148, 273
canons, *see* law, canon
Canterbury 14–15
canticles 216
  canticle of Mary, *see Magnificat*
Caratnia Teiscthe, False Judgments of 144

Carney, James 276
Carthach of Saigir 197
Cas Corach 9–11
Cashel 15–16
Cassian, John 231, 275
Caucasus 90
Céili Dé 14–16, 24, 219, 232, 246–58, 279–80
Celestine, pope 148
celibacy 15–16, 250
Cell Chuilinn 173
Cell Fhinnenn 172
Cell Guilbín 251
Cellach mac Aedo 16
'Celtic Christianity' 14
'Celtic church' 14
Cenél Conaill 201
Cephas, shore of 86
Chaldaeans 224
charity 121, 149, 167, 233, 239, 244, 271
Charybdis 40
chastity 154–5, 159, 201, 233, 237, 250
Cherubim, angelic order 34, 115, 119–20, 131
Christ, *see* Jesus Christ
Christmas eve 63, 84, 86, 94
Cianán of Doimliac 208–9
    law of 209
Ciarán, as generic name for a saint 191
Ciarán of Clonmacnoise 190, 202
Ciarán of Saigir 197–9
Circe 40
Cistercians 11, 16
Clann Shínaig 16
classical learning 10, 22, 97, 127
Clonard 169, 171
Clonmacnoise 190, 254, 256–7
clouds 38–9, 40–1, 60–1, 67, 69, 80, 82
Cluain Chorcaige 171
Cluain Chredal 195
Cluain Eidnech 183–4
Cluain Mór Maedóic 164, 197
Cluain Moescna 171
Cobthach Coel Breg 183
Cocytus, river 40
Coemgen of Glendalough 150, 167, 227

Cogitosus 162, 278
Colcu 254
Colcu of Slane 246, 256
'Colloquy of the Two Sages' 144
Colmán descendant of Fiachrae 208
Colmán Duib Chuilinn 208–9
Colmán Elo, *see* Colmán mac Beógnai
Colmán mac Beógnai 150, 231, 279
Colum Cille of Iona 14, 29, 31–3, 35, 162, 200–2, 206, 209, 219, 254, 261, 275
Columba, *see* Colum Cille
Columbanus of Bobbio 13–14, 23–5
Comgall of Bangor 209, 254
Comraire 128
Conaille Muirthemne 148
Conall 198
concealment, supernatural 83, 85–7, 128, 135, 200
Conchess, mother of Patrick 128
Conchobar son of Nes 144
Condmach, abbot of Armagh 182
confession 170, 216, 233, 250, 252–4
confessors 131
Conlaed of Kildare 177
Connacht 167, 197, 200
Connor 49
conscience 142–3, 183, 254
Constantine, emperor 273
constellations 104–6, 272
    see also zodiac
conversion of Ireland 10–12, 140
Copar, sister of Mo Laisse 252
Corc son of Lugaid 143
Corcu Loígde 198–9
Cornán of Glenn Essa 247, 249
corpse, treatment of 253–4
cosmology 22, 29, 75, 97, 127, 275
Cothraige, another name of Patrick 148
Counter-Reformation 17–18
creation 29, 32, 36, 52, 76–7, 81–2, 93, 97–108, 161, 182
    days of 32, 51–2, 54, 75, 87, 89, 182
Creator, God as 22, 24, 30, 33, 37, 52, 55, 130, 134, 235
Crimthann, original name of Colum Cille 200

Croaghpatrick, *see* Cruachán Aigli
Cromwell, Oliver 17–18
Crónán, as generic name for a saint 191
Cross 46–7, 85, 154, 187, 198–9
  sign of the 148, 171, 257
crosses
  as symbols and instruments of suffering
    95, 156, 186, 218
  used in worship 31, 109
cross-vigil 167, 253
Cruach, *see* Cruachán Aigli
Cruachán Aigli 11, 151, 160–1
Cruachán Brí Éle 166
Crunnmael 255
Cú Roí 254
Cualu 248
Cúil Bennchuir 183
Cuilenn, near Belach Con Glais 209
Cuilenn (modern Slieve Gullion) 205
Cuimmíne, sister of Colum Cille 201
Cuirrech Life 169, 171, 173, 179
Cúl Dreimne 31
Culdees, *see* Céili Dé
Cullen, Paul 19
curses 160, 203, 255

Dairchell, original name of Mo Ling 202
Dáire of Ulster 143
Dál mBirn 197
Dál nAraide 148, 200
Dál Riatai 200
Dan, river 85
Daniel 33, 225
Dante Alighieri 261
Dar, stream of 84
Dar Ercae, original name of Mo Ninne 205
Dar Í, law of 207
Darachel, archangel 123
Dard, lands of 83
Dark One, *see* Devil
darkness 81, 98
  spiritual 240
Dathan 69
David son of Jesse 62–4, 225–6, 263
dead, intercession for 161, 216, 250, 256–8
Dead Sea 77
Decius, emperor 188

Déisi 249
demons 34–5, 37–8, 54, 69, 71, 79, 93–4,
  128, 130, 133, 141, 160, 178, 180,
  192, 214, 216, 226, 245, 254–5, 261,
  264, 270–3
Derrynaflan 15
desire 231, 234, 235, 241–6, 252
  for God 245
  see also flesh, nature
Devenish 252
Devil 32, 34–5, 37–8, 54–6, 66–8, 81, 94,
  158, 192, 202–3, 215, 236, 241, 243,
  250, 254, 269, 272
  fall of 34–5, 37–8, 54–6, 81, 93, 124,
    141
devils, *see* demons
'devotional revolution' 18–19
dew 60, 217
Dian Cécht, Judgments of 144
Diarmait of Iona 254
Diarmait son of Cerball 31
diet 62, 199, 201, 246, 248–52, 255, 257,
  279
  see also fasting
disbelief 23, 61–2, 86–7
disciples 218, 265
distances, cosmic 91, 101–2, 111
Doet Nemthine, Judgments of 144
Doimliac 208
Dominations, angelic order 34, 115,
  119–20
Domnach Mór 169, 208
Domnach Sechnaill 148–9
Domnall
  as generic name for a king 191
  three students named 49
Donnán of Eig 199–200
Donnchad son of Domnall 182, 191
Doomsday, *see* Judgment, Day of
dove
  Colum Cille as 31, 201
  Holy Spirit as 65–7, 73
  soul appears as 50
Down 16
dragons 77, 80, 84, 207
  aquatic 84
  beneath the earth 88

dragons *(contd)*
　celestial 82, 88–9
　infernal 269, 272
　the Devil as a 35
　see also monsters
dreams
　revelatory 148, 198, 201–2
　sexual 246, 255
druids 11–12, 58, 128, 133, 140, 167–8
Dublin 15, 247
Dubthach moccu Lugair 139, 141, 143, 277
Dubthach son of Deimre, Brigit's father
　166, 170
Duiblittir of Finglas 246, 248–9, 257–8
Dúilem, see Creator
Dumbarton 148
Dún Cuair 182
Dún Reichet 209

earth 23, 41–2, 58, 60, 79–81, 93, 101–2,
　132, 263–4
　affected by human sin 66, 255
　as a name for the lower air 60–1
　as dwelling of mankind 53–5, 141
　creation of 36, 77, 79, 82, 98–9, 107–8,
　　182
　dwellers beneath the 43, 88
　inhabited by demons 35, 36, 68
　regions beneath the 87–8
　size of 107
Easter 160, 207
　Easter controversy 13–14
　vigil of 23, 75–6, 78–9, 84, 94, 262
Ebia, island of 90
Ebian, island of 83
Ebión, spring of 83
Ebothen, islands of 89
Echdruimm 200
Échtguide 251
Echu ua Tuathail 257–8
Edessa 206
Egypt 22, 57–60, 70, 75, 83, 93, 226, 261
Egyptians 14, 56, 261
Eig 199
Eithne daughter of Dímma, mother of
　Colum Cille 200–1

elders
　in religious communities 167, 189,
　　202, 231, 236, 251, 255
　twenty-four heavenly 47–8, 116, 120,
　　123
elements 36, 79, 98
Elijah 65, 68, 70–1, 206, 224, 262, 273–4
Elisha 65, 206
Elizabeth, mother of John the Baptist
　61–2
Elizabeth I of England 17
Emain Macha 144, 190
England 17–18, 276
Enoch 224, 274
　Book of 97
Eochaid grandson of Flannucán 149
Eochu son of Luchta, Judgments of 144
Eógan son of Durthacht, Judgments of
　144
Eóganacht Locha Léin 49
Erc of Domnach Mór 208
Eriugena, Johannes 14, 24
ether 37, 101, 118
Etna, mount 40
eucharist 84, 149–50, 207, 216, 221, 254,
　257
Eusebius of Caesarea 214
Eutychus 71–2
evangelists 48
Eve 37–8, 85, 276
Ever-new Tongue 77–8, 80–2, 85–8, 91–3
exegesis 13, 75
Ezekiel 57, 97

Fachtna of Ros Ailithir 199
Fachtna son of Sencha, Judgments of 144
Faeth Fiada 127–35, 277
Fafigial, archangel 123
Faichnech, bog of 166
fairies, *see sid*
faith 233, 239–40
falsehood 54, 84, 271
Fanat 206–7
fanes, a stone 84–5
fasting 14, 50, 67–8, 70, 201, 203, 205,
　216, 235–6, 241, 250–2, 254, 256

as means of coercion 11, 160, 255
see also diet
Father, God the 48–9, 52, 54–5, 66–8,
70, 77, 95–6, 117, 141, 152, 191,
221, 263, 274
Fathers of the Church 10, 29, 51, 97
feeding, miracles of 69–70, 163, 167–71,
175–8
Féilire Oengusso 15, 30, 180–227, 247,
278–9
Fer Dá Chrích 251, 253
Fer Fio 128, 136
Ferchertne the poet 144
Fergus son of Conall Gulban 200
Feidlimid son of Fergus, father of Colum
Cille 200
Fergus the poet 143
Ferns 190
Ferta Fer Féicc 135
Fiacc, a strong man 175
Fiachra of Iraird 197
Fid Gabla 175
Finglas 15, 247, 249
findruine 111, 137, 204
Fine Gall 172, 176
Fínnechta Fledach 273
Finnio mac Fiatach 254
Finntrácht Gléire 198
Fir Thuirbe 167
Fir Thulach 166
fire 56–7, 79, 132, 257
aerial 65
angelic 57, 65
creation of 36, 108
heavenly 82, 148, 166, 265–6
Holy Spirit as 65–6, 73
infernal 40, 42, 54, 91–2, 141, 251, 269–73
mountains of 88, 93, 272
of judgment 47–8, 88, 93, 161
purgatorial 239, 243–5, 249, 268
sacred 162
sea of 83, 88–9, 93, 272
firmament 65, 81, 99, 101–4, 106–7, 271–2
Fís Adomnáin 22, 261–74, 280
fish, creation of 36
flesh

battle against the 119, 243, 264
nature of human 68–70, 79, 87, 141
see also body; desire; nature
'Flight of the Earls' 18
Flood 93, 224
Fones, tribes of 90–1
forgiveness 55–6, 68, 140–2, 241
Forrach Pátraic 173
Fothad na Cánóine 182–3
Fothairt Tíre 174
France 14
Friday 182
Fursa 250, 279

Gabriel, archangel 61–2, 123
Gabuen, stars of 88
Galilee 68
Gallgaídil 199
Gallichiel, archangel 123
Gehenna, *see* hell⁴
generosity 233, 235, 237, 239
see also almsgiving
George 218
Gerald of Wales 12
Germanus of Auxerre 148
giants 39–40
Gilboa 225
Gilgal 65
Glaucus 40
Glendalough 167, 190
glés 100–1, 161
Gnosticism 22, 75, 261
God
descriptions of 80–1, 94–5, 266
see also Abbot; Creator; Father;
Governor; Jesus Christ; King;
Physician; Son; Spirit, Holy;
Trinity
gods
classical 40, 162
Irish 9–11, 128, 162
Goliath 225
Gorianus 148–9
Gospel 140–1, 153–5, 157–8, 166
books 21, 203, 256–7
oaths sworn upon the 49–50
government, God's 52–3, 70

Governor, God as 53, 58–9
'Great Jewel', a cross on Iona 31
Greek language 33, 35, 41, 156, 159
Greeks 14
Gregory the Great, pope 13, 29, 31–2, 97

Hab, lands of 84
hail 60–1
healing
    miracles of 68–9, 73, 149, 180, 217
    properties of nature 83–5, 89, 171
heaven 66, 89, 97, 132, 150, 155, 164, 166, 179, 258, 263–4, 273–4
    as a name for clouds 60
    as dwelling of the angels 34, 37, 49, 53–4, 56, 67–8, 94, 116, 124, 141, 212, 221, 264
    as reward 9, 50, 67, 90–1, 114, 124, 131, 151–3, 157–8, 161, 178, 180, 233–7, 239–44, 249, 258, 263–4, 274
    creation of 36, 77, 79, 98
    descriptions of 95–6, 108–19, 261, 265–7
    destruction of the heavens 79
    household of 50, 78, 161, 245, 264–5, 267, 269, 273
    in this world 243
    lower heavens 101–2
    music of, *see* angels, singing of
    of angels 118
    of the Lord 118
    of water 118
    seven heavens 80–2, 93–4, 104, 118, 184, 213, 222, 261, 267–9
    third heaven 264
    upper heaven 61
    see also ríched
Hebrew language 33, 41, 80, 147, 151, 154, 159
Hebrews 14, 32, 78–83, 85–8, 91–3, 148
    see also Israelites, Jews
heir (Irish *comarbae*) 159, 182, 195
Helair of Loch Cré 248, 250
Helena, mother of Constantine 273
hell 42, 75, 79–80, 88, 91–3, 102, 152, 225, 227, 257, 263–4

as dwelling of the demons 35, 37–8, 68, 94, 124
creation of 81
descriptions of 91–2, 261, 269–73
harrowing of 94
in this world 243
location of 42
sinners tormented in 39–40, 42, 50, 73, 90–3, 95, 160–1, 242, 274
    see also torments
Henry VIII of England 17
heretics 128, 133, 162, 271
Hermichel, archangel 123
hermits 16, 218, 249, 251, 254, 256
Herod Antipas 181, 187
Herod the Great 64, 218
Hevilath 64
hibien, a stone 84
Hilary of Poitiers 214
hiruath, a bird 86
Holy Innocents 218
Holy Land 97
Holy Spirit, *see* Spirit, Holy
Honoratus 218
Horeb, mount 56, 58, 65
hospitality 31, 165, 169–70, 176, 249, 270
households, the three 42, 161
hymnals 31
hymns 13, 29, 31–2, 78, 130, 147–51, 159, 161–2, 164, 248, 266, 275, 278

idolatry 83, 85, 128, 133, 227
Immirge Chiaráin 199
In te Christe 32
India 83–4, 86, 90
inexpressibility topoi 91–2, 94–5, 114, 118, 124, 214, 266, 272
Inisfallen 50
Instructions of Cormac 162
Iona 13–14, 31, 201, 207, 246, 252, 254, 256–7, 261, 275
Ior, river 85
Irish language 13, 15, 247
Isaac 71, 224
Isaiah 217
Isidore of Seville 34, 275

Israel 44, 56, 59, 64, 68, 70, 157–9, 225, 226
Israelites 56, 64
  see also Hebrews; Jews
istien, a stone 84
Italy 14, 40, 149, 165
Íte of Killeedy 195–6
Ithier, tribes of 90

Jacob 62, 64–5, 225
James the apostle 218
James I of England 17
James II of England 18
Jerome 57, 159, 214
Jerusalem 49, 64–5, 78, 218
  heavenly 96
Jesus Christ 36, 52, 62–74, 127, 134–5,
    151–9, 165, 179, 184, 186–7, 189,
    192–3, 195, 201–3, 207, 210, 212–13,
    215, 218–27, 245, 254
  as Child 94, 196
  as Judge 42–3, 45, 47–8, 131, 209, 265,
    274
  as Priest 156
  as Sacrifice 156
  as Saviour 21, 25, 49, 55, 64, 79, 84,
    93–4, 135, 138, 157
  as Shepherd 63, 156
  as Sun 95, 184
  ascension of 131
  baptism of 66–7, 131, 206
  incarnation of 55, 62–3, 67–70, 79, 84,
    94, 131, 163, 221
  passion of 55, 72, 79, 85, 94, 131,
    141, 187
  resurrection of 72–3, 75–6, 79, 84,
    93–4, 131
  transfiguration of 70–1
  see also Lamb of God; Son, God the;
    Son of God; Son of Man; Son of
    Mary; Word of God
Jews 52, 64, 271
  see also Hebrews; Israelites
Job 226
John the Baptist 55, 61–3, 66, 187, 206–7,
    264
John the Evangelist 225, 227

Jonah 24
Jordan, river 65–6
Joseph, husband of Mary 62
Joseph, the patriarch 56, 226
Joshua 65
Judaea 49, 64, 68, 94
Judah, tribe of 42, 86
Judas Iscariot 86
Judas Maccabaeus son of Gomer 86–7
judges 143–4, 271
Judgment, Day of 29, 44–50, 75, 78–9,
    88–94, 97, 131, 159, 161, 198, 206,
    245, 249, 265, 267, 270–2, 274,
    276
Jupiter 101
Justin, emperor 31
Justinian, emperor 31

Kadesh 58
Kells 16
  see also Book of Kells
Kildare 162, 169–70, 172–3, 175, 177–8
kin-slaying 83, 85, 93, 256, 270
King, God as 9, 22, 44, 64, 77, 81, 93,
    96, 98–109, 111, 114–24, 128, 137,
    141–2, 157, 164, 167–70, 174, 184–5,
    187, 189–90, 193, 196, 198, 203–4,
    210–13, 215, 217, 219, 222–4, 226–7
King of mysteries 23, 98, 104–5, 108, 115,
    224

labour, as religious discipline 241, 243, 257
Laisrén, breastplate of 128, 136
Laisrén of Clonmacnoise 254–5
Lamb of God 47, 63, 66, 84, 117
  see also Jesus Christ
Land of Promise 169
  see also Promised Land
languages 91, 95
  of the angels, *see* angelic language
  of birds 86–7
  of demons 95
  of sea-monsters 95
  see also Greek; Hebrew; Irish; Latin
last rites 50, 253
Latin language 13, 15, 33, 35, 41, 80,
    153–4, 156, 159, 276

law
    canon 12–13, 158
    Irish 12, 21, 139, 142, 277
    'New Law' 63, 139, 142
    of forgiveness 140
law *(contd)*
    of nature 139, 143
    of Scripture 143, 156
    of the prophets 143
    'Old Law' 48, 60, 62–3, 70, 143
Lazarus 71
Leabhar Breac 275, 278–80
learned families 17–19
Lebor na hUidre 280
Lecc Brénainn 169
Léiníne 208
Leinster 164, 166, 169–70, 173–7, 182,
    197, 209, 249
Lent 160, 257
Lent, summer 251
lepers 171–2, 174, 177, 203
leprosy 57, 68
Leth Cuinn 175
Letha 177
Levi, tribe of 56
Liadaine, mother of Ciarán of Saigir 198
Liber Hymnorum 275, 277–8
Libya 83–4, 90
Liffey, river 173
light 81, 98
    angelic 80–1, 95
    divine 23, 35, 65, 69–70, 95–6, 113,
        155, 265
lightning 80, 82, 93, 132
Lihigiel, archangel 123
Lismore 51
Loch Cré 248
Loch Lemnachta 169
Loch Rudraige 207
Loegaire son of Niall 11, 130, 135, 139–40,
    143, 149, 164, 189
Lombards 149
Lonachel, archangel 123
lorica 30, 127–38, 151, 180, 212, 216, 277
Lot 65, 224
Luachair Dedad 202

lubrum, a tree 35
Lucifer
    as collective designation for angels 66
    see also Devil
Lugaid, a strong man 175
Lugaid, former inhabitant of an
    abandoned settlement 190
Lugaid son of Loegaire 164
Lugnae, father of Ciarán of Saigir 198
lugubrium, a tree 35
Luna 101
    see also moon
Lupait, sister of Patrick 148
Lynally 231

Mac Caille 166
Mac Midrui 167–8
Maedóc of Ferns 190, 197, 250, 279
Maedóc ua Dúnlaing 197
Mael Díthruib of Terryglass 246, 248–51,
    257
Mael Maedóic Ua Morgair, *see* Malachy
Mael Phátraic son of Mael Shuthain 50
Mael Ruain of Tallaght 184, 191, 212,
    232, 246–51, 253, 255–6
Mael Shuthain ua Cerbaill 49–50
Mag Coel 176
Mag Fea 173–4
Mag Fenamna 167
Mag Léna 246, 255, 280
Mag mBreg 207
Mag Reichet 184
Magi 64–6
magic 58, 99, 127–8, 133, 137
    see also witches
Magnificat 248
Magonius, another name for Patrick 148
Maistiu 173–4
Malachy 16
Mamre 73
mankind 53–6, 60–1
    as tenth order 118–19
    creation of 36, 90, 93, 182
    extraordinary races of 90–1
manna 60–1, 154
Manoah, father of Samson 65
Mark the Evangelist 218

marriage 9, 15
Mars 101
Martin of Tours 218, 227
martyrs 78, 150, 185–6, 199–200, 212, 218, 220, 226, 270
Mary 62–4, 94, 163, 178–9, 188, 192, 205, 218, 248, 264–5
mass 149–50, 161, 180, 200, 207, 215, 253–4
matins 78, 85, 124, 251
matter, first 34, 36–7, 52, 80–1, 93–4, 98–9, 102
Maundy Thursday 209
Maurice, emperor 31
May 89
May Day 83–4
Meath 128, 182, 191, 247
Mel, Bishop 166
Mellifont 11, 16
Mercury 101
metre 32, 37, 151, 183, 277
Meyer, Kuno 128
Michael, archangel 49–50, 123, 217, 267–8
Midian 56
midnight 75, 78, 89, 93–4
Míliucc moccu Buain 148
Mínchloth, sister of Colum Cille 201
Mirachel, archangel 123
Mo Cholmóc ua Litáin 250
Mo Chua of Ros Cré 248
Mo Chuaróc of Echdruimm 200
Mo Chutu of Lismore 256
Mo Laisse of Devenish 252
Mo Ling 202–4, 207, 279
'Mo Nanna', nickname of Mo Ninne 205
Mo Ninne of Killeevy 205
monks 15, 31, 130, 183, 198, 202, 218, 231–2, 236, 246, 254, 257, 280
monsters
    aquatic 40, 79–80, 82–3, 86, 89–90, 94, 107, 169–70, 224
    beneath the earth 88
    infernal 91, 261, 269–70, 272
    see also dragons
moon 23, 29, 72, 77, 81–2, 105–5, 132
    creation of 36, 107, 182
    darkening of 47, 93

size of 107
    unnecessary in heaven 95
    see also Luna
Morann, Judgments of 144
Moses 11, 29, 44, 52, 56–9, 62, 65, 68, 70–2, 79, 160, 226
Muccrama 200
Mugdorna 257
Muirchú moccu Macthéni 135, 147
Muired, a strong man 175
Munster 167, 195, 202, 253
Muses 182
music 9, 90, 247, 249, 266
    fairy 9–10
    heavenly 91, 117–18, 249, 265
    of precious stones 85
    of water 84
    see also angels, singing of; singing

Naboth, island of 89
Nabuan, mountain of 84
Nad Fráich, Brigit's lector 167, 173
Nathaben, a tree 85–7
nature
    'hidden depths of' 51–2
    integrity of 51–2, 58–9, 61
    to be resisted 133, 235
    see also flesh
Nebuchadnezzar 187
Néde son of Adna 144
Neptune 40
Nero, emperor 181, 187–8
Nineveh 225
Ninne the poet 205
Noah 141, 217, 224
nocturns 124, 251
nó-fis 143
none 83, 88, 94, 161
Northumbria 13
Nuadu, condemned by Dubthach's judgment 142
Nuall Fir Fhio 13, 21, 127–9, 130, 135–8, 215, 277
numbers, used in counting angels 121–2
nuns 166, 179, 195, 198, 205, 207, 249

Octavianus Augustus Caesar, emperor 61, 64

Odaib, islands of 90
Odrán 208
Oengus mac Oengobann 15, 180, 182-4,
    247
offices, religious 9, 162, 165, 251, 265,
    273, 279
'Old English' 17-18
Olympus, as third heaven 102, 118
On the Miracles of Holy Scripture 12, 23-4,
    51-75, 275
Onchú of Cluain Mór Maedóic 197
Orion 46
Osraige 197
Otherworld 10, 29

pagans 64-5, 78, 186
    Irish 128, 135, 152-6, 189-90
paganism 133, 141, 240
    Irish 9-10, 12-13, 18-19, 21, 128-9,
        139, 162, 181, 191, 231
Panachel, archangel 123
papacy 16-18
Paradise 43, 85, 88, 93, 95, 211, 262, 273-4
Passover 93, 206
patriarchs 48, 131, 143, 210, 217, 265
Patrick 9-12, 16, 128, 130, 135, 139-43,
    147-62, 172, 182, 189, 198, 209,
    219, 227, 273
    law of 143, 207, 209
patristic learning, *see* Fathers of the Church
Paul, the apostle 71-2, 127, 150, 154, 165,
    188, 218, 226, 264, 273
Paul the First Hermit 187, 218
penance 24, 31, 62, 87, 141, 150, 243,
    249-50, 254, 257, 266, 280
penitentials 12, 24, 255
penitents 112, 116, 166, 270
Peter, the apostle 55, 69, 73-4, 150, 165,
    187-8, 218, 226-7, 264, 273
Peter the Deacon 199
Petrie, George 128
Pharaoh 56, 58-9, 93, 226
Philip, the apostle 78, 80
Philip the Presbyter 39
Phlegethon, river 40
Phocas, emperor 31
Phoenicia 206

Phorcys 40
Physician, God as 54-5, 68-9
Picts 31
Pilate, Pontius 187-8
pilgrimage 14, 49, 177
pilgrims 266
Placentia 165
plagues 59, 82, 85, 88-9, 94, 207, 216,
    225
Plain of Life 136
planets 65, 101, 104
plants, creation of 36, 108
Plea 165
Pleiades 46
Pliny the Elder 97
poets 16-18, 29, 139, 141, 143-4, 162,
    176, 182, 197, 205
poison 40, 84-5, 130, 134, 225, 227, 272-3
poor, gifts to, *see* almsgiving
popular tradition 18-19, 128, 163
Potitus, grandfather of Patrick 148
poverty, apostolic 73, 233
Powers, angelic order 34, 115, 119-20
prayer 14, 159, 166, 184-5, 212, 215-16,
    219-23, 234, 241, 246, 253, 274, 277
priests 11, 19, 50, 61, 78, 183-4, 196, 218,
    271
Principalities, angelic order 34, 115, 119-20
prior 231, 236
Promised Land 71
    see also Land of Promise
prophets 62, 107
    false 128, 133
    Hebrew 33, 48, 61-2, 64, 70, 131, 143,
        210, 217, 265
    Irish 33
    pagan 64
prostrations 50, 203, 249, 251
Protestantism 17-18
psalms, recitation of 159, 180, 200, 215-16,
    249-50, 253, 255
Pseudo-Dionysius the Areopagite 14
'Pseudo-Historical Prologue to the *Senchas
    Már*' 21, 139-44, 277-8
purgatory 267
    see also fire, purgatorial; souls,
        redeemed from punishment

Quiricus 188

Raguel, archangel 123
rain 39–41, 61, 80, 99
Ráith Breasail 15
Ráith Chatháir 170
Ráith Chruachan 190
Ráith Derthaige 170
Rameses 93
Raphael, archangel 123
Red Sea 77, 86, 93
reform, ecclesiastical 11, 14–16, 18–19,
    246–7
Reformation 17
Reilec Aingel 197
relics 21, 150, 186, 197, 216, 220, 270
Renna 209
repentance 56, 62, 87, 234, 243
requiems 250
resurrection
    of Christ, *see* Jesus Christ
    of mankind 45–6, 55, 71–3, 76, 97, 131,
        245
    of the world 77, 79
    see also bodies, resurrection
Riagail of Muccinis 207
ríched 79–82, 95, 97, 102, 108–20, 123
    see also heaven
rinnard 183, 212
rivers 77, 80, 83–4
    infernal 40, 273
    of Paradise 43
    of wine 89
Roman Empire 13, 31
Romans 31, 152, 159
Rome 10, 13–14, 16, 197, 273
    abbots of 273
    as term for an ecclesiastical settlement
        190–1
    bishops of 14
    travel to 150, 162, 165, 177
Rónchenn 177
Rónait, mother of Adomnán 207
Ros Ailithir 199
Ros Cré 248
Ros na Ferta 173, 175
Ros son of Trechem 143

roscada 143
roundness
    of the earth 81–2, 99
    of the firmament 103, 106
    of the heavens 81
    of the seas 81, 91, 94
    of the soul 81
    of the universe 41, 80–1, 93
Rule of the Céili Dé 279–80
rules, monastic 24
Rumiel, archangel 123

Sab, islands of 83, 85, 94
Sabairn, islands of 77
Sabbath 52, 60
Sabes, birds of 89
Saigir 197–9
saints 71–2, 95–6, 112, 131, 150, 157,
        159, 180–1, 184, 213–15, 219, 221,
        225, 253, 264–6, 268, 270, 274
    feasts of 106, 180–227
    land of the 112, 116, 265, 273
    lives of 13, 162, 262, 275, 278
    of Ireland 12, 150, 162, 169, 178, 219,
        246, 255
    patron 236, 246, 248, 256
Saltair na Rann 22–4, 75, 97–124, 276–7
Sames, a tree 85
Samthann of Cluain Brónaig 253
Samson 227
Samuel, prophet 71
Sapphira 74
Sarachel, archangel 123
Sárbile, original name of Mo Ninne 205
Sariel, archangel 123
Sarmichiel, archangel 123
Satan
    angel of 71
    see also Devil
satirists 271
Saturday 151, 160–1, 182
Saturn 101
Saul 226
Saxons 161
Sciaich 177
Scotland 13, 31, 199, 219
Scylla 40

Scythia 69
Scythians 14
sea 23, 39, 80–3, 93, 107, 132
    celestial 83
    creation of 36, 82
    daughters of the 128, 136
    dwellers beneath the 91, 162, 165
    infernal 82
    inhabited by demons 35
    at Judgment 161
Sea of Wight (Irish *Muir nIcht*) 165
Sebasten 206
Sechnall son of Restitutus 147–51
'Sechnall's Hymn', *see Audite omnes amantes*
Sechnasach, bishop 251
Sechmaide, king of the Britons 148
Secundinus, *see* Sechnall
Segiel, archangel 123
Senach 128, 137–8
Senbotha Fola 208
Senchas Már 139, 143, 277
Seon, spring of 83
Seraphim, angelic order 34, 115
sermons 261–2
serpent, in Paradise 35, 37–8, 54, 56
serpents, varieties of 91
sexual sins 50, 246, 254, 271
Sicily 40
síd, people of the 9–10, 137–8
silver warrior 128, 137
sin 66, 130, 133, 234–5, 237, 240, 245
    angelic 53–6, 81, 141
    original 53–6, 66, 72
    see also Adam, fall of; Devil, fall of
Sinai, mount 29, 44
Sinech, sister of Colum Cille 201
singing
    of angels, see angels, singing of
    of birds 89–90
    of stars 89
    of the sleepers of Fones 91
    of trees 86–7
    of water 83
    see also music
Slane 257
slavery 158, 226
slaves 11–12, 148, 163, 166, 176, 183

Sliab Bladma 164
Sliab Mis 148
snow 60–1, 80, 82, 89
Sol 101
    see also sun
Solomon 36
Son, God the 33, 49, 66–7, 77, 96, 274
    see also Jesus Christ
Son of God 71, 155, 158, 164, 173–5, 179,
        202, 204
    see also Jesus Christ
Son of Man 45, 71
    see also Jesus Christ
Son of Mary 165, 168, 186, 189, 196, 222
    see also Jesus Christ
sons of death 243, 268
sons of life 116, 149–50, 224, 242–3, 248,
        251, 253
souls 68, 142, 219, 234, 239–40, 261,
        267–9
    appear after death 50, 81, 257–8
    in hell 94, 242, 269, 271–3
    in relation to the body 72, 240
    leaving the body 81, 264, 267–9
    of the blessed 95, 262, 269, 273–4
    prayers for 130, 133, 223–4
    redeemed from punishment 73, 94, 147,
        150–1, 160–1, 250, 256–8, 270, 272
    returning to the body 46, 71–3, 93
soul-friend (Irish *anmchara*) 15, 24, 49,
        199, 249–50, 253, 257
Spain 51, 75
spectres 136
Spirit, Holy 21, 33, 49, 62–7, 73, 79, 96,
        121, 128, 138, 139, 141, 143, 154–5,
        158, 178, 221, 245, 248, 254, 263,
        274
spring 41, 78, 207
springs 77, 83–4
star
    evening 46
    of the Magi 64–6
stars 77, 79–82, 87–9, 102, 106–7, 121, 272
    angels described as 34–5, 65
    as portents of Christ 46
    creation of 36–7, 65, 87
    fall of 47, 93

shooting 65, 82
unnecessary in heaven 95
varieties of 88–9, 91
see also planets
Stephen the Protomartyr 218
Stichiel, archangel 123
stones 79, 132
virtues of precious 75, 78, 84–5, 138,
204, 267
study, as devotion 203
Styx, river 40
Succat, another name of Patrick 148
successor, *see* heir
summer 41, 77–8, 89
Sumsagial, archangel 123
sun 23, 29, 72, 77, 79–82, 87, 102, 105–6,
116
creation of 36, 107, 182
darkening of 47, 93
father of Circe 40
night journey of 87–8
size of 107
unnecessary in heaven 95
see also Sol
Sunday 150, 251, 272
law of 207
portents on 83–4, 89
sunrise 83, 235
superior, of a religious community 236,
246, 270–1
see also abbot, prior
Susannah 225
Sylvester, pope 273

Tabitha 74
Tallaght 15, 246–8, 255
Tamlachta Librén 183–4
Tara 11, 130, 135, 139, 189, 227
Tartarus, angel of, *see* Devil
Teaching of Mael Ruain 279
Tebe, islands of 84
Temple, in Jerusalem 61
Tenga Bithnua 22–4, 75–96, 262, 276
terce 83, 88, 94, 206, 257
Terryglass 248
texts, tampering with sacred 31–2, 50
Thecla 225

Thrones, angelic order 34, 115, 119–20
thunder 80, 82, 93
Thursday 151, 161
Thurles 19
tides 23, 29, 83, 106
Tigris, sister of Patrick 148
time
God in relation to 33–4, 53, 57, 59,
70, 80–1, 98, 181, 257
reckoning of 103–6, 180–1, 193–5, 210
see also calendars
Tír ind Éoin 174
Tír Lugdach 201
Tír na mBennacht 169
Tobias 226
togairt 113
torments 87, 90–1, 242, 264, 270–3
island of 84
lakes of 92
valley of 88, 91–2
see also hell
travel literature 75
tree of life 43, 85, 117, 273
trees
extraordinary 85–7
sacred 200
varieties of 91
trembling-beasts 82
Trent 17, 19
Trinity 32–4, 47, 49–50, 66–7, 87, 96,
130, 134, 142, 148, 159, 164, 166,
168, 221, 274
truth 54, 237–40
Tuesday 182, 207
Tulach Dubglaisse 201
Tulach na nEpscop 169
Tulach Tinn 198

Ua Néill, Aodh 18
Uachtar Gabra 173–4
Uar 198
Uí Briúin Chualann 169
Uí Chennselaig 174, 208
Uí Cherbaill 176
Uí Chúlduib 177–8
Uí Fhailgi 166, 170–1, 175, 183
Uí Muiredaig 174

Uí Néill 166
Ulster 18
Ultán of Ard mBreccáin 164
Uriel, archangel 123, 268

valley of tears 89
veil, heavenly 81, 103, 265, 267, 273
Venus 101
vespers 83
Vesta 162
vice, *see* sin
vigils 216, 235, 241, 250–1, 255, 257
Vikings 15, 199, 247
Virgin, *see* Mary
virgin birth 62–3
virginity 201
virgins 112, 117, 131, 205, 218–19, 265–6,
    270
  celestial 267–8
virtues 237, 239, 245
Virtues, angelic order 34, 115, 119–20
visions 57, 65, 70–1, 148, 198, 257, 261
vision literature 261
Vita Adae et Evae 276
Vita Columbae 275
Vita Prima Sanctae Brigitae 165, 278
Vita Secunda Sanctae Brigitae 278
voyage tales 280

Wales 13, 127

warriors, retired (Irish *athlaích*) 184, 248
water 38, 40–1, 59, 66–7, 69, 82, 99
  creation of 36, 108
waters, celestial 81, 107, 118
Watkins, Calvert 128
Wednesday 182
Whitby 13–14
'white language' 143–4
winds 29, 38–9, 79–80, 82–3, 93, 99–101,
    132
  colours of 39, 99–100
  glésa of 100–1
wine-flowers 88
winter 41, 77–8, 83–4, 89
wisdom literature, Irish 162, 231
witches 271
  see also magic; women
withershins 87
women 162, 206–7, 246, 252–4, 271, 273
  magic of 128, 133, 137
Word of God 68
world, form of 77, 80–1, 182

Zacharias, father of John the Baptist
    61–2, 66
Zion, mount 66, 77–8, 85–7, 161, 193
  spring of 83
zodiac, signs of 65, 104–6
zones, the five 82, 102–3